More than a Muckraker

More than a Muckraker

Ida Tarbell's
Lifetime
in Journalism

Edited, with an Introduction,
by Robert C. Kochersberger, Jr.

The University of Tennessee Press
Knoxville

"The Economic Test" from the "Onward and Upward with the Arts" section of
the *New Yorker*, Feb. 12, 1937, © 1937, 1965 The New Yorker Magazine, Inc.
(formerly the F-R Publishing Corp.).

"Man-Afraid-of-the-Cars" from the *New Yorker*, July 3, 1937, © 1937, 1965
The New Yorker Magazine, Inc. (formerly the F-R Publishing Corp.).

The paper in this book meets the minimum requirements of the American National
Standard for Permanence of Paper for Printed Library Materials. ∞ The binding
materials have been chosen for strength and durability.

Library of Congress Cataloging in Publication Data

More than a muckraker: Ida Tarbell's lifetime in journalism / edited,
   with an introduction, by Robert C. Kochersberger, Jr.—1st ed.
      p.   cm.
   Includes index.
   ISBN 0-87049-829-0 (cloth: alk. paper)
   ISBN 0-87049-934-3 (pbk.: alk. paper)
   1. Tarbell, Ida M. (Ida Minerva), 1857–1944.
   2. Women journalists—United States—Biography.
   I. Kochersberger, Robert C., Jr. 1950–
PN4874.T23M67   1994
070'.92—dc20
{B}   93-41331
                   CIP

To my family—Janet, Charlie, and Anne—
and to the memory of Cathy L. Covert

Contents

Foreword

Until the publication of Kathleen Brady's excellent biography, *Ida Tarbell: Portrait of a Muckraker,* the name Ida Tarbell was little more than a hazy memory, even for aficionados of journalism and journalistic practice. True, virtually all accounts of the legendary muckrakers who practiced their craft at the turn of the century mentioned her, but only fleetingly and always in the company of her better-known colleagues Lincoln Steffens and Ray Stannard Baker.

Perhaps her obscurity can be attributed to the power of the publicity machine. Several years ago, Edward L. Bernays, one of the founding fathers of public relations, told me how he had represented Steffens in the early 1930s, when Steffens had completed his memoirs. At the time, Steffens, like Tarbell and Baker, was no longer trendy and had been forgotten by most Americans. Bernays arranged a grand reception and banquet for the Steffens' book and invited many of its protagonists. The event made news and, Bernays said, helped to spur sales of the autobiography, which became both a bestseller and a classic in the literature of American journalism.

Tarbell wrote her own autobiography, *All in the Day's Work,* published in 1939. Upstaged by the war in Europe, it received little attention. The exploits of a journalist who had taken on the Standard Oil Company, among other targets, seemed a quaint artifact of another time. Years later—in 1986, to be exact—Kathleen Brady and I decided over lunch one day to do what we could to increase Ida Tarbell's visibility among journalists. We would nominate the site where she did her work to be designated a National Historic Site in Journalism, an honor awarded by the Society of Professional Journalists (SPJ). We put our proposal before the SPJ committee and were gratified by the reaction. The group agreed to mark the spot where Ida Tarbell had done her work and asked for our help in finding it.

Kathleen Brady visited the owners of the building in lower Manhattan where *McClure's Magazine* was crafted. It was there that Tarbell's investigative journalism had been developed. Brady was turned away by people who did not want landmark status accorded to a building they might later want to raze. Undaunted, Brady located the apartment house where Tarbell had lived during this seminal period in her life and to its owners made the same plea that the SPJ plaque be placed on the building's wall. She was again rebuffed. Finally, she and I went to the American Society of Magazine Editors and the Magazine Publishers Association and pleaded with them for some wall space in their midtown Manhattan headquarters where the plaque might be displayed. They agreed enthusiastically.

So, a few months later, at a ceremony at what was then the Gannett Center for Media Studies at Columbia University, the plaque was presented, and we celebrated Tarbell and her contribution to American journalism and American life. On that proud day, leaders of journalism and the feminist movement (Betty Friedan was there) joined in a symposium and a party which featured a ragtime band. Most of the press ignored the event, but a *Washington Post* columnist noted that he was glad that there were still people who cared about Tarbell and the values she espoused. Little did he know that the same mean-spirited business interests that Tarbell had opposed had almost blocked the historic designation.

Why should anyone care about a journalist who was most active in the early years of this century and who died in 1944? The answer is quite simple: Tarbell helped to invent modern journalism and in fact was a more rigorous, systematic journalist than almost anyone before or since. Trained in the sciences (she had taught science for a time), Tarbell brought the rigor of scientific inquiry and a penchant for facts and accuracy to detailed investigations of large topics, especially those involving government corruption and the excesses of big business. She wrote with passion and conviction, always supporting her statements with painstaking research and powerful evidence.

Tarbell also was a gifted biographer, producing short biographical sketches for magazines and full-length books about Lincoln and Napoleon, for example. While her work on Lincoln is rarely cited today, she was one of the last writers actually to interview many of Lincoln's contemporaries. Indeed, she acted as a scout for biographers and historians. Along with her muckraker colleagues, Ida Tarbell discovered what many journalists, even famous ones, learn—that writers are hired hands, unless they own their own publications.

Taking that belief to heart, she and the others founded their own magazine. But eventually they discovered that, as owners, they too were susceptible to the caution of the counting house. Without publisher S. S. McClure to rail against, and without his goading them toward courageous journalism, the independent effort foundered, and Tarbell and her colleagues went back to working for others.

Ironically, in all that has been written about Tarbell (most of it in biographical notes), there has been little direct presentation or analysis of her journalism and other writing. Historians of the press sometimes speak glibly about her importance in press history or in the history of women in journalism, while rarely citing even a single sentence from her writing. In fact, when Kathleen Brady published her biography of Tarbell in 1984, she worried that the book would receive little press attention and discussed this prospect frankly with an editor at the *New York Times.* "If you can prove that she had an affair with Teddy Roosevelt, I'll get you on the front page," he said, "but otherwise you'll have to be satisfied with the *Book Review.*"

What Tarbell gave to the method and substance of American journalism has its sensational moments in her battles with Standard Oil Company and the fight for antitrust legislation, but a sizzling sex story hers is not. In fact, Tarbell never let her gender get in the way of her professional interests, and she championed women's rights in a *de facto* sense, without ever being an active feminist. During the fight for women's suffrage in the 1920s, Tarbell, then well past middle age, was alienated by the tactics of activist women. Her own rejection of this first wave of feminism probably accounts for modern feminists' lack of enthusiasm for her, even though by any standard her achievements were impressive, if not monumental. They had nothing to do with women's rights in a narrow sense, but everything to do with demonstrating that, in every respect, women could be exemplary achievers.

In an era when the best-known journalists are often the least substantial, it is profoundly pleasing to contemplate Ida Tarbell's writing. In this volume, Robert C. Kochersberger, Jr., a historian of journalism and literature, offers a compendium of Ida Tarbell's work that is both pleasurable and systematic. Here we are treated to Tarbell's lively biography and biographical journalism, as well as her stolid muckraking and business reporting. Along the way we encounter Tarbell's commentary on women and womanhood, including what she saw as the contradictions between career achievement and motherhood. Finally comes an excursion through her vivid world, her journalistic and literary reactions to the passing show that she had the privilege to observe.

When one revisits material that originated between eighty and one hundred years ago, an inevitable question arises: Is the exploration worth it? In Tarbell's case, the answer is a resounding "yes," because the first-hand accounts and analytical reports are fascinating, both as lively and agreeable reading and as models of literary and journalistic style. One cannot truly understand Tarbell or the role of any writer or journalist in her period (or any other period) without looking at the substance of the particular body of work. With Professor Kochersberger's well-chosen and well-organized treatment, here we are accorded that opportunity. We see the intellectual product of a great journalist who was, in addition, a great woman, whether she chose to acknowledge it or not. She was also a consummate American living the American dream, rising from humble beginnings in western Pennsylvania and becoming one of the best-known individuals of her time. That her work was so strong and helped make magazines instruments of social change kept her name alive, in spite of all the forces that normally conspire to relegate mere journalists to obscurity.

It is curious, perhaps, that while Tarbell worked in biography and concerned herself with such monumental figures as Lincoln and Napoleon, it is her more ephemeral journalism for which she is best known. It is fascinating that perishable news should have formed a lasting basis for her reputation and for her impact on American life. One suspects that Ida Tarbell might have preferred that her niche in history be connected to literary more than to journalistic output, but in the latter area she was truly distinguished, while in the former she had to compete with other writers and critics who have given the world an avalanche of material about, for example, Lincoln and Napoleon. When one thinks of investigative journalism, one immediately thinks of the muckrakers—among whom Tarbell was probably the preeminent figure, despite Steffens' greater fame. When we examine Tarbell's journalism closely and note the time she took for her investigations, in some cases years, we realize that she was not just an early practitioner, but a far better investigator and analyst than many of today's leading adversarial journalists. In fact, when it comes to maturity of thought, rigorous research, and systematic analysis, Tarbell, who lived decades before the computer and the modern database, stands out as a profoundly important figure. Even today few can match her.

In creating and editing this book, Robert Kochersberger has rendered a public service. Having been an Ida Tarbell fan since I began to research utopian practices in American journalism, including the muckrakers, I am delighted at last to find myself and others the beneficiaries of this compact collection. The work of this great journalist and author gives real texture and meaning to the term "founding mother" of American journalism.

Everette E. Dennis
Executive Director
The Freedom Forum Media Studies Center
Columbia University
January 1993

Preface

Ida Tarbell was among the most prolific of American writers, and selecting the twenty-six pieces included in this collection was a challenging task. The Tarbell Papers Collection in Pelletier Library at Allegheny College, in Meadville, Pennsylvania, holds a wealth of material, with many magazine articles and manuscripts for other articles and speeches. (Some manuscripts are annotated in Tarbell's own hand, and seeing her handwriting was a thrill for me.)

I initially envisioned a collection of more than forty articles, chapters, and other pieces—such was the volume and range of what Tarbell did—but I quickly realized that half that amount would have to suffice. What I include here, then, represents a careful culling from the huge body of work available.

I first considered a chronological approach, arranging pieces in the order in which they were written. But that scheme, while revealing a steady change in tone and feeling, obscured the variety of the topics Tarbell chose. So instead I used a topical arrangement, with the selections in each topic arranged chronologically.

Examples of Tarbell's biographical work represent her first serious writing for publication and the material for which she initially became nationally known. This work additionally reveals some of her fascination with French women and, later, with her attention to social causes.

The section on business-related subjects shows Tarbell's fact-finding abilities and her concern with both the success of business and the humane treatment of workers. It was in this area, with the Standard Oil work, that Tarbell became genuinely famous.

The section on women's issues is necessary because Tarbell wrote extensively on the woman question of her time, and because her writing often appeared in direct opposition to what her life suggested. It might seem that Tarbell, the crusading, professional woman, would have supported the feminist causes of her day. In fact, she did not, strongly believing that a woman's main place was in the home, carrying out her God-given duty of bearing and rearing children. Tarbell never directly addressed this contradiction, preferring to be known in terms of her work rather than her personal life.

The final section, an eclectic sampling of Tarbell's writing on social issues, is my favorite. These articles show Tarbell's deep and thoughtful approach to life better than the other selections, and in doing so they reveal more of the personal Tarbell than any of her other writing. In these pieces she is thoughtful, outraged, compassionate, wistful, enthusiastic, and even funny.

Following standard bibliographic practice, the references do not contain volume numbers for newspapers and popular magazines, except for *The Chautauquan,* which, because of its unique service to the Chautauqua Literary and Scientific Circle, was a quasi-academic journal.

Readers interested in learning more about Tarbell have two excellent recent sources in Kathleen Brady's *Ida Tarbell: Portrait of a Muckraker* and Mary Tomkins's *Ida M. Tarbell.* The autobiography, along with Tarbell's other books, is readily available in major libraries, as are some of the magazines, especially *The American Magazine* and *McClure's.* A number of libraries in the Northeast have *The Chautauquan.* The best source of unpublished or otherwise hard-to-find material is Pelletier Library's Special Collections at Allegheny College, Meadville, Pennsylvania, the source of a number of pieces in this collection.

Assembling these samples of Tarbell's writing was made easier by a number of persons, especially Stella Edwards, of the Pelletier Library Special Collections, and Alfreda Irwin, Chautauqua Institution historian. Ida Tarbell's grandniece and eldest surviving relative Caroline Tarbell Tupper was warmly cooperative in granting me permission to use Ida's works. I also want to acknowledge the support of my wife, Janet C. Watrous, and of my colleagues Rod Cockshutt, Larry Rudner, Nancy Penrose, and Nancy Margolis. Their encouraging words at my low points were welcome indeed.

R.C.K.
Raleigh, N.C.
August 24, 1993

Introduction

Ida Minerva Tarbell was an author obsessed by facts and accuracy, and her early work was so fact-laden it was almost ponderous. During a lifetime of writing, however, Ida Tarbell eventually was freed by facts. She moved from specific, painstaking articles, including her muckraking and biographical work, to essays on broad social issues, moving almost inductively as she progressed from the particular toward the general. A career of fact-based writing gave her the confidence to strike out in writing that was broader, more thoughtful, and much more interesting in its range and compassion than that which she first practiced.

An early and continuing goal for Tarbell was finding her niche, her unique approach to life and work, and then sticking with it. She once said, "Now after all is done and said in this world, there is nothing so precious as the sincere expression of self. Even the dull person who is frankly content to be dull is better than the most brilliant imitator. We like things because they are perfect specimens of their kind, not because they are trying to be some kind that is not natural to them."[1] This philosophy truly was hers. Tarbell never was flashy or superficial. The force of her being was devoted to doing the things she did as well and as thoroughly as was humanly possible. With that she was content.

Early on, peering at tiny animals through a microscope brought Tarbell much happiness. In the same way, in the 1880s, her writing began with intense study of the details of her subjects and their lives. From this focus on particulars, her writing steadily widened in scope until, in the 1930s, she wrote essays on social issues—poverty and temperance among them—and the autobiography.

During the first decade of the twentieth century, immediately after her precedent-setting research and writing on John D. Rockefeller and the monopoly Standard Oil, Tarbell was widely known in America; she was identified predominantly as a muckraker, although her biographies of Napoleon and Lincoln had attracted attention first. Journalism historians Arthur and Lila Weinberg write that her Standard Oil work "catapulted her into national fame and her name became a byword in many homes throughout the country."[2]

From 1902 to 1904, the "History of the Standard Oil Company" was published in serial form in *McClure's* magazine, followed by its appearance as a book. The series, which depicted in damning detail the predation of Rockefeller's oil monopoly, made Tarbell virtually a household name. S. S. McClure biographer Peter Lyon writes, "Month after month, her reputation grew." McClure himself wrote, "The way you are generally esteemed and reverenced pleases me tremendously. You are today the most generally famous woman in America. People universally speak of you with such a reverence that I am getting sort of afraid of you."[3] Lyon adds that the "best-grounded, most careful, most substantial, and most devastating contribution made by the muckrakers to the general enlightenment was by Miss Tarbell."[4]

One commentator on Tarbell, Mary E. Tomkins, says that "an enthralled public followed her serial account in *McClure's* for two years as she tirelessly communicated to tens of thousands of readers 'a clear and succinct notion of the processes by which a particular industry passes from the control of the many to that of the few.'"[5]

Tarbell seemed to be indifferent to her fame; while she was best known as a muckraker, Tarbell didn't much care for the title. Even though her work clearly went beyond muckraking to a kind of literary journalism, she probably would have thought that description overly prideful, too.

To read her journalism with understanding today requires a brief discussion of the era of muckraking; of Tarbell's own work before, during and after the period of muckraking; and of her upbringing, education, and first experiences in journalism.

She was a woman of remarkable ability and complexity. Understanding her professional work begins as this collection begins, with her first job in journalism. We then move on to her biographies and other articles, then to the muckraking, and finally to Tarbell's consideration of very different topics, most concerned with the social problems of her era.

The Muckrakers

Theodore Roosevelt became president of the United States upon the assassination of McKinley on September 14, 1901, when Tarbell was forty-three years old. Roosevelt was a tough-talking, charismatic man who is credited with giving the name "muckraker" to the investigative journalists of the first decade of America's twentieth century. In so naming them, he gave them and their successors a title indelibly linked to their actions. This christening occurred on the afternoon of April 14, 1906, as Roosevelt spoke to the members of the Senate at the laying of the cornerstone of the new House of Representatives office building in Washington, D.C.

Since 1902, a group of dedicated, inquisitive magazine journalists had been digging into misdeeds, corruption, and injustices in American society, often concentrating on the large corporations that were beginning to dominate the American economy. The journalists even attacked the Senate, a group of men so corrupt, Fred Cook wrote, that "hardly any of them recognized the odor of their own corruption."[6] The attacks on this Senate had become too much for Roosevelt, who felt called upon to defend the corrupted against those who exposed their corruption:

> In Bunyan's *Pilgrim's Progress* you may recall the description of the Man with the Muckrake, the man who could look no way but downward, with a muckrake in his hands; who was offered a celestial crown for his muckrake, but who would neither look up nor regard the crown he was offered, but continued to rake to himself the filth of the floor.
>
> In *Pilgrim's Progress* the Man with the Muckrake is set forth as an example of him whose vision is fixed on carnal instead of spiritual things. Yet he also typifies the man who in this life consistently refuses to see aught that is lofty, and fixes his eyes with solemn intentness only on that which is vile and debasing. . . . But the man who never does anything else, who never thinks or speaks or writes save of his feats with the muckrake, speedily becomes, not a help to society, not an incitement to good, but one of the most potent forces of evil.[7]

Roosevelt's criticism did not slow the journalists. The muckrakers flourished from 1902 until 1912, stimulating the wave of reform that marked the first sixteen years of the century. The group changed things, and few writers can claim that.[8] The most important muckrakers were Lincoln Steffens, Upton Sinclair, David Graham Phillips (author of the *Cosmopolitan* series, "The Treason of the Senate," that angered Roosevelt), Ray Stannard Baker, and a lone woman, Tarbell, the subject of this book.

Tarbell and the other muckrakers, working for magazines (primarily *Munsey's, McClure's,* and *Cosmopolitan*), gave the public a new understanding of what journalism could accomplish, along with a stunning picture of the corruption and greed that characterized many of the country's major industries, industrial giants, and politicians. The articles, of course, also generated large circulations (estimated at a combined maximum of three million a month)[9] and attendant profits for the publishers. "Some of the muckraking magazines were run by such unabashed practitioners of the art as Frank Munsey and S. S. McClure. Their muckraking ran its profitable course as an adjunct of the Progressive movement, where their influence counted," according to magazine historians John Tebbel and Mary Ellen Zuckerman.[10]

In an editorial in the January 1903 issue of his magazine, McClure wrote that society was being corrupted, with "capitalists, workingmen, politicians and citizens" all breaking the law. He claimed that lawyers, judges, churches, and colleges all were failing to uphold the law, leaving "no one left; none but all of us." The burden of correcting the scandals fell to the people, McClure wrote: "We have to pay in the end, every one of us. And in the end the sum total of the debt will be our liberty."[11]

McClure was hyperbolic, of course, a victim of his own energy and enthusiasm for his magazine's contents and the profits the latter brought. He did not envision muckraking magazines as political weapons in the class struggle, to paraphrase one of Tebbel and Zuckerman's chapter titles. These authors write, "Although the object of the muckrakers and others was to expose the evils of capitalism, they did not have the slightest intention of overthrowing the government and installing communism even before the revolution occurred in Russia. Their goal was reform of a system they saw as both corrupt and unbalanced economically."[12]

As noted, muckraking had a short life. Causes of its decline included the changing nature of the United States, especially as the magazines themselves became big business and could no longer afford to antagonize advertisers, and the aging of the muckrakers themselves. Norman Hapgood, a newspaper reporter in Chicago, Milwaukee, and New York City before becoming editor of *Collier's*, wrote in 1930, "In journalism men are likely to worsen as they grow older, and as they lose excitement. There are not many pen-men who . . . are most effective in old age."[13] An exception was Tarbell, who continued to write into her eighties and to marvel about the very fact of growing old.

For some writers, nonfiction also entailed frustrations, and they sought release in fiction. According to Shelley Fisher Fishkin, such diverse writers as Whitman, Twain, Dreiser, Hemingway, and Dos Passos chafed at the limits of conventional journalism. "The move [to fiction] made sense. Liberated from what Douglass Cater once called the 'straitjacket of straight reporting,' these writers produced the masterworks of fiction that help to define the American literary tradition."[14] Tarbell herself once tried a novel, *The Rising of the Tide,* but, as Tomkins says, Tarbell had no aptitude for fiction.[15]

The investigative writers, primarily those who wrote nonfiction, did help to change the United States. But, after a decade, their muckraking came to an end. Tebbel and Zuckerman note that the middle class began to feel that government regulation would take over from muckrakers in exposing and controlling wrongdoing, and Woodrow Wilson's idealistic vision of the country was a good deal more comfortable than constant gloom. It was astonishing how quickly *Cosmopolitan, McClure's,* and the other muckraking magazines switched back to their old—and profitable—"formula of offering good fiction, romance, pictures of pretty girls, short stories and articles about successful men."[16]

As Robert Miraldi writes, "When this generation of Progressive era muckrakers gradually moved from journalism to other forms of writing and other ways to earn a living, the flame of muckraking flickered."[17] Tarbell moved on, too, but she did not falter, instead continuing to write on a broad range of topics, including business issues such as tariffs, factory efficiency, and work conditions; and social issues, on which the force of her writing remained undimmed.

Ida Tarbell's Professional Development

"Sociologist"

Though they never mention her name, authors Paul Baker and Louis Anderson seem to have been thinking about Ida Minerva Tarbell, when, in 1987, they described journalism and sociology in reciprocal terms. Both professional fields frequently proclaim their "objectivity and professional detachment" from the passions of partisan affairs and often claim "neutral ground in the swirling debates of the moment." Sociology and journalism both function as knowledge-producing enterprises within the larger context of changing common-sense constructions of human affairs. But the relationship is not one of simple harmony; for many reasons, "sociologists and journalists often find themselves in conflict with varied segments of the public."[18]

Tarbell's biographers do not describe her as a sociologist; she probably would have been horrified at the term. But the appellation does have striking applicability to her investigative and journalistic pursuits. With a falcon's eye for detail and a dedication to thoroughness, she watched her world and reacted to it, often taking on important social issues with her own version of muted passion. Tarbell skillfully used the tools of the sociologist and the journalist—observation, research, and interviewing—to marshal facts and paint convincing and, indeed, often damning pictures of her subjects.

Her early work, especially the first few pieces in *The Chautauquan* magazine, was a bit turgid, drowning in facts. But her biographical work, which is well-represented in this collection and for which she initially was hired by McClure, breathes life into her subjects and offers new perspectives on them. Tomkins writes that Tarbell "possessed a flair for illumination of character through anecdotes which enlivened her works."[19] For instance, in the selection on the life of Josephine, wife of Napoleon, Tarbell writes, "The tact and good sense with which Josephine conducted herself in her exacting and slavish position—the grace and patience with which she wore her royal harness—are as pathetic as they are marvelous."[20]

Muckraker

Tarbell is best remembered for her work on Standard Oil and its Rockefeller. Starting in November 1902, Tarbell, in nineteen installments in *McClure's* magazine, displays her merciless fact finding at its best. Magazine historians Tebbel and Zuckerman write that her "research was thorough, her writing sober, and the end result was an inexorable march of facts that showed in impressive detail how Standard Oil conducted its business. But she was also fair, in a sense. She displayed Big Oil in all its legitimate greatness but argued that too high a price had been paid for it."[21]

In writing about Standard Oil, Tarbell was signaling that the needs and practices of big business no longer were superior to the needs of the people. She fit appropriately into the era described by historians Michael and Edwin Emery:

> The industrial concentration that was maturing between 1880 and 1900 was of vital significance, but it was only a part of the enormous change in American life. Mechanization, industrialization, and urbanization brought swift and extensive social, cultural, and political developments. People were being uprooted physically and mentally by the effects of the economic revolution, and in the new environment no social institution could remain static.[22]

Muckrakers appeared on the scene to probe this new environment, motivated by perceived wrongdoing and injustice and their own new sense of the power they could wield. Their magazines—*Munsey's, McClure's,* and *Cosmopolitan*—recognized the new role given to mass media by enhanced education and the public's thirst for knowledge; they responded by cutting prices, first to fifteen cents and then to a dime, to obtain true mass circulations. By 1900 *Munsey's* had achieved a circulation of 650,000, with the other two in hot pursuit. All three followed a formula of popular fiction, general articles, and illustrations.[23]

According to David M. Chalmers, during the decade between 1903 and 1912, nearly two thousand articles of a muckraking nature appeared in the popular magazines, complemented by editorials, cartoons, and serials. "But of this vast outpouring, close to a third were written by a small group of 12 men and one woman who concentrated on and professionalized this kind of journalism."[24]

Professional

The comment about professionalism has particular meaning for any discussion of Ida Tarbell, the "one woman" in Chalmers' list. For her, professionalism was among the highest ideals. Professionalism led to her painstaking search for facts. It helped her tackle different subjects with equanimity. And professionalism helped her, in her own mind at least, to remain above the fray: "My point of attack has always been that of a journalist after the fact, rarely that of a reformer, the advocate of a cause or a system. If I was tempted from the strait and narrow path of the one who seeks for that which is so and why it is so, I sooner or later returned."[25]

Tarbell's obsession with facts and accuracy was not unusual for the muckrakers, who took it as a point of honor to spend "months of investigation before printing a brief article of five or six thousand words. They investigated everything, confirmed everything."[26] Philip Lawler writes, "One of the most cherished tenets of American journalism is the belief that a reporter should follow his story wherever it may lead."[27]

Robert Miraldi contends that "if, for example, one of the Ten Commandments of objectivity is the separation of 'values' from 'facts,' then the turn-of-the-century muckrakers were, at the least, trying not to be sinners. Being thorough and establishing facts were fetishes for most of these journalists."[28]

Tarbell was a paragon of thoroughness; she could have written a sentence in a handbook published by the Center for Investigative Reporting, founded in 1977: "Probably the simplest rule to remember in requesting any record is to know as precisely as possible what it is you want and where, and then proceed as though you deserve it."[29] For Tarbell, in writing about Standard Oil, the main question was this: "Was it possible to treat the story historically, to make a *documented* [emphasis added] narrative?"[30]

Worker

The collection of Tarbell's work in this volume, including magazine articles, book chapters, speeches, and other works, attempts to demonstrate the range and depth of Tarbell's journalism and to locate her life and achievements within the context of her times and her own personality. Tarbell was focused on work—one article in this collection is her answer to the question, "What interests you most in this cosmopolitan world of today?" Her answer, not un-expectedly and almost grimly: "Work." It was this seriousness of purpose that led Tarbell to college, to her first job as a teacher, to journalism, to Paris, and, ultimately, to a hard-hitting career in journalism that reached its zenith in the beginning years of the twentieth century.

Tarbell's early years, during which, almost frivolously, she took her first editorial job (on *The Chautauquan* magazine), introduced her to a life of self-conscious dedication to research and learning that informed virtually all of her writing and, indeed, most of her life. Tarbell biographer Kathleen Brady writes, "What she sought was accomplishment. Hers is the story of how one person handled the human dilemma of daring great things, despite galling limitations, and succeeded admirably."[31]

Editor and critic John Chamberlain, discussing muckraking, refers to Tarbell and Lincoln Steffens as the "scholars of the movement."[32] His comment hardly surprises; Tarbell's relentless pursuit of facts is continually evident in what she wrote, and it shows clearly in the examples of her writing in this collection.

Key Influences

To introduce this collection of Tarbell's works requires discussion of Tarbell's professional preparation—her "journalism internship" at Chautauqua—and of the range of individuals who served as models for her understanding of professionalism. It also requires us to examine events and persons of impor-tance in Tarbell's time. Her unexpected ideas on women's rights and roles, for instance, were colored by the suffrage movement.

Tarbell's first journalistic position exposed her to a group of women working professionally and to the variety of writing done by other women. Much of Tarbell's writing was on the so-called "woman question," and these early associations clearly influenced what she wrote later. Several of the selec-tions in this volume deal with the woman question, giving particular atten-tion to women in the workplace, a theme popular in *The Chautauquan*.

Tarbell's first forays into journalism came at Chautauqua Institution, a remarkable, unique place that had been a haven for thousands of persons dedi-cated to education, recreation, and contemplation since 1874. Ohio businessman Lewis Miller and Methodist Bishop John Heyl Vincent had founded it on the western shore of long, narrow Chautauqua Lake in the westernmost area of New York State, as an institution for Sunday school teachers.

Almost from its inception, Chautauqua Institution (or Chautauqua Assembly, as it first was known) gave publications and journalism important roles. During the third season, 1876, the *Daily Assembly Herald* began carrying full accounts of events and lectures at the institution, enabling those who could not attend the summer sessions to keep abreast of Chautauqua happenings. The *Herald* was edited by Rev. Theodore L. Flood in offices on institution grounds.[33] Flood, who left the pulpit to edit the newspaper, played a substantial role in managing Chautauqua publications and was Tarbell's first editor. In 1880, he started *The Chautauquan* magazine. Three years later, Tarbell joined its staff.

Flood, *The Chautauquan,* and Tarbell remain related in complex ways. Of the three, hers is the famous name, but the man and the magazine live, too, as forces that instilled in Tarbell her understanding of journalism and the role of facts within it. After all, she once said in response to a question, "Chautauqua? Why, that's where I learned my trade."[34] (For more on Chautauqua and the Chautauqua Literary and Scientific Circle, see appendix A.)

Tarbell learned her trade at the magazine by starting at the bottom, but she recognized that her beginning as a low-ranking editorial assistant had been important in her eventual development as a journalist. Tarbell once told an audience at Wellesley, "When you enter this great house of the writer's world, unless you are willing to begin at the bottom and take the stairs in rooms as they come . . . I am afraid this talk will be useless."[35]

For Tarbell, the orderly, neat, almost compulsive reporter and writer, such thinking was crucial. People and ideas had their origins in the past, and she recognized that each personality develops in relation to what has gone before and is understood in relation to what follows. He or she is at once product and part of the particular environment. In the autobiography, Tarbell wrote, "Nobody begins or ends anything. Each person is a link, weak or strong, in an endless chain."[36]

A Brief Biography

Tarbell was born November 5, 1857, in the Erie County, Pennsylvania, home of her maternal grandfather. Her parents were teachers, but her father's pioneering spirit led him to attempt to settle a piece of land in Iowa. His efforts were time-consuming and arduous, but by the time he was ready to move his family, which had been waiting all the while, oil had been discovered in northwestern Pennsylvania, and Franklin Sumner Tarbell returned.

. He started an oil tank business, and the family settled in Rouseville, Pennsylvania, a rough-and-tumble oil town where young Ida was surrounded by the rich sights and sounds of the booming oil business. Her father was one of the founders of the Methodist church in Rouseville, and the Tarbell family was active in it. Although Tarbell did not practice Methodism as an adult, her strong religious background "instilled in her a sense of discipline and purpose that never was lost."[37] The senior Tarbells, with increasing income, wanted to give their children a taste of the "advantages" they themselves had been denied. One such advantage was music; another was travel. The grandest excursions the family made were to Chautauqua Lake, where the Tarbell parents and children would ride steamers, eating and taking in the sights. These trips took place before Chautauqua Institution existed.

When Ida Tarbell was thirteen, the still-prosperous family moved to Titusville, Pennsylvania, where she attended high school. Shortly thereafter, the town's new growth was stifled by Standard Oil, which would strive for monopoly control of northwestern Pennsylvania's oil business. These developments were deeply disturbing, and the previously jovial Franklin Tarbell turned silent and stern.

Ida Tarbell admits that she could not comprehend the events then, but they nonetheless created in her a hatred of privilege. At fifteen, she perceived that privilege, at least that version of it accorded to owners of expanding oil companies, badly upset her world. As time passed, other currents had their impact on the developing teenager. She heard a series of lectures on the reconciliation of geology and the Book of Genesis and staggered away confused about the universe; she felt she ought to leave the church, because she found its tenets unbelievable. She would later recall that the growth of this doubt in her religion, in which she had placed great faith, gave rise to uncertainty: "Nothing was ever again to be final."[38]

In the midst of this uncertainty, Ida Tarbell set out to search for the beginnings of life. She acquired a microscope through which she peered at the world of the minuscule. In the Titusville house, a room was set aside for her, where she could be alone with her scientific study. But being alone was not enough, and she decided that in order to become a microscopist, she must attend college. Her determination to attend college, she later recalled, grew out of the crusade then going on for women's rights. Her parents, hospitable to crusaders, opened their doors to the women's rights activists. Tarbell recognized the divisive nature of the struggle, and some of its reverberations did not increase her regard for her sex. She noted that the women crusaders who visited her home, Mary Livermore and Frances Willard among them, never paid attention to her. On the other hand, the men the Tarbell family entertained did speak with Ida, and she mentally noted that men were nicer to her than women. But the women's rights struggle had its effect on her—it convinced her that educational and economic independence were goals worth pursuing.

The only way to assure this independence, as she saw it, was to secure an education. In fall 1876, the lone woman among forty "hostile or indifferent boys," she enrolled at Allegheny College, Meadville, Pennsylvania. Her inquisitive mind was stimulated by contact with her teachers, and at one point she studied a "missing link," a mud puppy with both gills and a lung, at home in water or mud, while at another she spoke on one of the first telephones. (Dealing with new technology was in her blood; she later became the first woman to fly in an airplane and write about it. See "Flying—A Dream Come True" in this volume.) At college Tarbell also had social contact with men but maintained her determination to be independent, to avoid any "entangling alliance."

She graduated from Allegheny College in spring 1880, taking a job as "preceptress" of the Poland Union Seminary, Poland, Ohio. She assumed a staggering teaching load—two classes in each of four languages, as well as classes in geology, botany, geometry, and trigonometry—but was so eager to teach that she did not recognize the overwork. After two years, though, exhausted, she retreated to her parents' Titusville home, where she dusted off her beloved microscope and resumed peering at hydrozoa. But the pursuit of microscopy was not to last long, for in her parents' home she soon met a guest, Theodore L. Flood, editor of *The Chautauquan.*

Meeting Flood stirred Ida's recollections of the family visits to Chautauqua Lake (and later Chautauqua Institution), of her exposure to the microscope there, and of Bishop John Heyl Vincent, who had impressed her as "handsome, confident, alert, energetic, radiating well-being."[39] She also recalled the worst mischief in which she had taken part—playing tag up and down a giant relief model of Palestine. The model had been built on the lake shore to resemble Palestine on the Mediterranean. The model was spotted with small versions of various communities of the days of Christ, and Tarbell recalled that tag-players could not be tagged if they were straddling Jerusalem.

It was to this place, full of memories, that Flood asked Tarbell to return, to work on *The Chautauquan.* Bishop Vincent had perceived that some references in the magazine needed explanation, and it was to strengthen the magazine in this regard that Tarbell was hired. As she said, "I was quick to accept, glad to be useful, for I had grown up with what was called the Chautauqua Movement. Indeed, it had been almost as much a part of my life as the oil business, and in its way it was as typically American. If we had a truer measure for values we would count it more important."[40]

She annotated parts of the monthly texts, answering questions before readers had a chance to ask them. Because most readers did not have access to libraries, it was Tarbell's job to provide, for instance, the proper pronunciation of certain words, translations of foreign phrases, identification of characters, and definitions of words. Doing this job, she began to think about facts; reading proofs, she said, was "an exacting job which never ceased to worry me. What if the accent was in the wrong place? What if I brought somebody into the world in the wrong year?"[41]

Tarbell started working for the magazine in 1883. In her seven years there, Tarbell took on a variety of editorial duties, attained a position of prominence on the magazine's staff, and began some writing of her own. But *The Chautauquan* was only a starting place for Tarbell's journalism. As she became more skilled, she worried that complacency would take its toll and she would end up in a comfortable corner at *The Chautauquan* for the rest of her life. Such a fate she did not want.

Paris held a special attraction for her, and in 1890 Tarbell quit *The*

Chautauquan to move to France. Her departure has never been satisfactorily explained; biographer Brady believes it came over Flood's refusal to promote her. After that, she never was casual about Flood.[42]

Tarbell studied at the Sorbonne and the College de France, and did research on the French Revolutionary figure, Madame Roland. Tarbell supported herself by the sale of articles about Paris to American newspapers.

While Tarbell was in Paris, in spring 1893, she first encountered Samuel S. McClure. McClure had sought Tarbell out in Paris, because a sample of her writing convinced him that her abilities could be put to good use on his magazine. Under an agreement with McClure, Tarbell wrote several articles from Paris for *McClure's Magazine.* In spring 1894, McClure offered Tarbell a salaried, full-time position. She accepted.[43]

Her first major assignment for *McClure's* was a biography of Napoleon, which ran from November 1894 to April 1895. Some historians have claimed that this hugely popular biographical series ensured the success of the magazine. In 1895, Tarbell started work on a biography of Abraham Lincoln, which was published in *McClure's* in 1896. Tarbell soon became associate editor of the magazine, and in 1900 she began research for a another series on the Standard Oil trust.

Disagreement on the staff of McClure's in 1906 led Tarbell to join John S. Phillips, Ray Stannard Baker, Lincoln Steffens, Finley Dunne, and William Allen White in buying the *American Magazine.*[44] At least some of the capital Tarbell contributed to the purchase is likely to have come from the substantial block of S. S. McClure Company stock she was given by S. S. himself during the Standard Oil series.[45]

Reflections on Tarbell from her contemporaries are enlightening. Peter Finley Dunne, who wrote as "Mr. Dooley," told Tarbell she sputtered like a woman.[46] Lincoln Steffens viewed Tarbell as a peacemaker. He recalled that when disagreement broke out and divided the office, it was Tarbell who moved in to quell the trouble:

> Sensible, capable, and very affectionate, she knew each one of us and all our idiosyncrasies and troubles. She had none of her own, so far as we ever heard. When we were deadlocked, we might each of us send for her, and she would

come to the office, smiling, like a tall, good-looking young mother to say, "Hush, children." She would pick out the sense in each of our contentions, and putting them together with her own good sense, gave me a victory over S. S., him a triumph over Phillips [an associate editor of *McClure's*], and take away from all of us only the privilege of gloating.[47]

In the same vein, Ray Stannard Baker's biographer referred to Tarbell's ability to calm rebellion.[48]

Baker himself wrote that he had "never known a finer human spirit in this world" than Tarbell. His paean described her as beautiful, generous, modest, full of kindness, gallant, possessing a good sense of humor, fearless, honest, interesting and having a "shining love of truth." Baker provided a glimpse of Tarbell's living quarters when he described her "book-lined study with the comfortable little tea table in front of the fireplace."[49]

Tarbell lived through a turbulent period of United States history, one that dripped with blood, she said. People struggled to get at causes, to find correction, to humanize and socialize the country; for at that time there were those who dreamed of a good world, although at times the world seemed to them to be going mad.

At one point during her years on *The Chautauquan*, Tarbell set out to write the novel, but she abandoned the attempt when she realized that she needed to know more about women before she could construct society. The women's rights movement was at least partly responsible for Tarbell's inability to continue with the novel. Staunch feminists insisted that men had made a mess of the world, and only women could set it right. While Tarbell believed that women were capable persons, she was troubled by the contention that women must be given suffrage if the world were to be improved. "I did not feel the confidence of my courageous friends," she wrote.[50] Tarbell refused to cast her lot with the active feminists, for she felt too strongly that women, like men, were only human.

To the individuals who vigorously denounced the Standard Oil trust, Tarbell's writing indicated she, too, hated the oil giant. She dealt with the label "muckraker" in a thoughtful chapter called "Muckraker or Historian?" In it she refers to "this classification of muckraker, which I did not like."

Tarbell seemed to try to avoid being included in this group of muckrakers when she wrote, "All the radical element, and I numbered many friends among them, were begging me to join their movements. I soon found that most of them wanted attacks. They had little interest in balanced findings. Now I was convinced that in the long run the public they were trying to stir would weary of vituperation, that if you were to secure permanent results the mind must be convinced."[51]

Tarbell's painstaking fact finding about the Standard Oil case indicted the company. But the opponents of the oil conglomerate, instead of accepting Tarbell's writing as an example of thorough journalism, clung to it as support for their own position. When they recognized that Tarbell was even-handed in her consideration of the oil business, they cast her aside. As she put it, "I saw I had ruined my reputation as the Joan of Arc of the oil industry."[52]

Tarbell's professionalism and reason might have cast her as Joan of Arc for the feminists, too, but her completely independent life as a successful woman conflicted with her oft-stated belief that the best place for a woman was in the home, caring for a family. Articles addressing the apparent contradiction are included in this collection. In time, Tarbell emerged as a forceful defender of nineteenth-century views of women and their social roles. Suffragists were upset to see Tarbell's name cited in antisuffrage literature and were dismayed when she, a successful, emancipated woman, accepted speaking engagements with local antisuffrage societies.[53]

Tarbell's arguments against the women's-rights movement were expressed as early as 1909, in a series she wrote for the *American Magazine,* and then more fully in a 1912 series, later compiled in book form as *The Business of Being a Woman.* Robert Stinson suggests two possible causes of her apparent conversion to an antifeminist posture. First, perhaps Tarbell at mid-life resented that, at an early age, she had been pushed into a professional career that made a domestic life impossible. Second, Tarbell's stance may have manifested an old ambivalence regarding women's social roles, which might be traced back to her childhood.[54] Focused on the future, Progressives nevertheless discovered that the past could not be wholly rejected. It may be that Tarbell tried to cope with this problem on an individual level by maintaining an independent professional life while rejecting the feminist ideals that had led her to become a professional in the first place.[55]

It is not easy, however, to pinpoint where and when Tarbell decided to become a professional, if in fact she made such a decision consciously. Her work on *The Chautauquan* was hardly a professional breakthrough, and when she settled into her first journalism job on *The Chautauquan*, the move seemed almost frivolous, as she calculated that it would take little time and provide "pin money." Compared to the resolution she demonstrated in her forays into biology and teaching, her start in journalism seemed out of character.

She wanted, first, to be a professional in the broadest sense—not a professional biologist or teacher, but someone who possessed a profession that could be practiced to provide income. The details of the profession—biology or teaching, for example—could come later. The goal was freedom, and it entailed never marrying.

At one point in the 1920s, Tarbell toured as a speaker on one of the Chautauqua circuits in the Midwest. During one of the introductions preceding her talk, Tarbell heard a long explanation of why she had never married. She mentions this in her autobiography without comment and, unfortunately, does not repeat the explanation.

The mention of Tarbell's spinsterhood suggests that one difference between Tarbell and the feminists was that they insisted on literal equality between men and women, while Tarbell advocated a complementary, relative equality. Tarbell's version of equality likely reflected her childhood experience in a home with cooperating parents in her hometown of Rouseville.[56]

As Tarbell observed her parents' successful cooperative efforts, she saw and heard a great deal about the women's suffrage movement's goals and participants. She also perceived the movement's lack of unity, forming her own impressions of it and developing her own position relative to it. Some of her earliest journalism appears to have been an attempt to puncture feminists' claims that women had no creativity because they were a slave class. Tarbell's article, "Women as Inventors," published in the March 1887 issue of *The Chautauquan* and reprinted here, documents the thousands of patents held by American women. She said that such inventiveness showed that women had creativity.[57]

In Tomkins' appraisal of Tarbell's world view, she was interested in promoting the interests of the white, Anglo-Saxon middle class of which she was a part and which feared being overrun on one side by industrialists and on the other by immigrants. Tarbell saw America as an industrialized nation that held onto, yet also renewed, pre–Civil War institutions:

> The vision implicit in Tarbell's work was compounded of nostalgia for the past and a plan for a future that was to be organically evolved from it; and the vision revealed her belief in a human nature sufficiently perfectible to base actions as well as prayers on the Golden Rule. Thus would come into being a social order that would be assuredly the product of much sweat, but of no blood and few tears.[58]

As a child whose parents appreciated their church life and were generous in opening their doors to the advocates of new causes or to destitute oil-field workers, Tarbell indeed had been exposed to the Golden Rule. She saw its observance in Chautauqua founder Vincent, who advocated the Chautauqua Literary and Scientific Circle so that others, like himself unable to receive formal schooling, could be educated. And she demonstrated the rule in her journalism, working to get all the information on all sides of the topic she was addressing. Her point of view, she said, was that of a journalist pursuing facts and rarely that of a reformer, an advocate of a cause or system. Others would say that Tarbell exhibited a great deal of indignation in her writing about Standard Oil, but her interpretations were always supported by excellent documentation and had at least the appearance of objectivity.[59]

In 1939, at the age of eighty-two, Tarbell looked back over her life in the autobiography, a readable, entertaining, but often exasperating book, as Tarbell writes in it that she cannot remember why she did or thought certain things. On January 6, 1944, she died of pneumonia in a Bridgeport, Connecticut, hospital and was buried in Titusville, Pennsylvania.

Tarbell's lifetime drive to find the facts, to uncover, as she called it, reliable information, was her way of relating to truth as a haven amid uncertainty. As the people, events, ideas, and points of view surrounding Tarbell changed, her facts did not. As early as her first position on the staff of *The Chautauquan,* she worked with information, and she wanted to be sure it was correct.

An American Editor and His Magazine

Ida Tarbell's first editor, Theodore L. Flood—founder of *The Chautauquan,* a Methodist minister, a politician—was a complex and contradictory man who undoubtedly influenced her development as a journalist. The best biographical information is provided by Frank Chapin Bray, Flood's successor as editor of *The Chautauquan.* Bray describes the magazine in an article for the May 12, 1938, sesquicentennial edition of the *Tribune-Republican,* the Meadville, Pennsylvania, newspaper.

Flood was born February 20, 1842, in Blair County, Pennsylvania, and was educated at the academy of Blair County and at Dickson Seminary. Later he studied at the Concord Biblical Institution, which was to become the School of Theology of Boston University. Flood fought for the North in the Civil War and achieved the rank of lieutenant.[60] When he reached the age of eighteen, Flood was licensed in the Methodist Episcopal Church and served in several New England pastorates. He also served churches in southwestern New York State and northwestern Pennsylvania and was pastor of the Methodist Episcopal church in Jamestown, New York, at the time he left the pulpit to found *The Chautauquan.* Working in collaboration with Bishop John W. Hamilton, Flood wrote the book, *Lives of the Methodist Bishops.* He was politically active as an 1892 nominee for Congress, and he belonged to the Grandsons of the American Revolution. Flood was a trustee of Allegheny College in Meadville and was president of the board of directors of the Meadville Commercial College and of the Pennsylvania College of Music, which he had helped to found. He also helped organize the Meadville Country Club.[61]

Flood, then, was, to all appearances, a civic-minded citizen. But he had political aspirations, too—aspirations that some felt were in conflict with the demands of his ministry. Jesse Hurlbut noted that an early visit to Chautauqua Institution by President Ulysses S. Grant was arranged by Flood, "who although a successful Methodist minister was also somewhat of a politician."[62]

While questions about Flood's plans for the magazine's finances remain difficult to answer, his heart seemed to be in the right place in connection with the women's rights movement. In Meadville on April 4, 1880, he delivered a lecture in which he staunchly defended the cause of women's rights. The talk was reprinted in the *Daily Assembly Herald* soon after. According to an editor's explanation, the speech was given in response to an anti–women's rights talk reprinted in the *Herald*. The editor also noted that the opinions expressed in Flood's speech were his alone and did not reflect any Chautauqua dogma.[63]

In the article, Flood quickly made two points: that women ought to be granted the right to vote, and that they ought to be given the privilege of joining the clergy. "The Christian pulpit," Flood said, "cannot afford to longer neglect the claims of woman as a teacher and worker in the world." He asked the question, "What is the difference between the sexes? Is it so radical that man and woman cannot work in the same places in the world unitedly and harmoniously? . . . We have conquered prejudice to color and race, to a large extent, but we have not conquered political and ecclesiastical prejudice against women to the same extent."[64]

Flood publicly supported the cause of women, both in this address and in his enthusiastic employment of women as editorial staffers on *The Chautauquan*. Tarbell profited in no small way from her association with women who worked for the magazine, even if most were in the lower ranks of the magazine's staff.

Flood's connections with journalism and Chautauqua began in 1876, during the institution's third season, when the *Chautauqua Assembly Daily Herald* began publication. The newspaper, later renamed the *Chautauquan Daily*, carried day-by-day accounts of lectures and other events, schedules, and miscellaneous tidbits of information dealing with the institution. It was operated by Flood as a private venture, under the approving eye of the institution's leadership.[65]

The Chautauquan magazine, started in 1880, announced itself as "A Monthly Magazine, devoted to the promotion of true culture, organ of the Chautauqua Literary and Scientific Circle." The magazine had a captive audience. Much of the content was required reading for the Chautauqua Literary and Scientific Circle (CLSC), and as the membership list of the circle ballooned, so did the circulation of *The Chautauquan*. From an initial printing of fifteen thousand copies for the first issue in September 1880, circulation rose to fifty thousand five years later.[66]

Journalism historian Frank Luther Mott perceives one great advantage that the magazine had over all other general magazines of the time: it could use "a strong and successful self-culture organization to draw into its net all— or nearly all—the big fish in the intellectual sea. Its table of contents soon became a distinguished roll call." Mott also suggests that the editor feared the magazine might grow dry and dreary and accordingly devoted less space to the circle's required readings and more to increasingly varied nonrequired content.[67]

The magazine was not above carrying advertisements, some for books or patent medicines. Typical was the advice that "a sallow complexion, a languid, spiritless state of mind, and an exhausted, debilitated condition of the body, is always remedied by taking Barosma, and Dandelion and Mandrake pills."[68]

The guaranteed flock of subscribers and the advertising content make it unlikely that the magazine lost money; a brand-new printing plant is further evidence of financial well-being. But Flood's own discussion of the magazine in 1899 emphasized the financial risk he felt he had taken in starting it; he liked to stress the service provided by the magazine and not its revenues. Flood recalled that he felt the magazine to be a bold undertaking. He dwelt at length on his own poverty and that of the institution, but said he had finally concluded that there was

> no hope for my magazine financially, save in the constituency of the
> Chautauqua Assembly, but I had faith in the people and believed that
> Chautauqua was a growing cause and that it would draw many and strong
> friends who would stand by it in years to come. Besides I considered it a safe
> undertaking to build *The Chautauquan* as a pulpit from which to teach history
> and science, religion and philosophy, and the practical duties of human life.[69]

While Flood maintained in retrospect that he had started *The Chautauquan* as a clergyman with few resources, a contemporary of his at the institution had a different view. Jesse Hurlbut, Bishop Vincent's aide and eventual successor, recalled "Flood's already-established financial, business and editorial ability" and said that Flood had "ventured his capital boldly and won deserved success."[70]

Flood was fifty-seven years old when he quit *The Chautauquan*. There is no record of what he did in the remaining sixteen years of his life, but it is likely that Flood spent it in his characteristic civic activity in Meadville. He died June 26, 1915, in his Meadville residence.

Whatever questions can be raised about Flood's motives, it is clear that *The Chautauquan* was a fine magazine. Examination of its content for successive decades shows that it was by no means indifferent to changing tastes and interests.[71]

The Chautauquan also contributed a great deal to Meadville, Pennsylvania, the community where it was printed and where Allegheny College was located. Over time, the growing magazine elicited increasing recognition from the town, at least in part because its publication provided work for approximately two hundred persons.

Many of these magazine employees were women. According to an article in which the magazine described its own printing, "In both these departments [business office and wrapper writers' room], the work is done entirely by women. The head book-keeper and cashier, assistants, advertising clerk, entering clerks and copyists are all women."[72]

The Chautauquan contained a wide variety of material. A typical issue, that of January 1883, contained articles on Russian and English history; Sunday readings; and feature stories on the driving of carriages, education for and against the caste system, Roumanian [*sic*] peasants and their songs, home life in Germany, the value of good food, tales from Shakespeare, and a tour around the world. There was also a lecture on thrift for women; articles on CLSC work and local circles; questions and answers on ancient Greece; the CLSC roundtable; columns entitled "Editor's Outlook," "Editor's Notebook," and "Editor's Table"; and a piece on the transit of Venus. One-quarter to one-third of the readings were required of the CLSC members as part of their ritual reading, and each issue separately indicated which articles were required.

In the articles not intended as part of the CLSC reading, variety was essential. Ample attention was given to science and etiquette, and not infrequently, households in foreign lands or ancient civilizations were portrayed. The geography of the continents was described, and references to physical exercise were aimed at keeping readers in good health. Many articles in the magazine appeared directed at its female readership. These articles ranged in subject from Mormon polygamy through social duties in the family and government employment for women to women's work in archaeology.

The forty-minutes-a-day reading regimen prescribed by CLSC founder Vincent would have meant a slow journey through each issue of *The Chautauquan*. But the person following it would have been exposed to the classics and fine literature, to other countries and interesting people, to the latest in science and the oldest in archaeology, and to information that would whet the appetite for more. The magazine was in itself an education, and its excellent editorial content, if slightly ponderous, was a boon to those craving knowledge.

For Tarbell, *The Chautauquan* was a further boon, offering exposure to a successful editor and to an unusually self-conscious approach to education. The success of the approach was not lost on Tarbell, who herself embraced a similarly dedicated pursuit of education.

American Women according to *The Chautauquan*

Tarbell was a rare woman, one whose personal life and journalistic accomplishments were guided by conventions different from those that governed the lives of most other women of her era. Her personality and professional work were colored by her environment, a crucial element of which was *The Chautauquan*; the people who surrounded her and their attitudes figured importantly in this formative stage of her career. The magazine carried a large number of articles by and for women and reflected a variety of viewpoints on the "woman question." Of particular significance when discussing Tarbell are the journal's pieces dealing with women in the workplace, women's wages, and women's education.

On the one hand, the magazine showed a home-and-motherhood point of view in Frances Power Cobbe's "Duties of Women as Mistresses of Households," while, on the other hand, it favored women's rights, as in "The Emancipation of Married Women."[73] As she worked for the magazine, Tarbell was surrounded by this variety of attitudes, as reflected in articles about women.

Author Pattie L. Collins observed in *The Chautauquan* in 1884 that the doctrine of "equal pay for equal work" was not enforced in America but that the prospects for its enforcement were improving.[74] Two years later, Mary A. Livermore echoed Collins in pushing the "equal work, equal pay" doctrine and went further, contending that if equality in pay were not afforded, women would be left with but one alternative—selling themselves.[75] An anonymous 1882 article argued that men could not keep education for themselves while denying it to women.[76]

In 1887, one author said that if a woman were willing to study humbly, earnestly, and thoroughly, success would be certain. But the author's scope was limited to such fields as small-fruit growing, market-gardening, and bee-keeping.[77]

Collins' article apparently drew many comments, and seven months later she offered a sequel, in which she criticized departments in the federal government as male bastions. In no way apologizing for her original article, Collins accused men of worrying that their free time would be threatened if women entered their lair.[78]

Another writer in *The Chautauquan* was Frances E. Willard, a vigorous opponent of liquor and proponent of women's suffrage, who recommended journalism as a good field for women. She said in July 1886 that journalism, next to philanthropy, was the best field for the intellectual woman, because the "woman question" could be settled in the "republic of letters." Moreover, the journalist was in good company and there was a smaller chance of discontinuity in income than in many fields. Journalism, Willard felt, was a calling in which specialties abounded and was a profession of "unbounded usefulness and power."[79]

In 1887, Tarbell, too, wrote about women in journalism for *The Chautauquan*.[80] What she wrote revealed her belief that men and women were suited to different roles. For instance, she wrote that the best kind of journalism for women included the household column ("which is growing in favor and only a woman can edit such a department with skill"), the social field ("she has the light, bright touch combined with the good taste which makes the social column so fascinating and so inoffensive"); and philanthropy and moral reform. Even though Tarbell specified these "soft" areas of journalism for women, she said that a woman's work must be as strong and finished as a man's in order for her to find a job.[81] And it is ironic, of course, that, in a few short years, Tarbell herself would be practicing journalism of the hard-hitting, male-dominated sort.

A minister who wrote in the magazine on the subject of women in art was nearly carried away by grandiloquence when he chastised men for hindering women:

> Had cruel man given woman a chance, and not imprisoned her in the
> kitchen or nursery, she would have written an Iliad, delivered an Oration on
> the Crown, composed an Oratorio like the "Creation" or the "Messiah," conceived a Novum Organum, built a Parthenon or St. Peter's, carved a Theseum
> or Laocoön, painted a Vatican State or a Sistine Chapel.[82]

An unsigned "Editor's Outlook" column in 1889 looked with pleasurable expectation on the progress women would make in the field of literature. Its author commented that the opening of doors to higher education to women was only just beginning and that it was one of the "stupendous" movements of the century.[83]

In winter 1889, *The Chautauquan* took note of the government's interest in women and their advancement and viewed as an encouraging sign a U.S. Commission of Labor report that was the first official recognition of working women by the government. The report was said to "inspire every working woman with the feeling that she is a citizen of government that seeks to promote her welfare; and that it is not simply a Government of men, for men, and by men."[84]

While such statements may seem empty oratory, it should be noted the magazine also could be serious and practical. An article by Julia Ward Howe, a prominent woman and author of "The Battle Hymn of the Republic," dealt with medicine, theology, and law. Howe warned:

> The woman . . . who takes up a profession takes up a burden which she is
> not at liberty either to carry lightly, or to lay down at pleasure. Let her refrain
> from it unless she is capable of true and persevering devotion to the interests
> of others, and willing to add to her zeal and creditable ambition all the skill
> and value which study and experience can give.[85]

While *The Chautauquan* carried articles in support of women's rights, it also affirmed the traditional role of women. Grace H. Dodge, in January 1889, wrote about societies established in urban areas for working girls, recounting the ways in which these societies served these women, who led squalid lives and were forced by necessity into factories. Some of the titles of talks addressed to the working girls were "Womanhood," "Purity," "Men Friends," "How to Get a Husband," "Money, How to Get It, How to Keep It," and "Home Life."[86]

One 1886 article, "A Business Education for Girls," at first glance appears to deal with a profession, but in fact it was intended to prepare women who might be left homeless, orphaned, or widowed to cope with life.[87] It did not allow that a woman might have wanted to pursue business as a profession.

One author in 1889 was willing for a woman to work, but "when a woman once begins to earn wages she seldom gives up her position for anything but marriage."[88]

The January 1884 issue of *The Chautauquan* carried the longest list of jobs suitable for women published in the magazine in the 1880s. It was from a review of "Work for Women" in Putnam's "Handy-Volume Series." Professions for women were: industrial drawing, dry-goods and house-furnishings salesperson, phonography, telegraphy, feather curling ("There is a serious drawback, however—the girls and women are not always moral, and the association is thus dangerous"), nursing, photography, proofreading, typesetting, bookbinding, lecturing, public reading, bookselling, dressmaking, millinery, beekeeping, poultry raising, market gardening, and cultivating flowers.[89] None of the jobs required higher education.

All the articles cited, plus others not mentioned, were carried in *The Chautauquan* while Tarbell was one of its editors. There is no evidence that Tarbell had any connection with them (Flood would allow only his name to appear on the masthead), but it is likely that she did.

So it was with some of the articles in *The Chautauquan* dealing with women's rights at the time Tarbell first was being exposed to journalism. The magazine, which had an important role in the journalism Tarbell would practice, seemed to strive for balance as it exposed her to a picture of women's rights. In this aspect *The Chautauquan* figured in the development of Tarbell's journalism.

Seven Years on *The Chautauquan*

One Sunday morning in Meadville in 1890, Tarbell was startled when an elderly Scotch Presbyterian minister leaned over his pulpit, shook a fist at his congregation, and shouted, "You're dyin' of respectability!" His accusation worried her, and Tarbell perceived that her pleasant complacency on *The Chautauquan* was a trap. The realization was part of her decision to leave the magazine, but her departure did not come before she had learned significant things about women as workers and friends and about journalism as her career.

Tarbell's years on *The Chautauquan* exposed her to women on a daily working basis. The staff's composition was largely female. In the autobiography, the first photo of Tarbell as an adult is with four other women, all members of the magazine's office staff. When she talked about the magazine's search for Allegheny College graduates for its staff, she named only women, even though there were vastly more men at the college. And when she found housing in Meadville, it was as part of a group of five women—known as the "co-ops"—who rented a house near the offices of *The Chautauquan*.[90] As part of this group and as part of the magazine, Tarbell was welcomed into other groups of women. As part of these groups, she recognized, perhaps for the first time, that women could constitute an intellectual force:

> We were taken into one of the most interesting and delightful little
> groups of women to which I have ever belonged. The group was made up of
> one or more from each of the three or four sets in town which rather prided
> themselves on being intellectual. They were not pretentious about it, if a bit
> solemn. . . . The Co-ops were rather proud of being accepted by these serious
> ladies and I think kept up their end rather well.[91]

Working for *The Chautauquan,* living as part of a group of women, participating in discussion groups—all these combined to sensitize her to women's issues and to help her form the attitudes toward women that she repeatedly addressed in her writing.

She also learned to appreciate journalistic routine that later would lend authority to what she wrote. Her mentor in this regard was Adrian McCoy, foreman of the magazine's print shop, who

> installed a proper respect for the dates on which copy was to be in, and forms closed; showed me the importance of clean copy by compelling me to see with my own eyes the time it took to make a correction, trained me until I could stand over the closing of the last form and direct the necessary changes. . . . When I could do that nonchalantly I felt as if I had arrived.[92]

Tarbell felt the satisfaction born of hard work. "I . . . threw myself heartily into an attempt to learn how to make up a magazine. . . . My willingness to take on loose ends. . . . I was not satisfied . . . with setting to rights and counseling the unhappy. . . . I became ambitious to contribute."[93]

Tarbell's interest in journalism was awakening. She was losing patience with the mundane tasks for which she was hired. She wanted to contribute articles to *The Chautauquan.* She noticed that, as her early, timid forays into journalism strengthened her position on the magazine, her capacity for self-expression grew. And as it did, so too did the drive that gave her work greater strength and prominence throughout her career. Tarbell began to write signed articles in the magazine, the first being "The Arts and Industries of Cincinnati," in the November 1886 issue. The article, which is in this collection, reflected Tarbell's rectitude and focused on the moral weaknesses of the city.[94]

During Tarbell's stint on the magazine, her social awareness blossomed and her interest in reform grew. Her particular editorial concerns on the magazine were its treatment of the problems and issues of the eighties, labor, slums, and temperance prominent among them.[95] She wrote that, by the time she left *The Chautauquan,* she had concluded that a trilogy of wrongs—all curable—were responsible for repeated depressions and poorly distributed wealth: discriminatory transportation rates, tariffs save for revenue only, and private ownership of natural resources.

Tarbell admitted that she might not be a writer, but she asserted that she was a good planner, had a sense of what mattered in a subject, and possessed a habit of steady, painstaking work that, she said, ought to count for something. As these traits developed, she began to think of what lay beyond her comfortable corner on *The Chautauquan*. And as she pondered whether to leave the magazine, she at last realized what she wanted to do: "It was no longer to seek truth with a microscope. My early absorption in rocks and plants had veered to as intense an interest in human beings."[96] She said she was becoming intent on observing people, and on collecting and classifying information about them. The detail-sorting routines Tarbell had practiced on the magazine were manifesting themselves in a way she could apply for a future in journalism.

As Tarbell grew dissatisfied with the direction her profession was taking on the magazine, she determined to leave its staff:

> I was scared by what *The Chautauquan* seemed to be doing to the plan I had worked out for the development of my mind. I had grown up with a stout determination to follow one course of study to the end, to develop a specialty. The work I was doing demanded a scattering of mind which I began to fear would unfit me for ever thinking anything through. . . . I did not want to be an editor. But to break with *The Chautauquan* meant sacrificing security. I had always had a vision of myself settled somewhere in a secure corner, simple, not too large. . . . I probably should not have been willing to sacrifice what I think I had honestly earned if there had not been growing upon me a conviction of the sterility of security.[97]

In the autobiography, Tarbell describes her departure from the magazine:

> When I told my editor-in-chief I was leaving, going to Paris to study, he was shocked. "How will you support yourself?" he asked, really anxious, knowing that I must depend on my own efforts.
> "By writing," I said.
> "You're not a writer," he said. "You'll starve."
> He had touched on the weakest point in my venture: I was not a writer, and I knew it.[98]

Flood said Tarbell was not a writer, yet, in a letter to her dated March 19,

1891, he said, "Permit me, however, to express my high appreciation of your abilities as a writer."[99] Further, in a letter of recommendation dated March 25, 1891, Flood described Tarbell as "an accomplished writer of scholarly habit."[100]

Tarbell's departure is shrouded in unknowns. In addition to the above discrepancies, Flood's letters make references to Tarbell's health. In the first letter to Tarbell cited above, Flood said, "I regret exceedingly that impaired health has forced you to detach yourself from *The Chautauquan*."[101] And in the second letter, while Flood lauded Tarbell as "a Christian lady of excellent character, fine reputation and high social position," he went on to refer to the "precarious condition of her health."[102] The autobiography does not refer to any ill health; the fact that she wrote *All in the Day's Work* as an octogenarian would seem to indicate a strong constitution.

Not only does Tarbell herself fail to mention any health problems, but she referred in an article to the need for health: "The power to work makes health an essential. Indeed, no ambitious woman should go into journalism without this qualification. While she may do the work of a department, she cannot carry the responsibility of higher positions without the steady nerve and the fire which health alone makes possible."[103]

When Tarbell walked out of magazine's offices in Meadville for the last time, she left little behind, but she took much with her. Tarbell left with seven years' experience on a magazine, experience that had directed her into journalism as her chosen profession. She had been exposed to a balanced point of view on women.

Tarbell was *The Chautauquan*'s legacy to American journalism. She and her work would be remembered for many years, while the magazine would suffer a largely unnoticed death. During her seven years in Meadville, Tarbell had developed confidence in her abilities as a journalist and had come to believe that no job or affiliation or conviction was so important that it could not be left behind. That confidence enabled her to take chances that most women of her time were unlikely to take.

Tarbell's editing and writing taught her three characteristics of good journalism: balance (*The Chautauquan* carried articles on both sides of the women's rights question), explanation (annotating articles for the magazine constituted further explanation of them), and accuracy (as composing room foreman Adrian McCoy drummed into her). As Tarbell increasingly dedicated herself to the practice of balance, explanation, and accuracy, her journalism more and more became a pursuit of "reliable information," a focus that guided her lifetime of research.

Why Read Tarbell Today?

Reading Tarbell's journalism is essential for understanding the muckraking or Progressive era in American history and opens new perspectives on issues important in the years that followed. A thorough reading is also important if one wishes to know Tarbell as an author; the autobiography and existing biographies do not give a complete picture of a person who was called the most popular woman in America. Tarbell lived for her writing, poured all her energies into it; through her writing we can see the essence of her intellect and glimpse the joint influence of her family, *The Chautauquan* and its editor, and the times.

The selections in this anthology reflect Tarbell's intensity, professionalism, and contradictions, and they show how a foundation in biography and muckraking led to Tarbell's later writing.

Thomas Connery calls muckraking a branch of literary journalism, and it is possible to see how Tarbell's work fits that description:

> Like its descendant of the 1970s and 1980s, literary journalism in the late nineteenth and early twentieth centuries often contained factual information common in conventional journalism, but focused on presenting impressions, details, and description not central to the typical conventional newspaper report. In the process, this created a different context as well. That is, such writing did not simply present facts, but the "feel" of the facts.[104]

Tarbell, then, was more than a muckraker; the biography that came before her muckraking work and the essays and articles that followed it are as valuable as her Standard Oil investigation. Her overall stance as a literary journalist provides a framework for examining her writing.

The divisions of this anthology—"Biography: Tarbell Looks at People," "A Woman's Eye on Business," "Issues of Home and Career for Women," and

"Tarbell Reacts to Her Times"—are intended to show how Tarbell approached the four principal topic areas of her nearly sixty years of writing. They are arranged roughly in chronological order, as the biographies are the first notable pieces she wrote and the general observations of life and social issues are the last.

Through this arrangement, it is possible to trace Tarbell's growth as a journalist and her changing understanding of how to approach not only assignments, but life. She began with very specific, particular topics, the biographies. Her muckraking and business writing dealt with subjects of increasing breadth; Standard Oil was not the only monopoly, and issues relating to the workplace were appropriate in many settings. Finally, as Tarbell approached the end of her career, her topics became virtually universal: religion, generosity, poverty, and old age. Her thoughts on these topics reveal a degree of compassion and outrage that would have seemed out of place for her years earlier, but those years of life experience richly equipped Tarbell to be as much a social observer as a reporter after the facts. One of the values of this collection is to enable readers to go beyond the muckraking, for which this extraordinary woman is best remembered, to broader topics in which her passion is as memorable as her facts.

Tarbell's writing paralleled the increasing complexity of life and society in the United States. As Baker and Anderson note, "Journalism is important in a complex society because only a minuscule portion of the social world is experienced directly."[105] Tarbell made it possible for her readers to experience in painstaking detail some of the important but distant issues affecting their lives. And, through her unmistakable fact-based approach, she still makes it possible for today's readers to gain insight into personalities, workplaces, and issues of her time.

Biographer Brady claims that Tarbell's tragedy was that she never knew the triumph of her success.[106] Tarbell did indeed succeed, and the fruits of her success—the articles she wrote—have to be read to understand her times and to know just how serious, indeed, was her work.

The Writings of Ida Tarbell

Part I
Biography

Introduction

Why would someone like Ida Tarbell write about dead French women? Three of the five biographical articles in this section deal with French women, and Tarbell obviously was fascinated by them. Her articles about Madame de Staël and Manon Phlipon Roland followed her article on women inventors, which had fired in her a desire to question the argument that men made the world.

In thinking about women and their roles in the world, Tarbell came to focus on the French Revolution and its women, who excited her most, she wrote. The excitement could have come from her own experience. Perhaps without knowing what to call it, Tarbell and her Meadville roommates, the "co-ops," constituted a sort of salon, where deep and layered conversations gave meaning to their experiences. When she came across Madame de Staël, who oversaw a brilliant salon in Paris, Tarbell must have felt that she had encountered a historical sisterhood. And when she found Madame Roland, according to biographer Brady, she found "the spark that exploded the frustration within her."[1] It was impossible to write about these personalities while holding her job in Meadville, so Tarbell left and began to study French women in the most appropriate of places.

It is in her biographical writing that Tarbell best shows her abilities in narration and description, and in the last selection here she gives readers a glimpse of the power of her feelings on social issues. The pieces in this section, while plodding in spots, generally do a good job of illuminating the lives—and deaths—of her subjects. Tarbell tried to depict her subjects' lives by showing not only what they did but also who surrounded them. This is particularly true in the article about Madame Roland, whose life was informed by her contemporaries.

These pieces reveal more than the others how well Tarbell could craft a narrative thread to unify her work. Biography required narration and chronology in ways that her examination of issues and situations did not, and Tarbell was able to write moving narratives that readily take the reader through the life she is describing.

A somewhat macabre aspect of these pieces is that three of them deal with persons who had unusual deaths—assassination, execution, and accident. It is unlikely that Tarbell had a fascination with death, but the unusual fates of her subjects add a luster to their lives that make them a degree more interesting.

The first piece, dealing with Madame de Staël, is a detailed look at a French revolutionary character, one better known for the quality of her *salon* than for the drama of her death. Tarbell's research ability is evident here; even though this work was written in the United States, the names, quotations, and locations in it show the kind of precision that marks her writing.

Madame de Staël's companions in *repartee* were among France's most colorful figures. Freed perhaps by the fact that she was considering things French, Tarbell let a dash of humor into this article, noting of Madame de Staël's husband: "The Baron's chief claim on posterity's attention is that he was the husband of his wife."

The second article here, "The Queen of the Gironde," is a thorough and in places literary account of the life of Manon Phlipon, later Manon Roland. The writing can be appealing: "The roofs of Paris are silvered by moonlight. The streets under the softening influence of night and weariness are quiet." But it could also be obscure: "To her always the highest virtue was to do the evident thing. It might be commonplace and irksome. But was it not her duty, and to do one's duty was it not to reach the heights of philosophy and to ally one's self with the Infinite Right which governs the universe?"

The writing could be a bit hyperbolic also: "Her bars free her. Her jailers are her deliverers. Death is her savior. The soul which dared to assert itself in a pure love can face the Eternal fearlessly. It is to society that it cannot reveal itself. *Comprendre, c'est pardonner. God understands. Society will not.*"

The description of Mme. Roland's death is stark: "At the foot of the guillotine she makes a last request of the bloody Sanson, to let etiquette go and spare her companion [a terrified man] the misery of seeing her die. And Sanson, a little shamefaced, consents. Then the ax falls. The beautiful head drops. Mme. Roland is free."

The next selection, Tarbell's account of the aftermath of Abraham Lincoln's assassination, ties together a number of vignettes from different people and places around the country, and in so doing gives the sort of perspective that Tarbell often used. Lincoln was assassinated when Tarbell was eight years old, and the feeling and depth in her report may have reflected her recollection of Lincoln. For her, from the time of his death, "the name spelt tragedy and mystery. Why all this sorrow over a man we had never seen, who did not belong to our world—*my* world?"

There is much detail about the funeral train and its thirteen-day trip to Springfield, Illinois, and burial. The trip took its toll on Lincoln's remains. She writes of the citizens of Springfield as they wept over his coffin:

> Their grief at finding him so changed was inconsolable. In the days after leaving Washington the face changed greatly, and by the time Springfield was reached it was black and shrunken almost beyond recognition. To many the last look at their friend was so painful that the remembrance has never left them. The writer has seen men weep as they recalled the scene, and heard them say repeatedly, "If I had not seen him dead; if I could only remember him alive!"

Tarbell surely realized what a distasteful image this was, but she used it none-theless, as it was a relevant aspect of Lincoln's funeral trip.

Tarbell's 1909 book on Napoleon includes a sizable section on Josephine, whose daily routines and travels seem to have fascinated Tarbell, so painstaking are the descriptions. It is a classic example of her prose. Sparing with adverbs and adjectives, Tarbell obviously sought just the right words to convey description and motion.

One section on Josephine demonstrates Tarbell's love of detail and com-prehensiveness. She describes Josephine's household: "There were a First Al-moner, a Maid of Honor, a Lady of the Bedchamber, numbers of Ladies of the Palace, a First Chamberlain, a First Equerry, a Private Secretary, a Chief Stew-ard—all of them having their respective attendants; and there were, besides these, valets, footmen, pages and servants of all grades."

Another passage also shows Tarbell's attention to detail: "In one year she bought one hundred and thirty-six dresses, twenty cashmere shawls, seventy-three corsets, forty-eight pieces of elegant stuffs, eighty-seven hats, seventy-one pairs of silk stockings, nine hundred and eighty pairs of gloves, five hundred and twenty pairs of shoes."

Josephine had profligate spending habits, but Tarbell perhaps viewed them in light of the hardships of being Empress of the French and Queen of Italy. Tarbell refers to "the fatiguing duties attendant upon official journeys in foreign countries and upon holding court in a strange city" and "her exacting and slavish position." In fact, Tarbell describes Josephine's one pleasure as acquiring items for her toilet.

The final biographical piece here, "A Noble Life," deals with Carola Woerishoffer, a prime player in what Tarbell called the "Revolt of the Young Rich." Tarbell writes with a strongly approving tone that makes clear her support of such worthy social causes as were pursued by Woerishoffer.

The year in which this piece was published, 1912, is generally considered the last year of the muckrakers' dominance, and in it Tarbell may be reflecting her own withdrawal from muckraking. The attention to detail remains strong, as always, and Tarbell uses relevant sources and quotes. But this piece seems to parallel the transition from muckraking to citizen-based activism, as it describes (as a muckraker might have) the woeful conditions that Woerishoffer tried to rectify, but then goes on to show how she succeeded in improving those conditions.

Woerishoffer, who died of injuries suffered in a car accident at age twenty-six, was born of a wealthy family and spent her few post-graduation years doing good works. She contributed large sums of money to important causes but did so modestly, avoiding attention or publicity in her philanthropy.

Particularly in the Lincoln and Woerishoffer pieces, Tarbell's biography goes beyond demonstrating a lucid prose style that can remain a model for good writing even today. The selections here identify people Tarbell found important not just in history, but in her own soul as well.

Madame de Staël

The time is one hundred years ago, the place a brilliant salon of Paris. Prominent in the company stand a couple in animated conversation. The lady is a plain person: her mouth is large, her features bold, her manners brusque, her voice harsh, her dress careless, and she twirls in her fingers a sprig of green. She has fine eyes, however, a splendid head of hair, and noble arms and shoulders. Her companion is an American, a handsome man in spite of the loss of a leg. He has a humorous, quizzical expression, a keen eye, full proud lips. His name is Gouverneur Morris and he is in Paris on business. He looks as if he would be a success at making either love or bargains. Madame de Staël, for this is the lady's name, is plying him with questions. Has he not written a book on the American Constitution? No, he did his part in aiding in framing the Constitution. How did he lose his leg? Unfortunately not in the service of his country. More of the same nature follows. Mr. Morris, who is studying French society as well as attending to business, goes home to record this conversation in his diary and to make comments on it which show him to think the lady a rather amusing character. Her position, however, Morris tacitly recognizes as prominent and important. She is, in fact, the wife of the Swedish minister in France, the Baron de Staël-Holstein. Her father, M. Necker, is the French minister of finance to Louis XVI, her mother, a woman who is famous in Paris for her beauty and culture, and, most unusual at that time, her austere virtue and active philanthropy.

The twenty-three years which Germaine de Staël has lived have been full of rich social and intellectual experiences. At her birth her father, a man of spotless character, was a partner in the most famous French banking house of the times, the Thellusons, and her mother, who had the distinction of being the heroine of the historian Gibbon's only love affair, was the center of a salon in which gathered weekly such men as Diderot, the encyclopedist, D'Alembert, the philosopher, Marmontel, the critic, Buffon, the naturalist, the Abbe Galiani,

From *The Chautauquan* 9 (July 1889): 579–82.

political economist, the German wit, Baron Grimm, Abbe Morellet, the *litterateur*, men of the brightest wits, quickest tongues, and most solid accomplishments in all France. As soon as little Germaine could sit squarely on a stool she was allowed to join the throng, and before she was twelve she made a fine reputation as a listener and a talker, the cleverest men of Paris paying her homage.

Madame Necker, enchanted with the brilliancy of her daughter, turned her mind to her education, a subject on which she had theories—not including natural development. She held Germaine rigidly to her system and encouraged her conversation with the *habitués* of her salon. The child's wonderful mind grasped everything laid before it; more, she transformed everything. Her heart was as sensitive as her mind; she was filled with despair at reproach or neglect, with the most passionate fondness at attention and appreciation. The pitch at which her nature stood had its effects. Her health began to fail. The physician ordered no books, and out-of-door life. She was turned loose at St. Ouen, a few miles from Paris, where the Neckers had a summer home.

Madame Necker, disappointed at the failure of her "system," looked coldly on her daughter's freedom. Germaine was deeply hurt at her mother's reproachful mien and turned to her father. M. Necker when his daughter was about six years old had given up private banking for public financiering. His wealth, integrity and his publications on finance led to his appointment as Director-General of the treasury, but the reforms he instituted made him enemies, and in 1781 he fell from power. This was at the time of Germaine's emancipation and the two soon became boon companions.

Five years pass and Germaine has become a woman of twenty. As a conversationalist she is considered unparalleled. Her *elogues* and portraits (it was the fashion of the day to write and read in the salons sketches of one's friends) were famous. She had done some respectable literary work. Every record left of her at this period is extravagant in her praises.

But a girl must marry. Madame Necker reasoned that as Germaine was a marvelous creature and would have seventy thousand dollars a year, she ought to marry so as to do a good deal for the family, which, though she had tried hard to prove otherwise, was purely *bourgeois*. Madame Necker's choice was young William Pitt of England, afterward so famous as a statesman and orator. But Germaine would not think of him. There were other equally desirable suitors. At last, after much negotiation, the matter was settled, and Germaine Necker became in 1786 the Baroness de Staël-Holstein. The Baron's chief claim on posterity's attention is that he was the husband of his wife.

When Morris met Germaine in Paris she was one of the most influential women of the city. She had the *entree* of the court. Her mother's salon was really hers, as Madame Necker was giving most of her time to the hospitals, and so brilliant had she made it that Morris calls it a chamber of Apollo, a *chambre ardente*. There was everything in the intellectual and social atmosphere of the time to stimulate a sensitive, vibrative nature like hers. The Revolution had begun, the Bastille had fallen. The wildest theories received applause. A party could be formed for any scheme. Philosophy and religion were in a chaotic state. Mesmerism was mystifying society. Madame de Staël's active mind grasped with extraordinary penetration and justice all the contradictory impulses and opinions afloat.

She was not less distinguished for the goodness of her heart and her intense friendships. For her father she had a devotion so idolatrous that it was romantic. Morris called it "exuberant vanity," and quotes her as saying that wisdom is a very rare quality, and she knows of no one who possesses it in a superlative degree except her father.

But he was far from comprehending the rich love which Germaine de Staël bestowed upon those dear to her. Her relations with the men of her salon he mistook as he did her attitude toward her father. Her marriage had been a purely business transaction. In no degree did her husband satisfy her ardent heart. Her conviction that the highest happiness is found in a satisfying marriage was not in harmony with her experience. In the men who thronged her salon and whose hearts and minds matched her own she sought a completer intellectual and spiritual union. The most devoted of her friends at this period was the gallant Count de Narbonne, who like herself was at the beginning of the Revolution a Constitutionalist. Morris always spoke of Narbonne as her lover and gives several anecdotes which sound very flippant. But Morris himself was flirting when he wrote and saw no deeper in those around him. Madame de Staël's relations were far from light or vulgar. They were in the best sense, friendships. Whenever she met a nature which appealed in any way to her own, she turned frankly to it. She claimed close sympathy as a natural right.

But the Revolution advances, and Madame de Staël begins to feel its power. Her father who had been called to his position as minister of finance in 1788 is obliged to resign in 1790. The atrocious outrages against the nobility begin. Madame de Staël sees her friends in danger of their lives, and she makes the most strenuous efforts to save them. Narbonne, Jancourt, and Lally-Tollendal are among those whom she saves at this time. But her activity endangers her own life. She attempts to leave Paris in a coach and six, is arrested and taken to the Hotel de Ville whence few now go save to the guillotine. After a short imprisonment she escapes and joins her father at his estate, Coppet, in Switzerland.

The chateau at Coppet stands above Lake Geneva. In the magnificent sweep it commands, fall the lake, the city, and the mountains of Savoy. Here, though surrounded by her family, the splendid beauty of the spot, and having access to the cultured society of Geneva, Madame de Staël can find no peace. Paris, its salons, its passionate vivacity, its impetuous, spontaneous naturalness have been her life since she can remember. Now she longs for its very horrors, since they drag down so many of her friends. Her exertions to secure passports for them are tireless. But her craving for conversation and companionship at last mastered her and she went to England to join a company of *emigrés* who had taken a country seat, Juniper Hall, at Mickleham in Surrey. Talleyrand, Narbonne, the Duc de Montmorency, and General D'Arblay, all from her circle of intimate friends, are there. This brilliant company was an amazement to the English who joined it, Fannie Burney, the fashionable novelist of the day, declaring that she had never heard conversation before.

Two classes of proscribed Frenchmen were scattered over Europe, the Royalists and the Moderate Republicans, who had encouraged the Revolution in its beginning as a method of reform. The Neckers were of the latter class and they gathered about them at Coppet many sympathetic friends. The place rapidly became famous for the brilliancy of its coterie. Madame de Staël, whose stay in England was but for a few months was doing for it what Goethe and Schiller did for Weimar, and Voltaire, for Ferney. Morris, who since we met him in Paris, has served a term as United States Minister to France, has seen the atrocities of the Revolution, and who is now only lingering in Europe because the situation is so interesting, comes there in 1794, and finds a "little French society which live at her expense and are as gay as circumstances will permit."

But a turn is coming. On the 28th of July, 1794, Robespierre fell. To the Reign of Terror succeeded a hysterical gaiety. Slowly, and not without spasms of revolt and murder, the nation regained self-control. Reason was firmly enough seated by August, 1795, to admit of a government. It was called the Directory. Sweden was the first country to recognize the new republic, and in October, '95, Baron de Staël was returned. Paris was once more opened to Madame. She came in haste and opened a salon which at once becomes powerful and popular. Her Republican principles—for she now avowed thorough Republicanism—governed the politics of her salon, and made it the headquarters of the best talent of that party. But a friend was always dearer than an idea to this woman of ideas, and all her friends of anti-Revolutionary days were welcomed. Many of those she loved were proscribed, and she intrigued incessantly to secure their return and with much success; among those she brought back were Talleyrand and Dupont de Nemours. This "pernicious activity" exposed her to new perils, and she was denounced from the Tribune, but defended. Later she was sentenced to leave France, but the Baron de Staël managed to save her.

After the fall of Robespierre, when Madame de Staël adopted Republicanism, she had said, "France can never become a mixed monarchy without passing through a military despotism." While the Directory is governing France, the armies of France, under Napoleon Bonaparte, are preparing the despot to carry out her prophecy. In 1799 the French army returned from Egypt. Its leader was the hero of the nation. It was a simple matter for him to make the *coup d'etat* by which the Directory was overturned and he made First Consul. Madame de Staël, who, in the earlier portion of Napoleon's career, had hoped to find in him liberal and patriotic principles, but had been bitterly disappointed, could not be too harsh against his usurpation. She inspired her circle, which had the importance of a party, with revolt, and she inflamed her brilliant and fascinating friend, Benjamin Constant, whom Napoleon had placed in the Tribunate, until he dared use his splendid eloquence openly against the government.

Napoleon had never admired Madame de Staël. Women were created for two purposes, in his opinion, to bear children, and to please men. When Madame de Staël, her bonnet crooked, her gown awry, her eyes aflame, came flying up to him, bent on discovering his opinion, he promptly concluded she was the kind of woman society had no use for, and he bluffly let his disapproval of her be known. Nevertheless, he knew her influence, and after he seized the government he sent his brother, to promise her anything she wanted if she would stand by him. Her reply is famous: "It is not what I *want* but what I *think*." Here was a new experience for the First Consul: a woman, and in his way. It was too subtle for him. He was a muscle, she an intellect. He had no guns for riddling ideas.

Constant's first speech of open defiance emptied Madame de Staël's salon. It was only for a time. In 1800 she published her "Literature in Relation to Social Institutions." It is a work of wonderful suggestiveness, of bold generalities and daring grasp, and it made a sensation. Prior to this time her main literary work had been a school-girl story, an immature set of reflections on Rousseau, and a promising study of the "Influence of the Passions on Literature;" but the new work was strong, original, bold. De Fontaine, De Gerando, and Chateaubriand discussed it. By the force of her genius she conquered Napoleon. Her salon was again full. She recovered what she declared to be the most exquisite pleasure of her life—conversing in Paris.

She had paid no tribute to Napoleon in the "Literature." Indeed, she had written sentences there which showed that she believed in forces more powerful and more permanent than the Little Corsican's bullets. He took his revenge in a Napoleonic way. Her friends were bullied into cutting her as Talleyrand—who owed his return to France and his position to her—did, or were ostracized socially. She herself was finally ordered to within forty leagues of Paris. The exile thus begun was continued until 1814.

Contemptible as was Napoleon's exile of Madame de Staël, her subsequent resistance to him was thoroughly undignified and unnecessary. She had the satisfaction of having made a heroic stand against him. She knew the power of her pen. The only limit put on her movements was to prevent her coming within forty leagues of Paris. But she wailed vehemently and melodramatically under this restraint. To most persons to live above Lake Geneva, the center of a devoted, almost adoring, circle of great minds, would be life at the best. Common sense would say that a woman who could go as an exile from Paris into the court of Weimar and Berlin as the honored guest of kings and queens, poets and savants, associating with Schiller and Goethe, and carrying away as tutor to her children such a man as Auguste Schlegel—all this she did in the winter of 1803-4—had still something to live for. But Madame de Staël could endure no limitations. She made no compromises. She refused to accept the semi-sensual, semi-intellectual solution to which most of the world agrees. She demanded the completest liberty and fullest satisfaction. When she failed she was openly inconsolable.

But without the struggle against exile it is doubtful if she would have left the world what she has. Her grief over her father's death, which occurred early in 1804, and her longing for Paris induced her to spend the winter of 1804-5 in Italy, the result of which was her novel "Corinne," her only great novel, for "Delphine," published in 1802, is feverish and unsatisfactory. "Corinne" set intellectual Europe aflame. It is a novel which, rare thing, is still readable. Though the sentiment is full an octave too high, and the style extravagant for present taste, its matter is of the deepest interest, the more so because in "Corinne" we have so much of Madame de Staël.

It is to exile, again, that we owe her finest production, the "Germany." This splendid survey of a country then unrecognized by Europe, was published in Paris in 1810. The censors let her book pass, and she read the proof sheets. When the first edition of ten thousand copies was ready for distribution, the police took them to cut to pieces. A MS. [manuscript] was saved. It had been her plan to leave for America as soon as "Germany" was out, but she was too overwhelmed now for that. "Trailing the wing like La Fontaine's dove," as she says, she went to Coppet, but not to struggle as we should expect. She seems a new creature. In a few months we find her writing to her beautiful friend, Madame Recamier, "I experience at times a sort of calm which certainly comes not from myself, but from God." Madame de Staël, like many another woman, had discovered the consolations of religion through the medium of a lover. She had been divorced from the Baron de Staël in 1797. In 1811 she was secretly married to a French officer, Rocca by name. He was a handsome man with an interesting story of bravery and honorable wounds, deeply in love with her and determined to make her love him. He succeeded, in spite of the fact that he was twenty-two and she forty-five. This union brought her the deepest happiness she had ever known. It is usually called a "ridiculous marriage," but if marriage be judged by the degree of contentment and of spiritual development it causes, Madame de Staël's was far from ridiculous.

But there was no peace for her while Napoleon lived. He feared she would go to England and write against the government, and he forbade her going more than two leagues from Coppet. The Prefect of Geneva was dismissed for kindnesses shown to her. Montmorency, Schlegel, and Madame Recamier were exiled for their friendship to her. It was intolerable, and she determined to fly to England by the roundabout route of Russia and Sweden, a feat she accomplished in the year 1812-13. After reaching Russia her flight became a triumphal tour. On reaching London she brought out the "Germany." What de Tocqueville and Bryce have done for American political institutions, Madame de Staël did for German literature and society. Indeed, her book introduced Germany to Europe, beginning the work which Carlyle finished.

Courted and honored in London she, nevertheless, hastened with joy to Paris when the powers of Europe drove Napoleon from France in 1814. Her salon was re-established in all its old glory. Louis XVIII covered her with honors. Her old friends flocked about her. Life was worth living again, save that her health was poor. Then, like a rocket, Napoleon dropped on the scene, in March, 1815. This was but for the Hundred Days. Then Waterloo opened France to her forever. Another terror stood in her way. Rocca was slowly dying and her own health was going. She sought Italy, hoping that the climate might benefit them both. It was in vain. Coppet sees her at intervals, and the company is more brilliant than ever for Byron is there. In the winter of 1816 she returns to Paris. A wonderful company gathered about her: the Duke of Wellington, Sir Humphry and Lady Davy, Humboldt, Lafayette, Chateaubriand, Talleyrand, Constant, Sismondi, Schlegel, Canova, Barante, Madame Recamier, Ticknor. But it was plain she was dying now and would go before Rocca. By spring she was confined to her chamber, and on July 14, 1817, she died.

Her restless, dazzling, unsatisfied life was done, but the world had not yet had the full fruit of her exile and her suffering. In 1818 her "Considerations on the French Revolution" was published, a marvelous work in many respects, and of great influence on modern French liberalism. It was begun as a defense of Necker, whose inadequacy for the situation in 1790 Madame de Staël could never see. When she had a point to make in favor of a friend, she was a capital practical politician, but she could never recognize that her father lacked this essential quality. "Ten Years of Exile" followed the "Considerations," a running, dashing account of Napoleon's treatment of her, and her wanderings in consequence. Both works she left unfinished.

Generous to the point of self-sacrifice, loyal to friends, just to foes, true to her own impulses, sincere in heart, and brilliant in intellect, Germaine de Staël is, nevertheless, an unsatisfactory character. Her constant state of expansiveness, her lavish admiration of everybody, her demand for sympathy, her "unconscionable instability of talking and shining," as Byron put it, her incessant thinking, were too much for the ordinary human nature, and, indeed, for most natures above the ordinary, for the first opinion great minds formed of her was usually like Heine's, a "whirlwind in petticoats." Though they all sooner or later recognized that what we might call the "gush" of her nature, was from no shallow pool, but the outpouring of a deep, pure, and stimulating fountain, and concluded, like Morris, that she was a "woman of wonderful wit and above vulgar prejudices of every kind." One quality she lacked, that repose of soul which finds in spiritual communion, in nature, in poetry, in art, the satisfaction which human fellowship almost always fails to give. She never comprehended this serene height. She longed for companionship, even in the presence of Mt. Blanc, and declared that she would go a hundred miles to meet a new mind, when she would not open the window to gaze on the Bay of Naples. Religion was a matter of the intellect to her, poetry a thing to be analyzed, art a subject for moral reflection and historical association. Ideas and friends, they alone satisfied her. When her exile limited them, she knew not how to open her soul to higher things. Then this woman, whose capacity for happiness was so magnificent, became, of all creatures, the most miserable.

The Queen of the Gironde

The roofs of Paris are silvered by moonlight. The streets under the softening influence of the night and weariness are quiet. It is a vastly different Paris from that of today—this Paris of 1763. Tall, stiff houses arise on all sides. The narrow streets are unpaved, unclean, unlighted, deserted save here and there by noisy revelers from whom the few belated foot passengers shrink. Cabriolets driven fast and furious dash by, splashing mud right and left. Now and then one of these "one-horse booby hutches" knocks down a man or child and kills him, but nobody gives the matter much attention.

Stop here at the heart of Paris—the point of the busiest life—the Pont Neuf crossing the Seine where it closes after opening its bosom to receive the Ile de la Cite. Just there where the famous bridge makes an angle with the quay on the right side of the island, stands one of the tall houses. An upper window is open and from the casement leans a young girl. She is not more than nine years of age, but her face as she looks toward the north kindled with the fire and purpose which one might expect to see in the face of an artist who had reached the culminating point of some great conception. Her head is nobly poised. Her blue eyes now dark and intense swim with tears. On the floor beside her lies a little book. It is a copy of André Dacier's Plutarch. All the Lenten season she has been reading it. Devout Catholic as she is, she has even carried it to church in the guise of a prayerbook, and while the priests chant their *aves* has read of Greek and Roman.

This is by no means her first reading. Already she has devoured an odd medley of books, the haphazard collection of an unintellectual household. But Plutarch! This is a new thing. Shakespeare found in the little volume the fire for Julius Caesar, for Coriolanus, for Anthony and Cleopatra. It begat in Rousseau the "Social Contract." That little book is to impregnate Charlotte Corday with a daring which will make her brave the command of the eternal God. The child at the window has discovered in the divine dream of noble minds—Republicanism.

From *The Chautauquan* 12 (Mar. 1891): 756–61.

There is nothing one would think in the family or surroundings of Manon Phlipon, for so the little girl is named, to induce elevation of the mind. Her parents—well, Lamertine calls them amphibious—a cross between peasant and bourgeois. Her father is a vain and clever man with a talent for making money at his engraving and enamel painting and by handling jewels; her mother is a serene and gently dignified woman, of such goodness and wisdom that she inspires a perfect love and devotion in her daughter—the only child of seven left her.

The ambition of the father and the wisdom of the mother led them to give Manon advantages unusual in her circle. She had masters for singing and dancing. She learned to play guitar and the violincello. Her father taught her engraving and designing. She studied Latin. She went to church, learned her catechism, confessed her sins. Into every thing she entered with a complete abandon. Her fervid nature knew no moderate emotions. Did she read? "I became Eucharis for Telemachus, Erminia for Tancred." Did she go to the field or wood? Her whole being was absorbed in that forest passion which characterizes reflective and ardent natures.

Religion was the deepest sentiment of her heart. The time of her first communion drew near. The solemnity of the step filled her imagination with awe, her heart with fearful rapture. She besought with tears to be put into a convent to prepare herself by a year's meditation—an appeal which her parents granted.

From such a childhood a rare womanhood was possible. At eighteen we find that the promise has been fulfilled. Form, face, and manner are characterized by grace, unconsciousness, vigor, mobility. A remarkable equipoise exists between her character and her conduct. She ceased to be a good Catholic, for her intellectuality prevented her long accepting such doctrines as the damnation of all the world outside of the church and of papal infallibility, but she still "goes to confession to set a good example to her neighbors and not to distress her mother." She has read all the great philosophers, Diderot, D'Alembert, Raynal, Malebranche, Descartes, Voltaire, Spinoza, Helvetius. Into each state she threw herself completely. She was a Stoic with the Stoics, a Materialist with the Materialists, an Atheist with the Atheists. Her purpose in thus abandoning herself to the system of each was to comprehend each fully. The result was a philosophy, wise, broad, and kind. No amount of philosophy ever uprooted her belief in and dependence upon God. In her girl-hood struggles with love she appeals to the Divine. In her womanhood when she is alone with nature she finds in communion with a Supreme Intelligence a deep and abiding satisfaction. A the end of her life she repeats, *Dieu juste, recois-moi!*

Her intellectuality does not absorb her emotions. But she has found a safe outlet for them. In her convent days Manon formed a passionate girl friendship. Sophie Cannet, her friend, lived at Amiens, and from the time that the girls parted until Manon's marriage, a voluminous correspondence was carried on. Every thought, every wish, every beat of her heart, Manon poured out to Sophie. The tenderness, the exquisite sentiment, the passionate longing of these letters is unexcelled in any love letters of the world. It was a friendship on her side which faithfully fulfilled Plato's love vision. Lovers, of course, were many. Her "Memoirs" contain an amusing catalogue of these suitors. There were her masters who all fell in love with her—one even going so far as to have a wen removed to recommend himself in her favor. There was a butcher who showed his heart's devotion by sending her juicy steaks when she fell sick, a jeweler looking for a third wife, and other tradesmen of the neighborhood. There was a doctor, too, to whom her father, now getting a little irritated at Manon's aversion to suitors in general, came near marrying her, and would, had he not himself been too officious in the doctor's affairs.

She had no thought of marrying a man for a home. Had she lived with Plutarch and the philosophers to sit her evenings out with a drowsy spouse whose only ideas were of his shop and Paris street gossip? In all the cortege only one seems to have touched her fancy, Pahin de Lablancherie. He had some claims to intellectuality, but she idealized him to an unreasonable de-gree. After a rough love passage, she was effactually cured of her illusion by learning that he was known in his circles as the *lover of the eleven thousand vir-gins*!

But this beautiful period of her life is ending. Her mother dies. Her fa-ther, always a weak man, soon consoles himself with a mistress and falls to squandering his money. Manon tries to recall him. But poor child, the un-equal contest can end only in failure.

In these troubles she devotes her leisure to study and writing. She pours out her thoughts to Sophie. She prepares a set of reflective papers, *Mes Loisirs*.

She corresponds with many eminent men of the day, but she allows nothing to interfere with the duty at hand. To her always the highest virtue was to do the evident thing. It might be commonplace and irksome. But was it not her duty, and to do one's duty, was it not to reach the heights of philosophy and to ally one's self with the Infinite Right which governs the universe?

Rousseau has been molding her mind, and from the *Nouvelle Heloise* she has received exalted ideas of marriage and motherhood. And so it comes about through the irksomeness of her life, and her belief that every woman ought to wed, that when, after an acquaintance of four years, Roland de la Platiere, a man of good family, some twenty years her senior, austere in mind and manners, learned in exact science, plain in person, careless in dress, rasping in voice, asks her to be his wife, she consents.

M. Phlipon comes in at this juncture in a very disgraceful way. He has squandered Manon's dowry, and now refuses M. Roland as son-in-law. This is the last drop. Manon writes Roland to dismiss his suit and goes to a convent to live. For six months this goes on. She visits her father weekly and mends his clothes—the last service which he now permits her.

Roland writes her—but does not rescue her. In spite of this cold-blooded treatment when he does come, and finds her fresh and blooming and brilliant as ever, he renews his suit, and on February 4, 1780, they are married. Years before she had written in referring to her father's importunities that she marry, "What I want is not a condition, but a *man*. I will die rather than prostitute my soul in a union with one who does not understand me." Roland is a good and true man—but how little he understands her! And she? In her philosophizing she had reached a conclusion that in marriage one party always gives himself for the good of the other. In the elevation of her soul such a sacrifice was glorious. She could do it honestly—for she had never loved.

During the next nine years of her life we find Mme. Roland an almost ideal wife and mother. After leaving Paris her home was Amiens, and here she was united with Sophie. Roland, however, was imperious and exacting and requested his wife drop the Cannets—which she dutifully did. She devoted herself to him completely, giving all her splendid vigor to copying notes, arranging his papers, and helping on his work.

In 1784 they moved to Lyons where with a skillful diplomacy she managed a household made up of such explosive elements as an austere husband long out with his family, a brother-in-law who possessed an exasperating piety, and an aged mother-in-law of irritable and domineering temper. By some strange magic she made and kept harmony among them. Her household cares were large. She kept always with her the "prattler full of mischief," little Eudora, her only child, whom, good disciple of Rousseau that she was, [she] braved French custom and nursed herself. She spent hours in her husband's cabinet, copying and compiling. "To work with Roland became as natural as to eat with him."

There was little time for study, but from 1782 to 1792 she carried on a vigorous correspondence with various young men of sentiments and principles similar to her own. Among them were Louis Bosc, Bancal des Issarts, and Francois Lanthenas. It is from her letters to the first that we know most of her life at Lyons. More charming letters could not be written. They sparkle with fun and raillery. They contain taking bits of description of home and life matters. They sometimes burn with eloquence, again show a tinge of coquetry.

In this correspondence her strong interest in public affairs develops. The condition of France was deplorable beyond description. In Lyons in 1789 Mme. Roland saw twenty thousand people daily fed at public expense. The abuses in the court, the church, in all departments of public administration had reached the limit of folly and excess. To cure all this Mme. Roland had one dream—Republicanism. When the States-General was assembled in 1788 she watched its acts with keenest interest. Many of her letters to Bosc and Lanthenas at this time were used for articles in the more radical Parisian journals. When the National Assembly began its work in 1789, her interest was intensified. A Declaration of Rights and a new Constitution! Surely France was saved. But the Assembly disappointed her. She declared that the Declaration of Rights was "garbled," and that the Constitution was a "poor piece of patch-work."

In February of 1791 Mme. Roland had the joy of going to Paris, her husband having been sent from Lyons to represent the city's interests before the Assembly.

She began at once to attend clubs and the sessions of the Assembly. Brissot de Warville, a leading Republican and journalist, had been in correspondence with the Rolands and had used many of Mme. Roland's ideas in his journal. He came to see them. Soon others, attracted by the learning and integrity of the man, by the beauty and brilliancy of the woman, and by the unadulterated patriotism of both, gathered at the house each week. Among her visitors were Robespierre, Buzot, Petion. Mme. Roland soon had the leading Republican salon in Paris.

She declares that she never said anything in these gatherings of men. "I knew what suited my sex"—but she managed to hold absolute sway. Her platform was clearly defined. It denied the divine right of kings and the justice of a privileged class. It proclaimed the rights of the people and even the right of insurrection. "It is a cruel thing to think, but every day it is more evident that we are retrograding through peace and that we will be regenerated only through blood." Many of her measures appeared at this time before the National Assembly, her friends being inspired to believe in them and to dare to present them by her enthusiasm and eloquence.

At the end of six months Roland's mission was ended and they went back to Lyons. The National Assembly soon dissolved. In October the Legislative Assembly, with a much younger and more radical membership, gathered. The Rolands decided to go to Paris for the winter. Once there, Mme. Roland immediately became the center of a Republican salon and of the party of the Assembly known as the Gironde.

What was the Gironde? It was a body of men dominated by pure Republican principles, recognizing the brotherhood of man and the universality of the principles of liberty and justice, and so elevated in sentiment and enthusiasm that they could discern no obstacles in the way of realizing their ideals. Such men illumine a century now and then. They purify it; it suffocates them. They give it their spirit; it destroys their bodies. The Girondes were not politicians. They were incapable of compromise. They had the vacillation of the idealist when he encounters the tools of politics and of society, and is driven to choose something. They had, too, the proud self-confidence and obstinacy, which is so irritating to men who cut and trim their consciences, and sell and buy back their souls as self-interest or party-interest dictates. But they were eloquent, young, honest, noble. They fulfilled the Republican ideals of the people and the Assembly, and the party came into power. Brissot was its leader, and through his influence Roland was called to the Cabinet as Minister of the Interior.

The situation with which they had to cope was this: a bankrupt monarchy with a king in semi-bondage; a court hostile to the people; a people starving for bread and maddened by the vision of a country where plenty and freedom prevailed; an Assembly of diverse opinion; a surrounding continent disgusted with the anarchy of the French, sympathizing with the king, and preparing for war against the people.

Roland entered the Ministry with hopefulness. Mme. Roland practically went in with him. He believed at first that a reconciliation with the king and court was easy and certain, but Mme. Roland would have none of it. She had an opportunity to make friends of the class represented by Dumouriez, who was a member of the Ministry—those who were for the constitution, the king, peace, order—but she suspected Dumouriez of self-interest and intrigue and kept aloof. One of her ideas which the Ministry had adopted called for a camp of twenty thousand men to protect Paris against the foreign foes and traitors within. The king did not accept it. Mme. Roland wrote a letter of exhortation and warning to his Majesty, which her husband had the temerity to present in his own name. It caused the overthrow of the Ministry.

Roland became more popular than ever by his fall and after the tenth of August, 1792—the effect of which was to strip the king of his authority, to make him and his family prisoners, and to summon a new national assembly, the Convention—was recalled to the Ministry.

The Gironde after the tenth of August was ready to stop. Insurrection had done enough—put the government in the power of the people's representatives. Now was the time to form a solid republic. But how? The foreign enemies of France were closing around her. Terror had seized the people. Suspicion was rampant. Worst of all there had arisen a mysterious tribunal, the Commune, which arrogated to itself the power of saying who were traitors to the country and of punishing them.

The frightful September massacres follow. Hundreds are killed without fair trial or judgment. Now if ever is Roland's time. To force order and justice is the only hope. This is no time for platitudes, but he gives the country words, words, words—never deeds.

The Gironde did demand the punishment of the parties guilty of the September crimes. They demanded order. But they had not reckoned with their host. When they preached the divine right of insurrection they preached it as to men like themselves lofty in purpose, pure in soul. They forgot that the same fire which kindles in a noble heart inspiration to virtue and courage may awaken in a cruel breast a very holocaust of fury and crime. When they had prepared the tenth of August, they had prepared the Commune.

In the Convention the Gironde was opposed by the party known as the Mountain. Through one man only was there any possibility of union between these elements, Danton. But Mme. Roland hated Danton. He inspired in her an uncontrollable physical repugnance. She believed him cruel. She mistrusted his motives. She refused to treat with him. Thus the only man who grasped the situation and could have helped the Gironde to victory was driven from an alliance with it.

There was another fact which, I believe, did no little to strengthen Mme. Roland's implacable attitude toward Danton. In the turmoil and woe of these fearful days there somehow had been born between her and Buzot a love whose intensity and purity never faltered. They had no right to love? Both were married? They had no right to yield and neither ever did. To love? God must be the judge. To her he was the incarnation of the Republican spirit, the only man in the Gironde who thoroughly appreciated her ideals and who had the courage to carry her measures into the Convention. The elevation of the experience only made her more incapable of political union with Danton.

Between the Mountain and the Gironde there soon became open war. Marat had in his room in those days a map of France flanked by a brace of pistols and above it scrawled in bold letters—LA MORT. It was the insignia of the Mountain. "A white Grecian statue," Mme. Roland, was painted on the banners of the Gironde. They could not meet each other for they did not understand each other.

There was no inevitable end. On the 22nd of January, 1793, Roland resigned. In April the expulsion from the Chamber of twenty-two of the Girondists was demanded by the Commune. To go or to appeal to the country was the alternative. The latter seemed to the accused perilous to the public safety. "Fling us into the abyss and let the country be saved!" cried Vergniaud. On the 22nd of June they were imprisoned, on the 31st of October executed. The remainder of the party were proscribed. A portion remained in the city to show their confidence in the people. The rest, among them Roland and Buzot, escaped to endeavor to raise an army in the departments and by union with sympathizers in the city to abolish the Commune, restore order, and reinstate the Convention.

Their enemies frustrated their attempts. One way only remained—to unite with the foreigners—but this was treason. They preferred defeat.

And where was Mme. Roland at this time? On the 31st of May, 1793, she was arrested and imprisoned. "In that black wreck of things," the five months she spent in prison are one serene, unsullied spot. Her life of meditation, of devotion to duty, of fidelity to ideals, now shows wonderful fruits—elevation of spirit, gentleness, courage. Nobility is not an impulse, serenity is not a mood, unswerving faith is not a spark. These things come into being like the worlds, by the struggling of whirling elements, the selection and the adjustment of the atoms of her life.

Her cell became a temple. Vile women grew quiet in her presence. She received unwonted favors. Flowers and books were allowed her. "With these," she declares, "I forget the injustice of men, their folly, and their evil-doing."

She began her "Memoirs," that delightful book in which she traces her life with a naïveté, a relish, a lightness of touch, a brightness of spirit, incomprehensible in her situation. Now and then the narrative breaks for a comment:

"France has become a vast carnage of blood," is her cry as news of a fresh horror reaches her.

Again, "One is not sure of living twenty-four hours."

And again, "I am interrupted by the news that I am included in the accusation against Brissot—I do not fear to die in such good company."

All her courage and serenity, her rational view of things, her contempt of death—are they the result of philosophy alone?

In 1863 in a heap of soiled papers which a Parisian bookseller had bought for fifty francs from somebody's garret, were found letters written in prison by Mme. Roland to Buzot. They revealed a secret of her heart which had long puzzled students of her life, and they helped explain why in her prison she lived as one who had entered within portals of eternal peace and joy. She loved Buzot, knew herself to be loved by him. Within her prison waiting death she feels that she dares yield her heart to her love, that in so doing she can commit no sin against what to her is the highest thing in human life—virtue.

The letters are veritable paeans of victory. Her bars free her. Her jailers are her deliverers. Death is her savior. The soul which has dared to assert itself in a pure love can face the eternal fearlessly. It is to society that it cannot reveal itself. *Comprendre, c'est pardonner.* God understands. Society will not.

On the 9th of November, 1793, there was a little stir in the yard of the Conciergerie. The black death-cart had come for its passengers to the guillotine. In the prison a group of weeping men and women were embracing a stately woman whose smiles and kindly chidings at their grief would seem to say that this was her marriage day. She leaves them at last and steps proudly out. Clad in white with her long black hair falling to her girdle, erect, serene, beautiful, she steps into the dreadful vehicle and is driven over the same quay on which a little below stands the house from which the young girl leaned. There is the same intense look in these blue eyes, the same divine purpose in this face. It is the little girl, now a woman and about to die for the principle born that night by the Seine—Republicanism.

There is a cringing man in the cart, weeping with terror. She smiles at him until inspired by her courage he lifts his head and smiles back. At the foot of the guillotine she makes a last request of the bloody Sanson, to let etiquette go and spare her companion the misery of seeing her die. And Sanson, a little shamefaced, consents. Then the ax falls. The beautiful head drops. Mme. Roland is free.

Six days afterward a little out from Rouen a peasant found a man sitting upright by a tree, dead. On a scrap of paper nearby he read:

"Not fear, but indignation, made me quit my retreat on learning that my wife had been murdered. I did not choose to remain longer in a land polluted with crimes."

It was Roland. He had taken his life.

In July 1794, not far from Castillon, the bodies of two men half eaten by wolves were found. One was that of Buzot. He had lived in a vain effort to obey the commands of the woman he loved, to save his country. He had failed, and hunted by his enemies and hers, had died in misery and despair.

Lincoln's Funeral

The first edition of the morning papers in all the cities and towns of the North told their readers on Saturday, April 15, 1865, that Abraham Lincoln, President of the United States, lay mortally wounded in Washington. The extras within the next two hours told them he was dead. The first impulse of men everywhere seems to have been to doubt. It could not be true. They realized only too quickly that it was true! There was no discrediting the circumstantial accounts of the later telegrams. There was no escape from the horror and uncertainty which filled the air, driving out the joy and exultation which for days had inundated the country.

In the great cities like New York a death-like silence followed the spreading of the news—a silence made the more terrible by the presence of hundreds of men and women walking in the streets with bent heads, white faces, and knit brows. Automatically, without thought of what their neighbors were doing, these men went to their shops only to send away their clerks and close their doors for the day. Stock exchanges met only to adjourn. By ten o'clock business had ceased. It was not only in the cities where the tension of feeling is always greatest that this was true. It was the same in the small towns.

"I was a compositor then, working in a printing office at Danville, Illinois," says Prof. A. G. Draper, of Washington, D.C. "The editor came into the room early in the forenoon with a telegram in his hand; he was regarding it intently, with a pale face. Without saying a word he passed it to one and another of the compositors. I noticed that as the men read it they laid down their sticks, and without a word went, one after another, took their coats and hats off the nails where they were hanging, put them on, and went into the street. Finally the telegram was passed to me. It was the announcement that Lincoln had been shot the night before and had died that morning. Automatically I laid down my stick, took my hat and coat, and went into the

---

Originally published as chapter 31 of Tarbell's *The Life of Abraham Lincoln* (New York: McClure, Phillips, 1900), vol. 4: 41–59.

street. It seemed to me as if every man in town had dropped his business just where it was and come out. There was no sound; but the people, with pale faces and tense looks, regarded one another as if questioning what would happen next."

Just as the first universal impulse seems to have been to cease all business, so the next was to drag down the banners of victory which hung everywhere and replace them by crape. New York City before noon of Saturday was hung in black from the Battery to Harlem. It was not only Broadway and Washington Square and Fifth Avenue which mourned. The soiled windows of Five Points tenements and saloons were draped, and from the doors of the poor hovels of upper Manhattan west of Central Park bits of black weed were strung. And so it was in all the cities and towns of the North. "About nine o'clock on Saturday the intelligence reached us of the assassination of Mr. Lincoln and the attempt upon Mr. Seward's life," wrote Senator Grimes from Burlington, Iowa. "Immediately the people began to assemble about the 'Hawkeye' office, and soon Third Street became packed with people. And such expressions of horror, indignation, sorrow, and wonder were never heard before. Shortly, someone began to decorate his house with the habiliments of mourning; and soon all the business part of town, even the vilest liquor dens, was shrouded with the outward signs of sorrow. All business was at once suspended, and not resumed during the day; but everyone waited for further intelligence from Washington."

And this was true not only of the towns, it was true of the distant farms. There the news was slower in coming. A traveller journeying from the town stopped to tell it at a farm-house. The farmer, leaving his plow, walked or rode across lots to repeat it to a neighbor. Everywhere they dropped their work, and everywhere they brought out a strip of black and tied it to the door-knob.

The awful quiet of the North through the first few hours after the tragedy covered not grief alone; below it was a righteous anger, which, as the hours passed, began to break out. It showed itself first against those of Southern sympathy who were bold enough to say they were "glad of it." In New York a man was heard to remark that "it served old Abe right." Cries of "Lynch him, lynch him!" were raised. He was set upon by the crowd, and escaped narrowly. All day the police were busy hustling suspected Copperheads away from the mobs which seemed to rise from the ground at the first word of treason.

"I was kept busy last night," further wrote Senator Grimes from Burlington, "trying to prevent the destruction of the store of a foolish woman who, it was said, expressed her joy at Mr. Lincoln's murder. Had she been a man, so much was the old Adam aroused in me, I would not have uttered a word to save her."

In Cincinnati, which had spent the day and night before in the most elaborate jubilation, the rage against treason broke out at the least provocation. "Some individuals of the 'butternut' inclination," says a former citizen, in recalling these days, "were knocked into the gutters and kicked, because they would make no expression of sorrow, or because of their well-known past sympathy with the rebellion. Others as loyal as any suffered also, through mistaken ideas of meanness on the part of personal enemies. Junius Brutus Booth, a brother of the assassin, was closing a two-weeks' engagement at the Pike Opera House. He was stopping at the Burnet House. While there was no violent public demonstration against him, it was well known that his life would not be worth a farthing should he be seen on the streets or in public. Of course the bills were taken down and there was no performance that night. Mr. Booth was well pleased quietly to escape from the Burnet and disappear."

In one New Hampshire town, where a company of volunteers from the country had gathered to drill, only to be met by the news, it was rumored that a man in a factory nearby had been heard to say, "The old abolitionist ought to have been killed long ago." The volunteers marched in a body to the factory, entered, and dragged the offender out into the road. There they held a crude court-martial. "The company surrounded him," says one of the men, "in such military order as raw recruits could get into, and questioned him as to his utterances. He was willing to do or say anything. 'Duck him!' was the cry raised on every hand. The canal was close at hand, but there were voices heard saying: 'He's an old man. Don't duck him. Send him out of town.' And so it was done. He was compelled to give three cheers for the Star and Stripes. I shall never forget his pitiful little 'Hooray!' He was made to kneel down and repeat something in praise of Abraham Lincoln that one of his officers dictated to him, and then he was marched to his boarding-place, given certain minutes to pack up his effects, and escorted to the railroad station, where he was sent off on the next train. This was a very mild example of the feeling there was. Had the man been a real American Copperhead, he would scarcely have escaped a ducking, and perhaps a drubbing also; but many said: 'He's only an Englishman, and doesn't know any better.'"

The most important expression of the feeling was that at a great noon meeting held at the Custom House in New York. Among the speakers were General Butler, E. L. Chittenden, Daniel L. Dickinson, William P. Fessenden, and General Garfield. The awful, wrathful, righteous indignation of the meeting is told in the following citations from the speeches.

"If rebellion can do this to the wise, the kind, the benevolent Abraham Lincoln," said Butler, "what ought we to do to those who from high places incited the assassin's mind and guided the assassin's knife? [Applause, and cries of 'Hang them!'] Shall we content ourselves with simply crushing out the strength, the power, the material resources of the rebellion? ['Never, never.'] Shall we leave it yet unsubdued to light the torch of conflagration in our cities? Are we to have peace in fact or peace only in name? [Cries of 'In fact' and applause.] Is this nation hereafter to live in peace, or are men to go about in fear and in dread, as in times past, when every man feared his neighbor, and no man went about except he was armed to the teeth or was clad in panoply of steel? This question is to be decided this day, and at this hour by the American people. It may be that this is a dispensation of God, through his providence, to teach us that the spirit of rebellion has not been broken with the surrender of its arms. [Applause.]"

"Fellow citizens," said Garfield, "they have slain the noblest and most generous spirit on this earth. [Applause.] It may be almost impious to say it; but it does seem to me that his death almost parallels that of the Son of God, who cried out, 'Father, forgive them, for they know not what they do.' But in taking away that life they have left the iron hand of the people to fall upon them. [Great applause.] Peace, forgiveness and mercy are the attributes of this government, but justice and judgment with inexorable tread follow behind, and when they have slain love, when they have despised mercy, when they have rejected those that would be their best friends, then comes justice with hoodwinked eyes and the sword."

The tense despair and rage of the people on Saturday had not broken when they gathered on Sunday for worship. Never, perhaps, in any sorrow, any disaster that this nation has suffered, was there so spontaneous a turning to the church for consolation as on this Sabbath day. Never, perhaps, did the clergy of a country rise more universally to console the grief of a people than on this day. Everywhere, from the East to the West, the death of the President was the theme of the sermons, and men who never before in their lives had said anything but commonplaces rose this day to eloquence. One of the most touching of the Sunday gatherings was at Bloomington, Illinois. Elsewhere it was only a President, a national leader, who had been lost; here it was a personal friend, and people refused to be comforted. On Sunday morning there were sermons in all the churches, but they seemed in no way to relieve the tension. Later in the day word circulated that a general out-of-door meeting would be held at the court-house, and people gathered from far and near, townspeople and country people, in the yard of the court-house, where for years they had been accustomed to see Lincoln coming and going; and the ministers of the town, all of them his friends, talked one after another, until finally, comforted and resigned, the people separated silently and went home.

On Monday a slight distraction came in the announcement of the plan for the funeral ceremonies. After much discussion, it had been decided that a public funeral should be held in Washington, and that the body should then lie in state for brief periods at each of the larger cities on the way to Springfield, whither it was to be taken for burial. The necessity of at once beginning preparations for the reception of the funeral party furnished the first real relief to the universal grief which had paralyzed the country.

The dead President had lain in an upper chamber of the White House from the time of his removal there on Saturday morning until Tuesday morning, when he was laid under a magnificent catafalque in the centre of the great East Room. Although there were in Washington many citizens who sympathized with the South, although the plot for assassination had been developed there, yet no sign appeared of any feeling but grief and indignation. It is said that there were not fifty houses in the city that were not draped in black, and it seemed as if every man, woman, and child were seeking some souvenir of the tragedy. A child was found at the Tenth Street house [where Lincoln was taken after he had been shot] staining bits of soft paper with the half-dried blood on the steps. Fragments of the stained linen from the bed on which the President died were passed from hand to hand; locks of the hair cut away by the surgeons were begged; his latest photograph, the papers of the day, programmes of the funeral, a hundred trivial relics were gathered together, and are treasured to-day by the original owners or their children. They

"dip their napkins in his sacred blood;
Yea, beg a hair of him for memory,
And, dying, mention it within their wills,
Bequeathing it, as a rich legacy,
Unto their issue."

On Tuesday morning, when the White House was opened, it was practically the whole population, augmented by hundreds from the North, who waited at the gates. All day long they surged steadily through the East Room, and at night, when the gates were closed, Lafayette Park and the adjoining streets were still packed with people waiting for admission. In this great company of mourners two classes were conspicuous, the soldiers and the negroes. One had come from camp and hospital, the other from country and hovel, and both wept unrestrainedly as they looked on the dead face of the man who had been to one a father, to the other a liberator.

Wednesday had been chosen for the funeral, and every device was employed by the Government to make the ceremony fitting in pomp and solemnity. The greatest of the nation—members of the cabinet, senators, congressmen, diplomats; representatives of the churches, of the courts, of commerce, of all that was distinguished and powerful in the North, were present in the East Room. Mr. Lincoln's friend, Bishop Simpson, and his pastor, Dr. Gurley, conducted the services. More than one spectator noted that in the great assembly there was but one person bearing the name of Lincoln and related to the President—his son Robert. Mrs. Lincoln was not able to endure the emotion of the scene, and little Tad could not be induced to be present.

At two o'clock in the afternoon, the booming of cannon and tolling of bells announced that the services were ended. A few moments later, the coffin was borne from the White House and placed in a magnificent funeral car, and under the conduct of a splendid military and civilian escort, conveyed slowly to the Capitol, attended by thousands upon thousands of men and women. At the east front of the Capitol the procession halted, and the body of Abraham Lincoln was borne across the portico, from which six weeks before in assuming for the second time the presidency, he had explained to the country his views upon reconstruction: "With malice toward none; with charity for all; with firmness in the right, as God gives us to see the right, let us strive on to finish the work we are in, to bind up the nation's wounds; to care for him who shall have borne the battle, and for his widow and his orphan—to do all which may achieve and cherish a just and lasting peace among ourselves, and with all nations."

The rotunda of the Capitol, into which the coffin was now carried, was draped in black, and under the dome was a great catafalque. On this the coffin was placed, and after a simple service there left alone, save for the soldiers who paced back and forth at the head and foot.

But it was not in Washington alone that funeral services were held that day. All over the North, in Canada, in the Army of the Potomac, even in Richmond, business was suspended, and at noon people gathered to listen to eulogies of the dead. Twenty-five million people literally participated in the funeral rites of that Wednesday.

On Thursday the Capitol was opened, and here again, in spite of a steady rain, were repeated scenes of Tuesday at the White House, thousands of persons slowly mounting the long flight of steps leading to the east entrance and passing through the rotunda.

At six o'clock on the morning of April 21, there gathered in the rotunda the members of the cabinet, Lieutenant-General Grant and his staff, many senators, army and navy officers, and other dignitaries. After a prayer by Dr. Gurley, the party followed the coffin to the railway station, where the funeral train which was to convey the remains of Abraham Lincoln from Washington to Springfield now stood. A great company of people had gathered for the last scene of the tragedy, and they waited in absolute silence and with uncovered heads while the coffin was placed in the car. At its foot was placed a smaller coffin, that of Willie Lincoln, the President's beloved son, who had died in February, 1862. At Mrs. Lincoln's request, father and son were to make together this last earthly journey.

Following the remains of the President came the party which was to serve as an escort to Springfield. It included several of Lincoln's old-time friends, among them Judge David Davis and Ward Lamon; a Guard of Honor, composed of prominent army officers; a large congressional committee, several governors of States, a special delegation from Illinois, and a bodyguard. From time to time on the journey this party was joined for brief periods by other eminent men, though it remained practically the same throughout. Three of its members—Judge Davis, General Hunter, and Marshal Lamon—had been with Mr. Lincoln when he came on to Washington for his first inauguration.

Precisely at eight o'clock, the train of nine cars pulled out from the station. It moved slowly, almost noiselessly, not a bell ringing nor a whistle sounding, through a mourning throng that lined the way to the borders of the town.

The line of the journey begun on this Friday morning was practically the same that Mr. Lincoln had followed four years before when he came to Washington for his first inauguration. It led through Baltimore, Harrisburg, Philadelphia, New York, Albany, Buffalo, Cleveland, Columbus, Indianapolis, and Chicago, to Springfield. The entire programme of the journey, including the hours when the train would pass certain towns where it could not stop, had been published long enough beforehand to enable the people along the way to arrange, if they wished, to pay a tribute to the dead President. The result was a demonstration which in sincerity and unanimity has never been equaled in the world's history. The journey began at six o'clock on the morning of April 21, and lasted until nine o'clock of the morning of May 3; and it might almost be said that during the whole time there was not an hour of the night or day, whether the coffin lay in state in some heavily draped public building or was being whirled across the country, when mourning crowds were not regarding it with wet eyes and bowed heads. Night and darkness in no way lessened the number of the mourners. Thus it was not until eight o'clock on Saturday evening (April 22) that the coffin was placed in Independence Hall, at Philadelphia. The building was at once opened to the public, and through the whole night thousands filed in to look on the dead man's face. It was at one o'clock in the morning, on Monday, that the coffin was carried from Independence Hall to the train, but thousands of men, women, and children stood in the streets while the procession passed, as if it were day. In New York, on the following Tuesday, City Hall, where the coffin had been placed in the afternoon, remained open the whole night. The crowd was even greater than during the day, filling the side streets around the square in every direction. It was more impressive, too, for the men and women who were willing to watch out the night in the flare of torches and gaslights were laborers who could not secure release in daytime. Many of them had come great distances, and hundreds were obliged, after leaving the hall, to find a bed in a doorway, so overfilled was the town. The crowd was at its greatest at midnight, when, as the bells were tolling the hour, a German chorus of some seventy voices commenced suddenly to sing the *Integer vitae*. The thrilling sweetness of the music coming unexpectedly upon the mourners produced an effect never to be forgotten.

Nor did rain make any more difference with the crowd than the darkness. Several times during the journey there arose heavy storms; but the people, in utter indifference, stood in the streets, often uncovered, to see the catafalque and its guard go by or waiting their turn to be admitted to view the coffin.

The great demonstrations were, of course, in the cities where the remains lay in state for a few hours. These demonstrations were perforce much alike. The funeral train was met at the station by the distinguished men of the city and representatives of organizations. The coffin was transferred to a stately hearse, draped in velvet and crape, surmounted by heavy plumes, ornamented in silver, and drawn by six, eight, ten, or more horses. Then, to the tolling of the bells and the regular firing of minute guns, followed by a vast concourse of people, it was carried to the place appointed for the lying in state. Here a crowd which seemed unending filed by until the time came to close the coffin, when the procession reformed to attend the hearse to the funeral train.

The first of these demonstrations was in Baltimore, the city which a little over four years before it had been thought unsafe for the President to pass through openly, the city in which the first troops called out for the defense of the Union had been mobbed. Now no offering was sufficient to express the feeling of sorrow. All buildings draped in black, all business suspended, the people poured out in a driving rain to follow the catafalque to the Exchange, where for two hours, on April 21, the public was admitted.

As was to be expected, the most elaborate of the series of funeral ceremonies was in New York. There, when the funeral train arrived on Tuesday, April 25, the whole city was swathed in crape, and vast crowds filled the streets. The climax of the obsequies was the procession which, on Wednesday, followed the hearse up Broadway and Fifth Avenue to Thirty-fourth Street and thence to the Hudson River station. For a week this procession had been preparing, until finally it included representatives of almost every organization of every nature in the city and vicinity. The military was represented by detachments from scores of different regiments, and by many distinguished officers of the army and navy, among them General Scott and Admiral Farragut. Companies of the Seventh Regiment were on each side of the funeral car. The city sent its officials—educational, judicial, protective. The foreign consuls marched in full uniform. There were scores of societies and clubs, including all the organizations of Irish, German, and Hebrews. The whole life of the city was, in fact, represented in the solid column of men which marched that day through the streets of New York in such numbers that it took four hours to pass a single point. Deepest in significance of all the long rank was the rear body in the last division: 200 colored men bearing a banner inscribed with the words, "Abraham Lincoln—Our Emancipator." A platoon of police preceded, another followed the delegation, for the presence of these freedmen would, it was believed by many, cause disorder, and permission for them to march had only been obtained by an appeal to the Secretary of War, Mr. Stanton. Several white men walked with them, and at many points sympathizers took pains to applaud. With this single exception, the procession passed through a silent multitude, the only sound the steady tramp of feet and the music of the funeral dirges.

At four o'clock the funeral car reached the station, and the journey was continued toward Albany. But the obsequies in New York did not end then. A meeting was held that night in Union Square, at which George Bancroft delivered an oration that will remain as one of the great expressions of the day upon Lincoln and the ideas for which he worked. It was for this gathering that Bryant wrote his "Ode for the Burial of Abraham Lincoln," beginning:

"Oh, slow to smite and swift to spare,
Gentle and merciful and just;
Who in the fear of God dids't bear
the sword of power, a Nation's trust."

Imposing, solemn, and sincere as was this series of municipal demonstrations over the bier of Lincoln, there was another feature of the funeral march which showed more vividly the affectionate reverence in which the whole people held the President. This was the outpouring at villages, country crossroads, and farms to salute, as it passed, the train bearing his remains. From Washington to Springfield the train entered scarcely a town that the bells were not tolling, the minute guns firing, the stations draped, and all the spaces beside the track crowded with people with uncovered heads. At many points arches were erected over the track; at others the bridges were wreathed from end to end in crape and evergreens and flags. And this was not in the towns alone; every farm-house by which the train passed became for the time a funeral house; the plow was left in the furrow, crape was on the door, the neighbors were gathered, and those who watched from the train as it flew by could see groups of weeping women, of men with uncovered heads, sometimes a minister among them, his arms raised in prayer. Night did not hinder them. Great bonfires were built in lonely country-sides, around which the farmers waited patiently to salute their dead. At the towns the length of the train was lit by blazing torches. Storm as well as darkness was unheeded. Much of the journey was made through the rain, in fact, but the people seemed to have forgotten all things but that Abraham Lincoln, the man they loved and trusted, was passing by for the last time.

At eleven o'clock on the morning of Monday, May 1, the funeral train reached Chicago, and here the mourning began to take on a character distinctly different from what had marked it through the East. The people who now met the coffin, who followed it to the court-house, who passed in endless streams by it to look on Lincoln's face, dated their trust in him many years earlier than 1861. Man after man of them had come to pay their last tribute, not to the late President of the United States, but to the genial lawyer, the resourceful, witty political debater who had educated Illinois to believe that a country could not endure half slave and half free, and who, after defeat, had kept her faithful to the "durable struggle" by his counsel. The tears these men shed were the tears of long-time friends and personal followers.

As the train advanced from Chicago toward Springfield the personal and intimate character of the mourning grew. The journey was made at night, but the whole population of the country lined the route. Nearly every one of the farms passed—indeed, one might almost say every one of the farms passed—had been visited personally by Lincoln on legal or political errands, and a vast number of those who thus in the dead of night watched the flying train he had at some time in his life taken by the hand.

It was at nine o'clock on the morning of May 3 that the funeral train entered the town where, four years and two months before, Abraham Lincoln had bidden his friends farewell, as he left them to go to Washington. Nearly all of those who on that dreary February morning had listened to his solemn farewell words were present in the May sunshine to receive him. Their hearts had been heavy as he departed; they were broken now, for he was more than a great leader, an honored martyr, to men of Springfield. He was their neighbor and friend and helper, and as they bore his coffin to the State House, in the centre of the city, their minds were busy, not with the greatness and honor that had come to him and to them through him, but with the scenes of more than a quarter of a century in which he had always been a conspicuous figure. Every corner of the street suggested that past. Here was the office in which he had first studied law; here, draped in mourning, the one before which his name still hung. Here was the house where he had lived, the church he had attended, the store in which he had been accustomed to tell stories and to discuss politics. His name was written everywhere, even on the walls of the Hall of Representatives in the State House, where they placed his coffin, for here he had spoken again and again.

During the time that the body lay in state—from the noon of May 3 until the noon of May 4—the place Lincoln held in Springfield and the surrounding country was shown as never before. The men and women who came to look on his face were many of them the plain farmers of Sangamon and adjacent counties, and they wept as over the coffin of a father. Their grief at finding him so changed was inconsolable. In the days after leaving Washington the face changed greatly, and by the time Springfield was reached it was black and shrunken almost beyond recognition. To many the last look at their friend was so painful that the remembrance has never left them. The writer has seen men weep as they recalled the scene, and heard them say repeatedly, "If I had not seen him dead; if I could only remember him alive!"

It was [on] May 4, fifteen days after the funeral in Washington, that Abraham Lincoln's remains finally rested in Oakland Cemetery, a shaded and beautiful spot, two miles from Springfield. Here, at the foot of a woody knoll, a vault had been prepared; and thither, attended by a great concourse of military and civic dignitaries, by governors of States, members of Congress, officers of the army and navy, delegations from orders, from cities, from churches, by the friends of his youth, his young manhood, his maturer years, was Lincoln carried and laid, by his side his little son. The solemn rite was followed by dirge and prayer, by the reading of his last inaugural address, and by a noble funeral oration by Bishop Simpson. Then, as the beautiful day drew toward evening, the vault was closed, and the great multitudes slowly returned to their duties.

The funeral pageant was at an end, but the mourning was not silenced. From every corner of the earth there came to the family and to the Government tributes to the greatness of the character and life of the murdered man. Medals were cast, tablets engraved, parchments engrossed. At the end of the year, when the State Department came to publish the diplomatic correspondence of 1865, there was a volume of over 700 pages, containing nothing but expressions of condolence and sympathy on Lincoln's death. Nor did the mourning and the honor end there. From the day of his death until now, the world has gone on rearing monuments to Abraham Lincoln.

The first and inevitable result of emotion which swept over the earth at Lincoln's death was to enroll him among martyrs and heroes. Men forgot that they had despised him, jeered at him, doubted him. They forgot his mistakes, forgot his plodding caution, forgot his homely ways. They saw now, with the vision which an awful and sudden disaster so often gives, the simple, noble outlines on which he had worked. They realized how completely he had sunk every partisan and personal consideration, every non-essential, in the tasks which he had set for himself—to prevent the extension of slavery, to save the Union. They realized how, while they had forgotten everything in disputes over this man, this measure, this event, he had seen only the two great objects of the struggle. They saw how slowly, but surely, he had educated them to feel the vital importance of these objects, had resolved their partisan warfare into a moral struggle. The wisdom of his words, the sincerity of his acts, the steadfastness of his life were clear to them at last. With this realization came a feeling that he was more than a man. He was a prophet, they said, a man raised up by God for a special work, and they laid then the foundation of the Lincoln myth which still enthralls so many minds.

The real Lincoln, the great Lincoln, is not, however, this prophet and martyr. He is the simple, steady, resolute, unselfish man whose supreme ambition was to find out the truth of the questions which confronted him in life, and whose highest satisfaction was in following the truth he discovered. He was endowed by nature with the vision of seer. His power of getting at the truth of things he had won by incessant mental effort. From his boyhood he would *understand*, though he must walk the floor all night with his problem. Nor had nature made him a saint. His lofty moral courage in the Civil War was the logical result of life-long fidelity to his own conscience. From his boyhood he would keep faith with that which his mind told him was true, though he lost friend and place by it. When he entered public life these qualities at first won him position; but they cost him a position more than once. They sent him to Congress; but in 1849, they forced him out of public life. They brought him face to face with Douglas from 1854 to 1858, and enabled him to shape the moral sentiment of the Northwest; but later they defeated him. They made him Illinois's candidate for the presidency in 1860; but they brought upon him as President the distrust and hatred of even his own party. It took four years of dogged struggle, of constant repetitions of the few truths which he believed to be essential to teach the people of the United States that they could trust him; it took a murderer's bullet to make them realize the surpassing greatness of his simplicity, his common sense, and his resolution. It is this man who never rested until he found what he believed to be the right, and who, having found it, could never be turned from it, who is the Real Lincoln.

Etiquette Regulating Josephine's Life . . .

Consecrated by the Pope, crowned by Napoleon, Josephine's position seemed impregnable in the eyes of all the world. It was one of dazzling splendor. The little creole whose youth had been spent in a sugarhouse, who had passed months in a prison cell, who many a time had borrowed money to pay her rent, now had become the mistress, not of a palace, but of palaces—of Fontainebleau, the Tuilleries, Versailles, Rambouillet. She who for so many years had begged favors at the doors of others, was now the center of a great machine, called a "Household," devoted to serving her. There were a First Almoner, a Maid of Honor, a lady of the Bedchamber, numbers of Ladies of the Palace, a First Chamberlain, a First Equery, a Private Secretary, a Chief Steward—all of them having their respective attendants; and there were, besides these, valets, footmen, pages, and servants of all grades. Her life, so long one of unthinking freedom, was now regulated to the last detail. The apartments in the palace devoted to her own uses were two—the apartment of honor and the private apartment. Before the door of the ante-chamber of the apartment of honor stood, day and night, a door-keeper; within were four valets, two *huissiers*, two pages (to do errands), from twelve to twenty-six footmen, ready to do honor to the incoming and outgoing guests. In the salons, where visitors waited, were other decorative footmen and pages—a retinue ten times larger than actual service required, but none too large to the eye accustomed to court etiquette. It was through this hedge of attendants that the supplicant, flatterer or friend who would see Josephine now must work his way—a slow way, often only to be made by fair address, strong relations, and judicious gifts. Josephine by nature the most accessible of mortals, was now obliged to turn away old friends because they did not please His Majesty, the Emperor. That he was oftentimes quite right, the following frank little letter shows:

Originally published as chapter 6 of Tarbell's *A Life of Napoleon Bonaparte, With a Sketch of Josephine, Empress of the French* (New York: Moffat Yard, 1909), 386–98.

"I am sorry, my dear friend, that my wishes cannot be fulfilled, as you and my other old friends imagine they can. You seem to think that if I do not see you it is because I have forgotten you. Alas! no, on the contrary, my memory is more tenacious than I wish. The more I think of what I am, the more I am mortified at not being able to obey the dictates of my heart. The Empress of France is the veriest slave in the Empire, and she cannot acquit the debt which Madame de Beauharnais owes. This makes me miserable, and it will explain why you are not near me; why I do not see Madame Tallien; why, in short, many of my friends would be forgotten by me, but that my memory is faithful.

"The Emperor, displeased at the prevailing laxity of morals, and anxious to check its progress, wishes that his palace should present an example of virtuous and religious conduct. Anxious to consolidate the religion which he has restored, and having no power to alter laws to which he has given his assent, he has determined to exclude from Court all persons who have taken advantage of the law of divorce. He has given this promise to the Pope, and he cannot break it. This reason alone has obliged him to refuse the favor I solicited of having you about me. His refusal afflicts me, but it is too positive to admit of any hope of its being retracted."

The apartment of honor was devoted to receiving, and Josephine's movements there were prescribed in detail. The costume she should wear, the chair in which she should sit, the rank of the person who should be allowed in the room when she received, who should announce, who carry a note, who bring a glass of water, all of this was ordered and performed precisely. In her private apartment there was greater appearance of freedom, though it was arranged by the code at what hour she should take her morning cup of tea and by whose hand it should be presented, who should admit her pet dog, what should be her costume for the morning, and who should arrange it.

When the Empress left the palace, the forms were multiplied. Attended by her ladies of waiting, she passed over a carpet spread for her passage, through the file of liveried servants which decorated all the apartments. Before her marched the younger of the two pretty pages always waiting in the outer salon, while the elder bore the train of her robe. At the door, the magnificent *portier d'appartement* struck the floor with his halberd as she passed. One of the dozen carriages in her stables drawn usually by eight horses awaited her. Before, beside, and behind her as she drove were servants in gorgeous livery, mounted or afoot; a brilliant spectacle for the passer-by, but a wearisome one for poor Josephine.

It was no better when she traveled, as she did a great deal, especially in the first two years after the coronation. Thus in the spring of 1805, she accompanied Napoleon to Milan, where he was to be crowned King of Italy. The journey was a long series of brilliant functions—at Lyons, a triumphal arch, a reception by the Empress, an entertainment at the theater; at Turin, flattering ceremonies; on the field of Marengo, mimic manoeuvres of the battle, led by Murat, Lannes, and Bessieres, and watched by Napoleon and Josephine from a throne, and after the manoeuvres, the laying of a cornerstone to those who lost their lives on the field; at Milan, on May 26, the coronation of Napoleon, which Josephine watched from the gallery of the cathedral, followed by splendid public fetes lasting for days; a mimic representation of the battlefield of Castaglione; visits to Bologna, Modena, Parma, Geneva, Turin, all attended by the most extravagant festivities. This journey lasted from April 4th to July 18th, the date of their return to St. Cloud, and through it all Josephine was scarcely free for an hour from the fatiguing duties of a great sovereign.

Napoleon returned to Paris from Italy to prepare for war with Austria, and in September he set out on the campaign. Josephine went with him as far as Strasburg, where she transferred her household to the Imperial Palace which had been established there for Napoleon's use. For two months, she remained at Strasburg, while Napoleon dazzled Europe by the campaign which, on Dec. 2nd, culminated at Austerlitz. Alone, she conducted her court as she would have done in Paris, magnificently and brilliantly. In November, she left Strasburg to go to Munich—a triumphal march, really, for everywhere she received royal honors. Her approach to every city through which she was to pass *en route* was announced by the ringing of bells and salvos of artillery; great processions of dignitaries went out to meet her; arches of triumph were erected for her; beautiful gifts were presented; there were illuminations, balls, and state performances of all sorts. She reached Munich on December 5th, and here remained until after January 14th, on which day another great ceremony, her son's marriage with Princess Augusta of Baden, was celebrated.

From the manner of arrangement one might have expected nothing but misery from this alliance. The young princess was violently opposed to it, and only consented at her father's entreaty—"a sacrifice to father, family, and country," she said. Eugene knew nothing of the proposed marriage until he arrived, at Napoleon's order, in Munich. The two young people never saw each other until four days before the wedding. Fortunately they fell in love at once, and their married life was one of exceptional devotion and happiness. Napoleon was so pleased with the course things took that he adopted Eugene at the time of the celebration of the marriage—a great blow to the Bonapartes and a new happiness to Josephine.

The fatiguing duties attendant upon official journeys in foreign countries and upon holding a court in a strange city were repeated again in 1806. In January, after Eugene's marriage, Josephine came back to Paris with the Emperor, but in September he left for the campaign against Prussia and Russia, and she went to Mayence to establish her court. This time the journey was not according to the code, for Napoleon had wished the Empress to remain in Paris during his absence, and it was only at the last moment that, overcome by her grief, he consented that she go with him in his carriage. Only a single maid accompanied her—the royal household not being able to start its cumbersome self for several days. At Mayence Josephine remained until January. Hortense, now Queen of Holland (Louis had been made King in 1806), was with her, with her two little sons, and in many ways the court was agreeable; but Josephine wished to join the Emperor, and it was only when he commanded her to go to Paris, that she consented to return and open her court there.

The tact and good sense with which Josephine conducted herself in her exacting and slavish position—the grace and patience with which she wore her royal harness, are as pathetic as they are marvelous. To rule her household, with all the jealousies and meanness natural to such a combination of women, so that there would be no scandals, and that the members would respect and love her, was a delicate task; but she never failed in it. She kept their love, and she kept her supremacy—even the supremacy of beauty. There were many of the young women received by the First Consul who were glad enough to try to outshine Josephine; but she almost always outwitted them. An amusing example of her skill is an encounter that occurred between her and her sister-in-law, Pauline. Pauline, who was young, vivacious, and very pretty, always resented a little the charm that Josephine exercised, and she took no small pleasure in trying to outdo her. In 1803, she was married to the Prince Borghese, at the chateau of Joseph Bonaparte, Mortefontaine. A few days after her marriage, she appeared in Paris, where she was presented officially at St. Cloud. It was natural enough that Pauline should desire to outshine everybody at this presentation, but Josephine desired particularly that she herself should not be so thrown into the shadow that Napoleon would notice it. She did a very clever thing. Although it was winter, she put on a light robe of white Indian muslin, the garment which always became her best and in which Napoleon delighted to see her. The gown was made very simply, and her only ornaments were enameled lion's heads which caught up the sleeves on her shoulder and which formed a buckle to her girdle. Her arms and neck were bare, and her hair was done on top of her head. She made an altogether charming picture; and when the First Consul saw her, he said, "Why, Josephine, what does this mean? I am jealous, you have gotten yourself up for somebody. What makes you so beautiful to-day?" Even after they were in the salon, his compliments continued. The Princess Borghese was a little late in arriving. When she did appear, she was resplendent; her dress was a bright green velvet, embroidered with diamonds; at her side was a great bouquet of brilliants; on her head, a diadem of emeralds and diamonds. Josephine in her simple robe stood at the end of the salon waiting exactly as if she had been a sovereign, to let her sister-in-law come to her. Pauline was obliged to go the length of the salon to salute her. After the presentation, she said to Madame Junot, who tells the story, "My sister-in-law thought she would be disagreeable when she made me cross the salon; in fact, she delighted me, because otherwise the train of my gown would not have been seen." Presently, however, Pauline was thrown into despair. She had forgotten entirely that the salon where they were received was furnished in blue, and that while it made a charming background for Josephine's white muslin, for her green velvet it was something deplorable. Josephine, of course, could not be accused of having planned this; it was Pauline's own forgetfulness that had wrought her confusion. The white gown and the regal manner were a favorite device of Josephine when she suspected that some young and fascinating woman was preparing to outshine her.

One very difficult task for Josephine in her court was holding her own with the women of noble birth who were gradually being admitted, but she did it with a combination of graciousness, deference, and majesty which was not to be analyzed, and which only an all but infinite tact explain. It was tact born of good will—a good will which everybody about her admitted. "No one ever denied the exquisite goodness of Madame Bonaparte," Mlle. Avrillon says. "She was extremely affable with everybody about her. I do not believe there was ever a woman who made her companions feel their dependence less than she." Madame de Remusat says that to goodness she joined a remarkably even disposition, and the faculty of forgetting any evil that anyone had done to her. Another member of her household has said of her goodness, that it was as inseparable from her character as grace from her person; "she was good to excess, sensitive beyond all expression, generous to prodigality; she tried to make everybody happy about her, and no woman was ever more loved by those who served her and merited it more. . . . As she had known unhappiness, she knew how to sympathize with the troubles of others. Her temper was always sweet, always even, as obliging for her enemies as for her friends; she made peace wherever there was trouble or discord."

Josephine was no less happy on her journeys than she was at home. She won everybody. No one was presented who did not go away feeling that in some way the Empress had especially distinguished him. As a matter of fact, she prepared herself carefully for her meetings with foreigners by employing an instructor who informed her about their families, their deeds, their books, their diplomatic victories. She mastered this instruction so thoroughly that she always had some flattering reference at her tongue's end. The diligence and energy she showed in preparing herself for official functions is the more surprising when one remembers her natural indolence.

Josephine had few resources in which she could find relief from her burden of etiquette. She cared little for books—out-of-door sports wearied her, and the hunt, on which she often accompanied the Emperor, was a sore trial. She was afraid, to begin with, and she never failed to cry over a wounded beast. She was a poor musician. She embroidered, to be sure, but not because she cared for it; she did like cards, and played tric-trac whenever etiquette allowed it. She played a good hand of whist, too; and she was very fond of telling her own fortune with cards—hardly a day passed, indeed, that she did not try to read the future from cards.

The one real pleasure in her life was undoubtedly her toilet. She had always been extravagantly fond of personal decoration—she loved brilliant stones, gay silks, fine laces, soft cashmeres; and when she found herself an Empress, with every reason and opportunity for indulging her love of finery, she abandoned herself to the pleasure until her wardrobe became the chief amusement of her life.

Almost every day, men and women, bearing stuffs of all sorts—jewels, models, laces, everything, in short, that French fancy could devise for a woman's toilet—found their way to Josephine's private apartments. Before these wily tradespeople she had no self-restraint—one should say, perhaps, no self-respect—for almost invariably she allowed herself to be wheedled into buying. The number of pieces added to her wardrobe each year indicates a startling prodigality. Thus, in one year, she bought one hundred and thirty-six dresses, twenty cashmere shawls, seventy-three corsets, forty-eight pieces of elegant stuffs, eighty-seven hats, seventy-one pairs of silk stockings, nine hundred and eighty pairs of gloves, five hundred and twenty pairs of shoes. If this had been an unusual purchase, it might be explained; but it was not. With every season there was the same thoughtless buying of all that struck her fancy. It was out of the question for her to wear all she bought, for Josephine was not one who prided herself on never appearing twice in the same costume. Many of the things she bought she never put on at all; and when her wardrobes were overburdened, she made a little fete of the task of lightening them, giving away piece after piece of uncut lace, pattern after pattern of velvet, silk or muslin, rich gowns, hats, stockings, shoes. Anything and everything was scattered in the same reckless fashion in which it had been acquired. Not that her giving of personal articles was confined to this occasional clearing out of stock; she gave as one of her royal prerogatives, whenever it pleased her to do so. Often she took from her shoulders a delicate scarf or superb cashmere shawl to throw about some one of her ladies whom she heard admiring it, and not infrequently she sent a gown to one who had complimented her on its beauty. Mlle. Ducrest says that one day she heard a gentleman of the household, in admiring a cashmere gown which the Empress wore, remark that the pattern would do very well for a waistcoat. Josephine picked up a pair of scissors, and cutting the skirt of her dress into three pieces, gave one to each of the three gentleman in the room.

Josephine's prodigality caused great confusion in her budget. She was allowed, at the beginning of her reign, $72,000 a year for her toilet, and later this was increased to $90,000. But there was never a year during the time that she did not far over-reach her allowance and oblige the Emperor to come to her relief. According to the estimate Mason has made, Josephine spent on an average $220,000 yearly on her toilet during her reign. It is only by going over her wardrobe article by article and noting the cost and number of each piece that one can realize how a woman could spend this amount. Take the simple item of her hose—which were almost always white silk, often richly embroidered or in open work. She kept 150 or more pairs on hand, and they cost from $4.00 to $8.00 a pair. She employed two hair-dressers, one for every-day, at $1,200 a year; the other for great occasions, at $2,000 a year; and she paid them each from one thousand to two thousand dollars a year for furnishings. It was the same for all the smaller items of her toilet.

Coming to gowns, the sums they cost were enormous. Her simple muslin gowns, of which her wardrobe always contained two hundred or more, cost from one hundred to four hundred dollars apiece. Her cashmere and velvet gowns were much more costly, ornamented as many of them were with ermine and with buckles, buttons, and girdles set with precious stones. One of her great extravagances was cashmere shawls. She never had enough of them—it is true she gave away many—and she rarely appeared without one within reach. Her collection of shawls is said to be the most valuable ever seen in Europe. Many of them were made after patterns which she sent herself to the Orient. They were of every delicate shade of color, and in texture they were like gossamer. Her coquetry with these beautiful drapes was like the coquetry of the Spanish signora with a fan. She said everything with them.

A large lump of Josephine's yearly allowance for dress went into jewels. Her extravagance in this particular was less justifiable than in any other, because she already owned a large quantity of precious stones of all sorts when she became Empress, many of them gifts to her in Italy, and because as Empress she had at her command the magnificent crown jewels—$1,000,000 worth of gems, in fact—and wore them when she wished. Nevertheless, she bought, evidently for the mere pleasure of buying and laying away—innumerable ornaments of every description, scores of which she probably never put on; rings, necklaces, girdles, buckles, all by the hundreds. No stone known to commerce but was represented in her collection. No form into which gold and silver can be fashioned which was not found there. She had specimens of the ornaments of all ages and all countries, and of the novelties of the times she bought by the score. She not only added incessantly, but she exchanged, reset, recut, carried on, in fact, a trade. To the end of her life she kept her interest in her jewels, and loved to show them to her companions, to play with them, to decorate herself with them. They were kept together for many years after her death, but were finally sold by Hortense. When experts came to value them, it was found that according to the prices they set—fully one-third below the cost price—the large pieces alone, such as her diadem of diamonds and her splendid pearl necklace, were worth nearly a million dollars; and as for the small pieces—the innumerable pieces of every size and kind and style—their value was never computed.

The effect on the Emperor of Josephine's prodigality can be imagined. He appreciated as she never could the lack of dignity in her reckless spending, and did his utmost to persuade her to keep her accounts in order. He even resorted to severe measures, turning out of the palace tradespeople who he knew hung about her apartments watching for an opportunity to show her a novelty in modes or in ornamentation, a rare jewel or a rich shawl. He ordered that her expenses be regulated by a person especially appointed for that purpose and that Josephine herself be not allowed to buy anything without supervision. None of these means affected anything. Annually there was a great debt run up by her, and when the settlement could be put off no longer, Josephine would confess. She always put the amount far below what it actually was, and only after much badgering could Napoleon get the real state of things. Then there was a scene, always ending in tears from Josephine. Invariably, they conquered Napoleon. "Come, come, pet, dry your tears," he would beg, "don't worry;" and he paid the debts, and raised her income. In twelve months the scene was repeated.

A Noble Life: The Story of Carola Woerishoffer

When we attempt to set down the social symptoms of our day we must include the Revolt of the Young Rich. All over the land it is going on—a questioning of the fortunes laid in their hands, a resentment at the chance for a life-fight of their own taken away, a rising passion of pain and indignation at meaningless inequalities and sufferings. They are not taking it out in talk, at least not all of them. An increasing number are offering themselves for actual every-day service, and offering themselves in humility as learners. Such a one was a young girl, Carola Woerishoffer by name, who four years ago suddenly appeared among the social workers of New York City. She had come "to learn and to help," she said.

A few months ago she was suddenly killed like a soldier at his post in the discharge of her self-imposed task of learning and helping. Brief as was Carola Woerishoffer's term of service, it has left an impression whose significance, those who now sit bewildered by the seeming meaninglessness of her death, will surely in time more and more fully realize.

The girl came into the social work of New York City direct from Bryn Mawr College, where she had been graduated in 1907. She was not one of the many girls who are sent to college. She was one of the few who go because they want its training for a special self-chosen undertaking. "Helping to improve social conditions" was the work she had set for herself—not probably in those words but certainly in their spirit. It was entirely logical that she have this ambition. It was in her blood and it was one of the strongest influences of her childhood associations.

Carola Woerishoffer was the grandchild of one of the rarest and most useful women this country has produced. "A woman great without aiming to be so," they said of her at her death—Anna Ottendorfer—to whose courage and intelligence the country owes one of its most fearless and liberal newspapers—the *New Yorker Staats-Zeitung*. Left a widow with six children in 1852, Mrs.

From the *American Magazine* (July 1912): 281–87.

Ottendorfer, then Mrs. Uhl, assumed the full management of the young daily which she and her husband had founded but not yet developed to a profitable point. It is said that when she had settled the bills of the week following Mr. Uhl's death she had sixty-eight cents left! But she had vision and courage. She refused to sell the paper. She took the full management and made it profitable and powerful.

In 1859 Mrs. Uhl married Mr. Oswald Ottendorfer, who was then an editorial writer on the paper. From that time the two shared the responsibilities of the enterprise and together made it the institution it is.

One of Mrs. Ottendorfer's daughters, Anna Uhl, married a banker famous in Wall Street for daring and successful operations, Charles Woerishoffer. To this couple were born two girls. The younger, Carola, was born about the time of Anna Ottendorfer's death.

Mrs. Woerishoffer inherited her mother's goodness and understanding, and she continued so far as in her lay all her innumerable efforts to make life more tolerable for the weak and the poor, more beautiful and significant for everybody. Her social and political views developed with the times. Among the rich women of the United States, it is doubtful if there is one to-day more truly radical. With her radicalism goes the strictest integrity; her attitude toward taxation is an illustration. Probably no property holder in New York City comes nearer to a literal fulfillment of the tax laws than Mrs. Woerishoffer.

Carola thus grew up in a circle alive with the memories of a noble grandmother and under a mother whose life was spent in active and intelligent service. She was thrown much, too, with Oswald Ottendorfer, a man of the highest principles and ideals, and saw and heard in his circle all of the great political and social leaders of the day.

The child responded fully to traditions and atmosphere. She was open-minded and open-hearted. She feared no one. She was insatiable in her curiosity and her love of adventure. She was full of passionate enthusiasm—a fiery patriot—a worshiper of every one who "did things." In the little collection of souvenirs, which those nearest to her have gathered since her death, is a *carte de visite* photograph taken when she was perhaps five years old. The vigorous little figure, the small proud head, the fearless, challenging eyes are not things to forget. Here is a child, a glance tells, whose respect would be an honor and whose love a treasure, one whom you would not attempt to wheedle or deceive, one to whom you would not lie. The wise would be humble in her presence—the foolish uneasy.

She always knew quite definitely what she wanted. At nine years of age, seeing a portrait of Miss Thomas, President of Bryn Mawr College, in a gallery, she hung before it, refusing to look at anything else and telling her mother, as she left, "When I grow up I am going to Miss Thomas' school." And this resolve she carried out.

Miss Thomas tells us that she has reason to believe that all of the girl's work from the start was chosen for the bearing it might have on the social work she hoped to do later, and she adds: "Her curriculum of study, as it is written on our college records to-day, is the very course I should recommend above all others for social workers." She did what is called "good work" in college; but it is the personality that counts in the group, not this or that bundle of achievements. Definite purpose and creditable scholarship are not unusual. Unfettered judgment, contempt of precedent, fearless expression— these are unusual and these Carola Woerishoffer had to a degree that startled, horrified or thrilled those who came in contact with her, according to their individual outlook.

It was not to her studies alone by any means that she turned her vigorous attention. She was eminently a lover of life, of people and things doing. As an athlete she was famous—probably the strongest and most daring a swimmer the college ever had. She was a spirited horsewoman—good at all games, most ingenious and energetic in college pranks of every sort. It will be long before Bryn Mawr girls will cease to tell of the day when Carola Woerishoffer, coming across a sophomore on the bank of the swimming pool, who seemed to show a trace of that cockiness, not to be tolerated in sophomores, picked her up and ducked her. It will be long before they will forget to tell of how one day when the question of the strength of a fire-net was brought up, she settled the question by diving straight into it from an upper window.

When she graduated from Bryn Mawr she merely transferred from that milieu to lower New York, her purpose, her habits of study and observation, her frank judgment and fearless conduct. She brought there, too, what was perhaps the strongest thing in her, a passion to depend entirely on herself, and to be judged by what she, the individual, Carola Woerishoffer, could prove herself to be. She wanted nothing, no recognition, affection, or position which she suspected to have come to her for any other reason than for what she herself was or might be. It was this passion of hers, in my reading of her character, which made her so unwilling to depend in any way on her wealth. Carola Woerishoffer was rich, very rich, I believe; that is, she had entirely in her own hands an annual income of many tens of thousands of dollars, but comparatively few of those who came in contact with her knew it.

Thus it was that she, who because she had a fortune, which she intended to give where it would be most useful, might have had practically any position which she desired, at the start refused all positions save those in the ranks where the hard work is done. "She wanted to work it out," she said. She wanted, no doubt, to take by actual contact her own measure of the undertakings already in operation in the town and no less of the workers themselves.

The first intimation of the kind of help they were going to get from the newcomer was in 1908, when the first Congestion Exhibit was planned for New York. It is said that the French were beaten in 1870 on their own territory because the Germans knew the country they were to fight in better than those who owned it! There has been many a social battle lost in New York City because the well-intentioned fighters have never realized that the first point of success is to know the lay of the land. A few people who saw this undertook to give the city of New York a lesson in its own social geography. It was a new idea and money was skeptical. It looked as if the exhibition might fail when Carola, whose quick intelligence had seen the awakening that might come from putting baldly before the city its own waste places, its hidden horror spots, came to the rescue.

"She made that thing possible," Mr. McAneny, President of the Borough of Manhattan, said at an impressive Memorial Meeting at Greenwich House, last November; and he added: "She taught us at the City Hall that there were things that the city had long neglected, that the city ought quickly to take up, and the city had taken up many of those things. I can tell you that this girl has led the City of New York to do things that will last for many, many years, and will continue to grow and to expand."

What she learned through the Congestion Exhibit and through various social organizations, each in its own way, trying to get at and correct some evil or other, seems to have intensified her desire to get to the bottom of things. It was this eagerness which led her to offer to go herself as a worker in the laundries of the city in order to get for the Consumers' League the facts it needed for an investigation it had on hand. She, of course, knew nothing about the processes of the laundry, nothing of washing, drying, starching and ironing, nothing of mangles and wringers and jiggers. Moreover, her appearance was against her for she had all the marks of her breeding and her full life. She went at the undertaking quite simply and practically, attempting no disguise, but dressing "poorly" and acting as unobtrusively as possible. Only in one case did she use influence to get work; that was at the beginning, when she obtained through a friend "a job as a learner on collars." After this preliminary instruction she trusted to answering advertisements, and although she changed at the end of every week, unless she was thrown out earlier by fault of her incompetency, short work, or some conflict with authority, she never was without work for more than a day during the full four months of the summer of 1909.

The report of what she learned in this experience is in the hands of the Consumers' League; but if anyone thinks to find on the face of it much about Carola Woerishoffer, he will be disappointed. He must read between the lines to see her at all. Then he realizes that she put in four months of as hard and trying labor as any man or woman could give to a cause.

As she was determined to shirk nothing she was regularly at her tub or mangle or feeding machine at 7:30 A.M. and whenever the work demanded it she stayed on into the night. There were no provisions for seating in the long work period, frequently the rooms were practically unventilated, always more or less stifling from steam and damp. In some places she found neglect and uncleanliness adding to the disagreeable features inevitable in the industry. She worked days over unguarded machines where the girls told her cynically: "You didn't get burned to-day or yesterday, but you sure will some time, everyone does." That she must have often suffered disgust, pain and fatigue is certain, but she makes no record of it. It is only by accident, indeed, that one learns that she was conscious that it was a hot summer! She is telling in her scrupulous, restrained way of the ventilating provisions in the different places she worked: "In one place where the investigator dipped shirts in hot starch at a breakneck pace," she says, she was first struck when she went out to lunch by the coolness of the day. That night she discovered that the thermometer had registered 96 degrees in the shade!

The entire naturalness of her attitude toward her fellow-workers, her apparent unconsciousness that there were any differences between her and them, made it possible for her to fall at once into friendly relations. She was one of them. Dozens of little comments like the following show this: "Upon entering a new place the investigator found, as a rule, a spirit of friendly interest and of cordiality, expressed occasionally in the accepted formula: 'Say, you got a feller?' 'Sure; ain't you got one?' 'Sure.'"

Or take this: "One of the ironers was eager to tell her past pampered life as a cook 'off Fifth Avenue.' 'Sure, and it was a fine time I had there, but,' she added with a sigh, 'it was there I met me misfortune.' 'And what was that,' someone asked. 'Me husband,' said she, and then explained how it was through his illness that she had been brought upon her present arduous days. 'Standing on your feet nine hours a day five days in the week when you are well on in life is no joke.'"

Her strict control of herself, the easy terms she fell into with the girls, gave her a reasonableness toward the work and an understanding of how and why they, as a rule, accept cheerfully and as a matter of course its hard conditions. That is, understanding and not emotion ruled her investigation. One has to read closely between the lines to realize that there was a stern, passionate little judge turning over the facts she was gathering. Mrs. Florence Kelly has told of a talk she had with Miss Woerishoffer in which she bared her soul as she rarely did.

"One day Carola came to my office," says Mrs. Kelley. "'I hope you have not been to lunch,' she said; 'I hope you are going to take me, because if you do not I shall not have any. I undertook, when I began working in the laundry, to find out as nearly as I could how it would feel just to have the amount of money that I could earn with my strength, without skill, and now I have been dismissed for taking the part of an old woman in a scrap with the foreman. If I were a real laundry worker, I should not have any money until next Wednesday.'

"We went out to luncheon at one o'clock," continues Mrs. Kelly, "and she talked to me until five, almost uninterruptedly, about the perfectly needless hardships of the people among whom she worked. I do not think she knew at all what she was eating. I do not think she realized when we walked back to the office. I do not think she knew that it was five o'clock, until the cleaners came to close the office. She talked all those hours perfectly absorbed. I have been haunted by that conversation. I have thought of it innumerable times, and the memory of her face is always the memory of an unsmiling one, absorbed, aflame with the passion of living and changing the things that ought to be changed. I cannot imagine saying anything that day that could possible have made her smile. She had not learned to write. She had written some notes about this work which she wanted published, and we went over them again and again. She was afraid they would not be accurate, afraid they might exaggerate, and when she finished they were so literal in their statement of facts that they did not present the picture at all."

Spirited, adventure-loving, eager as she was, she had great capacity for humdrum work, if she realized its need. That is, it did not require the excitement of an investigation like this of the laundry to keep her at work. At Greenwich House, the Social Settlement, under the direction of her friend, Mary Simkhovitch, where she lived when her own home was closed, as it was much of the time, she was always ready to help, whatever the task. First and last, she did a great deal of routine work in the Woman's Trade Union League, which she had joined when she first came to New York. Miss Marot says she could always be depended upon to address envelopes, serve on committees, canvass for the label, distribute circulars or do any other odd job at which the officers, all of them her friends, needed help.

It was not until the shirtwaist strike of the fall of 1909 that she had an opportunity to show what her loyalty to trade unionism really was. It will be remembered that at the very start of this strike the police began to arrest the girls generally and in many cases for practically no cause. It soon became evident that unless bail could be furnished at a moment's notice hundreds of young girls would be thrown into jail for indefinite periods. The courts demanded real estate security and there was a great hurrying to and fro among the officers of the League for help. Carola at once set out to relieve the situation. Her mother cooperated with her, and for $1 transferred to her daughter real estate to the value of $90,000. There was a sensation in the courtroom when she appeared with her $90,000 bond and made it known that she would remain in court as long as the strike lasted and would see that the girls got fair play.

Her success in escaping newspaper notoriety at this time was amazing. "There she was," says Helen Marot, "by all precedent the hero of the hour, a romantic personage, her bond a veritable fairy wand, releasing the girls from the dreaded confinement of prison walls and evil associations. But Carola's integrity was greater than her romanticism. Before the first day was over, by sheer force of character she had turned the attention from herself to the strikers. She disarmed the girls in their expression of gratitude. She even performed a superhuman feat with the press. Without exception every reporter sacrificed an opportunity to turn in 'copy,' and a copy which he knew would have first place and several days' run. They took from her instead stories about the strike, and during those thirteen weeks she promised and gave them material, telling them that if they published her name they would never have another story from her."

Her position as bondsman did not end with the shirtwaist strike. From that time to the time of her death she was appealed to by striking unions—boxmakers, cloakmakers, cordage workers, tailors, white goods workers—to go their bond. She let it be known where she could be found day and night and never refused a call at any hour. Her expression in the shirtwaist strike made her realize the need of a fund for emergencies in time of strike. "Don't you think it would be a good thing to have a strike fund started," she said casually one day to Miss Marot. "I have received an unexpected dividend, and will make the first contribution." From her tone, Miss Marot thought that her contribution would be possibly $500. She handed her a check for $10,000. It was with that check that the Strike Council was organized.

This intense grappling with things as they are in New York City, her incessant turning over in her mind of what she saw, always with the fixed purpose of getting at causes and of finding the best point of attack, led her to throw herself eagerly into new undertakings which her judgment approved. It was in the service of one of the newer efforts of the State to prevent injustice that Carola Woerishoffer lost her life—the Bureau of Industries and Immigration, founded in 1910.

The knowledge she had gained first hand, of the exploitation of ignorant newcomers in the country, had convinced her of the need of better inspection and fresh legislation, and she gladly accepted a place on the Bureau staff as a special investigator. Her interest and her activity soon were centered on studying the conditions in the colonies and camps of foreigners, particularly in the country. These settlements are frequently scattered in wild and isolated places. Visiting them is difficult and expensive work always and often really dangerous. Miss Woerishoffer attacked the problem with indomitable energy. That she enjoyed both the difficulties and the dangers is unquestionable. She had the spirit that carries a soldier into battle and it rose with the fight. Driving her own machine, often unattended, she scoured the country where the laborers were gathered, finding out facts of all sorts. No exploiting "boss" could escape her. She saw where the weak place was at a glance and her suggestions for immediate relief, as well as for preventive legislation, were always worth considering.

It was in this service, as I have said, that she lost her life. That she overworked persistently, all her friends knew, though her endurance was so remarkable that they had ceased to remonstrate. In September of 1911 she was inspecting the labor camps near Cannonsville, New York. She had gone to work at six that morning, had stopped at noon only to eat a sandwich, and this she had been doing for days. For the first time in her life, the friend with her heard her say that she was tired. She complained that her wrist seemed too weak to control her car. The road was wet and at a bad turn, when the car was at low speed the wheel skidded, the car went over an embankment, burying her beneath it and injuring her so seriously that she died the next morning. "The State has had no enrolled soldier," says Miss Kellor in her report of the first year's work of her Bureau, "who has responded to every call more promptly, who has performed the duties set him more unflinchingly, or who has given his life more utterly in the field of battle than she in the cause in which she believed."

Soldier is the word for her—a soldier of a new type, but a type which, unless all the signs are wrong, is to multiply and increase. Carola was a revolting soldier—one who refused the weapons those in authority put into her hands, refused the place in life they wished her to take, refused to march in the way they ordered her to go. The rich, who are humane, have approved methods of what we call philanthropy. They are founded on the belief that poverty is ineradicable and that relief, not prevention, is their duty.

Carola broke with this view of social service and with all its machinery. Its aloofness offended her deep, warm sense of human brotherhood. I believe it was nothing but an extraordinary consciousness of the oneness of man that enabled her to do the work she did in the way she did. She could move among men without consciousness of class. One of the most extraordinary evidences of a genuine democratic spirit that I have ever come across was the fact that she worked for four months in the steam laundries of New York, side by side with girls and women of all nationalities and colors, joined them in their lunches and recreations, got from them confidences of every sort and yet never but once was the question of her "belonging" raised. Once, and once only, a girl did say to her: "You are different. You do not belong here."

Another point where she could not follow her class was in using the emotional appeal which has served reformers and philanthropists so exclusively in the past and which unquestionably is one reason we have never gotten farther in preventive work. She would have none of it—"gush" was her abomination. She had a reverence for the facts quite unusual among men and women who seek to help. Her contention was that unless we know in cold figures—in personally verified observations—what the conditions are, we can never know the true point of attack—the laws and regulations necessary, the instruction necessary, the relief necessary.

The control of her emotion, which she exercised in her investigation and discussion, her openly expressed disdain of those who allowed themselves to be carried away by their feelings, was often set down by those who knew her but slightly to coldness of nature. But I do not believe it was a lack of sensitiveness or scant power of emotion which made her the stern little Spartan she was. It was rather an early realization that those who do things must learn control. I fancy she resolved very early in life to put under control a nature which those, who remember her in childhood, declare to have been extravagant in its demands for affection and in its sensitiveness to the opinion of others.

She sought to be just as she sought self-control. One of her friends told me this story: Carola desired greatly to be made the secretary of a certain organization in whose work she heartily believed and to which she had already promised a large sum. She believed herself fitted for the place and so did several of the leaders in the movement. But for some reason she was not appointed. She was greatly disappointed, and her friend thoroughly angry. "Promise," he said, "that you will give nothing to them." She looked at him quietly—"Oh, very well," she said and went away.

The next day she found her friend again in good temper. "There was no use in my arguing with you yesterday," she said. "You were angry and so unreasonable. You must see how silly it would be not to support an organization that does good work simply because they do not happen to like me."

Her attitude toward money was singularly indifferent. As I have said, she refused utterly to trade on it; she wanted to prove that she had a value quite apart from that. Her joy was great when Miss Kellor appointed her to the Bureau of Immigration at a salary of $1200 a year. She was worth something in her own right—a recognized producer—useful to society. Toward this money she had a feeling quite different from that which came to her in dividends. She kept it apart, and in buying presents for her mother or friends, used it exclusively.

Her gifts were always secret. It was only after death that it was known where the $10,000 which helped the Trade Union League so much, in the fall of 1910, came from. Her gifts to individuals in trouble were unending, and almost always anonymous. In her close contact with the very poor, every day forced on her some situation where immediate relief was imperative. She used often to send money by mail to the person, no name attached.

She was a growing person—one saw it in many ways. To her friends in social work this development was characteristically shown by her changing estimate of methods for achieving results. Shortly after coming from college she gave generously to certain charities which deal with the problem of consumption by palliative methods. Three years later she remarked: "I have stopped giving to that committee. They are not getting anywhere, and they can't, till they get at the economic causes of consumption."

So, too, while unstintingly giving personal effort in bailing out striking men and women, she came to believe that governmental regulation is essential to secure and maintain fair conditions of working. She admitted to a friend only a week before her death, that she was anxious to work for the minimum wage, and industrial commissions, which would determine with impartiality and for all workers what are fair conditions for working and fair pay for work. The knowledge that poverty cannot be exterminated so long as a few draw large unearned incomes, instead of daunting, seemed to inspire her. Her only objection to a certain progressive form of taxation was illuminating. "But mother and I won't have to pay any more taxes under that system," and she did not thoroughly approve of it until shown that both her mother and she would bear a heavier and proportionate share of taxes through the proposed change. When reminded once that most of the constructive work and legislation would gradually reduce her income, she replied: "Well, I am prouder that I can earn a living than that I don't have to now, and I'd rather give to people that are trying to bring about a fairer chance than to anything else."

A beautiful thing about the girl was the way she had with children; her gift for friendship with simple people. After her death many letters came to her friends, telling of her kindness. One of the most beautiful tributes is in a letter from a Maine guide to her friend, Vladimir Simkhovitch. "It seems such a pity that Miss Woerishoffer should have to die," he writes, "she had everything to live for, health, strength and beauty. Wealth with her did not seem to count, she was frank in speaking and absolutely fearless. I had formed such a liking for her on such a short acquaintance that it comes to me, now, as a surprise. I did not realize it until I heard of her death and nothing has ever upset me so much since my brother Will was drowned in the lake."

There were many to whom, as to this simple-hearted man, her death brought the surprise of their own affection—[but] more to whom it brought the realization of the meaning of her life. Twenty-six fuller years are rarely lived. Rarely, at such an age, has a purpose been better conceived, the attitude of mind and spirit more clearly manifested. She has set a pace for the new soldier, which the Revolt of the Young Rich is bringing into that most splendid of wars—the war on poverty and injustice.

Part II

A Woman's Eye on Business

Introduction

Ida Tarbell is best known for her writing about business. The *McClure's* series on Standard Oil and John D. Rockefeller, later published as a two-volume book, was a landmark in investigative business reporting (even though it also was correctly labeled muckraking), and Tarbell was widely applauded for the changes her work wrought. Magazine historian Frank Luther Mott believes that the estimated fifty thousand dollars the series cost *McClure's* was well spent, "for the Tarbell 'History of the Standard Oil Company,' which ran for two years, was one of the greatest serials ever to appear in an American magazine. It was a significant socioeconomic document; though subject to later correction in some respects, it represented good historical investigation; it was interesting reading for all, and for some it was nothing short of sensational."[1]

The writing she did was important, establishing a model that, even many years later, other reporters follow. As Baker and Anderson note:

> Numerous investigations of the workplace have been made by both academic scholars and free-lance reporters. Investigators collect field notes from the shop floor and office suites, interview workers on the job and in their homes, and then return to their typewriters to tell the story of work at the bottom of the occupational ladder. Their accounts can best be termed muckraking sociology, portraying workers as powerless, alienated, bored, angry, manipulated, trapped and deskilled.[2]

In this section, comprising business and investigative pieces, Tarbell concentrates on two themes. The first is that business is important, can be profitable, and is not inherently evil. The second is that business has certain obligations to its workers, with regard to their human needs, that in many instances it does not fulfill. Tarbell's goal, evident also in many articles not presented here, was to make business efficient and *profitable*—that is, to restrict governmental interference in business operations to the minimum feasible, but also to ensure that business treated its workers humanely. Of course, Tarbell believed that good treatment of workers would lead to increased productivity and profit, so she remained consistent within a pro-business stance.

Despite these perspectives, Tarbell was not blind, and the piece on Standard Oil shows clearly her conviction that business, if lacking morality, had to be controlled. But this indictment was dispassionate. Her work always appeared as fact-based reporting and not as advocacy, and she disappointed some northwestern Pennsylvania oilmen when she refused to step beyond the role of reporter to assume that of advocate.

The first selection here is taken from the beginning of the Standard Oil series. In it, Tarbell employs narration, description, and quotation to paint a chilling picture of Rockefeller and of the deliberate way he set out to squash competition and make as much money as he could through Standard Oil and the South Improvement Company. Rockefeller, in his early teens, had realized the force of money and reckoned that "it was a good thing to let the money be my slave." He lived by that motto, and Tarbell captures a number of scenes in which Rockefeller seems to be a person obsessed.

Quickly moving to the adult Rockefeller, the piece describes how the plan for dominating the oil industry was launched. Tracing the secrecy, the manipulation, and the ruthless, predatory, threatening behavior Rockefeller and his associates employed, Tarbell's account is as gripping today as when it first was written.

Elbert Hubbard, a Standard Oil executive, sought with a good deal of color to discredit Tarbell's work:

Ida Tarbell . . . is an honest, bitter, talented, prejudiced and disappointed woman who wrote from her own point of view. And that view is from the ditch, where her father's wheelbarrow was landed by a Standard Oil tank-wagon. . . . She shot from cover, and she shot to kill. Such literary bush-whackers should be answered shot for shot. Sniping the commercial cara-van may be legitimate, but to my mind the Tarbell-Steffens-Russell-Roosevelt-Sinclair method of inky warfare is quite as unethical as the alleged tentacled-octopi policy which they attack.[3]

S. S. McClure's biographer, Peter Lyon, applauds what Tarbell did: "When she was done, Miss Tarbell had drawn a formidable indictment. She had shown that almost every step the Standard Oil Company had taken toward trust and monopoly had necessarily trampled a competitor to death, and had been accomplished by fraud, deceit, special privilege, gross illegality, bribery, coercion, corruption, intimidation, espionage, or outright terror."[4]

A short time after the stunning Standard Oil success, Tarbell turned to another western Pennsylvania target, Pittsburgh, "A Tariff-Made City." Virtually one impassioned tirade against the so-called "Pittsburgh millionaires," this piece is a stunning criticism of iron and steel tariffs, showing how they created an enormous gulf between the heads of industry and the workers. Tarbell wrote: "The estimated tariff profit in the steel trust alone in 1907 was $80,000,000. Who got the money? Go look at the steel palaces and chateaux in New York and Paris. Go ask the Pittsburgh millionaires who fill the glittering places of pleasure in the great cities of Europe and this country." Of the wealthy she said: "Not even the child has touched them. The conditions under which the children of the poor are brought up in Pittsburgh are such that babies die like flies." This piece shows Tarbell at her outraged best.

"The Fear of Efficiency" is Tarbell's examination of "scientific management," as developed by Frederick Winslow Taylor. She gives the expected thorough description of scientific management, which was being touted as a way of increasing the speed of factory piecework. Tarbell then criticizes the approach, taking Germany as an example. In this post—World War I article, Tarbell claims that German military disregard for human factors led to its defeat in the war. Ever even-handed, Tarbell finds merit in scientific management's ability to increase production. And she emphasizes that the scientific approach is not necessarily in conflict with a concern for human needs in a business organization.

Those human needs earlier had been addressed by Tarbell in a piece called "A Fine Place to Work." Describing many workplaces, Tarbell claims that companies paying most attention to the human needs of their workers—for recreation, ease, cleanliness, and positive group activity—reap benefits in terms of increased production and greater employee loyalty. In one passage Tarbell even credits such humane treatment of employees with helping to ease racial prejudice, noting that in one plant "it was not infrequent for a white man deliberately to take a coloured man's table or invite him to his."

The final selection here, an undated, but probably 1925, typescript, is "The Floyd Collinses of Our Mines." Using as an example the seventeen-day ordeal of Floyd Collins, a Kentucky spelunker who was trapped and then died underground, Tarbell raises questions about American coal mine safety. "Must we engulf nine hundred men yearly in taking out soft coal?" she asks. The answer, of course, is no; but preventing the deaths would be costly, and Tarbell accuses mine management of being unwilling to spend the money required.

Written much in the style of a good newspaper editorial, this piece cites facts (British miners die at one-third the American rate) and argues for nation-wide enactment of mine-safety laws: "If at any moment of those seventeen days that young Floyd Collins lay pinned down by rock in his Kentucky cave, legislation could have saved him, can we doubt that it would have been worth it? An extra session, if necessary!"

These pieces, then, represent the ways in which Tarbell approached business. She was not hostile to profit, saw humane worker treatment as essential to both profit and human dignity, would accept government involvement when warranted, and strongly opposed tariffs. Also evident in these works are the range of sources Tarbell used and how extensive her research could be.

It is also possible to see in this group of pieces, from first to last, a subtle change in Tarbell's approach, as she gave less attention to assembling minute details and more to offering commentary and opinion. In the Standard Oil and Pittsburgh pieces, she piles fact upon fact to hammer home her points. But in time, she broadens her scope, arguing that scientific management is worthwhile but must not override human needs in the workplace. In the later pieces, then, Tarbell shifts from the sterile, fact-based reporting on Standard Oil to warmer and more compassionate pleas for attention to worker welfare.

The Rise of the
Standard Oil Company

Strung along the banks of Walworth and Kingsbury Runs, the creeks to which Cleveland, Ohio, frequently banishes her heavy and evil-smelling burdens, there lay in the early sixties a dozen or more small oil refineries. Why they were there, more than two hundred miles from the spot where the oil was taken from the earth, a glance at a map of the railroads of the time will show. No railroad entered the region where oil was first discovered. To bring machinery for refineries to that distant and rugged locality was practically impossible. The simplest operation was to take the crude to the nearest manufacturing cities. Cleveland was one of these. Great as was its distance from the oil field, its advantages as a refining center more than balanced that. Cleveland commanded the entire western market. It had two trunk lines running to New York, both eager for oil traffic, and by Lake Erie and the canal it had for a large part of the year a splendid cheap waterway. Thus, at the opening of the oil business, Cleveland was destined by geographical position to be a refining center.

Men saw it, and hastened to take advantage of the opportunity. There was grave risk. The oil supply might not hold out. As yet there was no certain market for refined oil. But a sure result was not what drew people into the oil business in the early sixties. Fortune was running fleet-footed across the country, and at her garment men clutched. They loved the chase almost as they did success, and so many a man in Cleveland tried his luck in an oil refinery, as hundreds on Oil Creek were trying it in an oil lease. From the start the refineries made money, even the rudest ones. Seeing this, and seeing, too, that the oil supply was probably permanent, men who loved the result rather than the gamble took up the business. Among these was a young firm of produce commission merchants. Both members of this firm were keen businessmen, and one of them had a remarkable commercial vision—a genius for seeing the possibilities in material things. This man's name was Rockefeller—

From *McClure's Magazine* (Dec. 1902): 115–28.

John D. Rockefeller. He was but twenty-three years old at the time, but he had already got his feet firmly on the business ladder, and had got them there by his own efforts. Frugality had started him. It was the strongest trait of his character. Indeed, the only incident of his childhood preserved by biographers illustrates his love for saving. When he was eight years old, so the story runs, he raised a flock of turkeys—his earliest business venture. The flock was a fine one, for the owner had given it close care, and it was sold to advantage. A boy of eight usually earns to spend. This boy was different. He invested his entire turkey earnings at 7 per cent. It was the beginning of a financial career.

Five years after this turkey episode, when young Rockefeller was thirteen years old, his father moved from the farm in central New York, where the boy had been born (July 8, 1839), to Cleveland, Ohio. Here he went to school for three years. At sixteen he left school to become a clerk and bookkeeper. He was an admirable accountant—one of the early-and-late sort, who saw everything, forgot nothing, and never talked. His earnings lie saved, waiting for an opportunity. In 1858 it came. Among his acquaintances was a young Englishman, M. B. Clark. Older by twelve years than Rockefeller, he had left a hard life in England when he was twenty, to seek fortune in America had landed in Boston in 1847, without a penny or a friend, and it had taken three months for him to earn money to get to Ohio. Here he had taken the first job at hand, as man-of-all-work, wood-chopper, teamster. He had found his way to Cleveland, had become a valuable man in the houses where he was employed, had gone to school nights, had saved money. They were two of a kind, Clark and Rockefeller, and in 1858 they pooled their earnings and started a produce commission business on the Cleveland docks. The venture succeeded. Local historians credit Clark & Rockefeller with doing a business of $450,000 the first year, a figure that somewhat taxes credulity. However that may be, the firm prospered. The war came on, and as neither partner went to the front, they had full chance to take advantage of the opportunity for produce business a great army gives. A greater chance than furnishing army supplies, lucrative as most people found that, was in the oil business (so Clark and Rockefeller began to think), and in 1862, when an Englishman of ability and energy, one Samuel Andrews, asked them to back him in starting a refinery, they put in $4,000 and promised to give more if necessary. Now Andrews was a mechanical genius. He devised new processes, made a better and better quality of oil, got larger and larger percentages of refined from his crude. The little refinery grew big, and Clark & Rockefeller soon had $100,000 or more in it. In the meantime Cleveland was growing as a refining center. The business which in 1860 had been a gamble, was by 1865 one of the most promising industries of the town. There were thirty refineries, big and little, with a capacity of from 1,800 to 2,000 barrels of crude a day, and the refined shipments of the year amounted to nearly 200,000 barrels. It was but the beginning—so Mr. Rockefeller thought—and in that year he sold out his share of the commission business and put his capital into the oil firm of Rockefeller & Andrews.

In the new firm Andrews attended to the manufacturing. The pushing of the business, the buying and the selling, fell to Rockefeller. From the start his effect on the business was tremendous. He had the frugal man's hatred of waste and disorder, of middlemen and unnecessary manipulation, and he began a vigorous elimination of these from his business. The residuum that other refineries let run into the ground, he sold. Old iron found its way to the junk shop. He bought his oil directly from the wells. He made his own barrels. He watched and saved and contrived. The ability with which he made the smallest bargain furnishes topics to Cleveland story-tellers today. Low-voiced, soft-footed, humble, knowing every point in every man's business, he never tired until he got his wares at the lowest possible figure. "John always got the best of the bargain," old men tell you in Cleveland today, and they wince though they laugh in telling it. "Smooth," "a savvy fellow," is their description of him. To drive a good bargain was the joy of his life. "The only time I ever saw John Rockefeller enthusiastic," a man told the writer once, "was when a report came in from the Creek that his buyer had secured a cargo of oil at a figure much below the market price. He bounded from his chair with a shout of joy, danced up and down, hugged me, threw up his hat, acted so like a madman that I have never forgotten it."

He could borrow as well as bargain. The firm's capital was limited; growing as they were, they often needed money, and had none. Borrow they must. Rarely if ever did Mr. Rockefeller fail. There is a story handed down in Cleveland from the days of Clark & Rockefeller, produce merchants, which is illustrative of his methods.

One day a well-known and rich businessman stepped into the office and asked for Mr. Rockefeller. He was out, and Clark met this visitor. "Mr. Clark," he said, "you may tell Mr. Rockefeller, when he comes in, that I think I can use the $10,000 he wants to invest with me for your firm. I have thought it all over."

"Good God!" cried Clark, "we don't want to invest $10,000. John is out right now trying to borrow $5,000 for us."

It turned out that to prepare him for a proposition to borrow $5,000 Mr. Rockefeller had told the gentleman that he and Clark wanted to invest $10,000!

"And the joke of it is," said Clark, who used to tell the story, "John got the $5,000 even after I had let the cat out of the bag. Oh, he was the greatest borrower you ever saw."

These qualities told. The firm grew rich, and started a second refinery—William A. Rockefeller & Co. They took in a partner, H. M. Flagler, and opened a house in New York for selling their oil. Of all these concerns John D. Rockefeller was the head. Finally, in June 1870, five years after he became an active partner in the refining business, Mr. Rockefeller combined all his companies into one—the Standard Oil Company. The capital of the new concern was $1,000,000. The parties interested in it were John D. Rockefeller, Henry M. Flagler, Samuel Andrews, Stephen V. Harkness, and William Rockefeller.

The strides the firm of Rockefeller & Andrews made after the former went into it were attributed, for three or four years, mainly to this extraordinary capacity for bargaining and borrowing. Then its chief competitors began to suspect something. John Rockefeller might get his oil cheaper now and then, they said, but he could not do it often. He might make close contracts for which they had neither the patience nor the stomach. He might have an unusual mechanical and practical genius in his partner. But these things could not explain all. They believed they bought, on the whole, almost as cheaply and with as great, or nearly as great, economy. He could sell at no better price than they. Where was his advantage? There was but one place where it could be, and that was in transportation. He must be getting better rates from the railroads than they were. One of the rival refiners, of a firm long in the business, which had been prosperous from the start, and which prided itself on its methods, its economy, and its energy—Alexander Scofield & Co.—went to the railroad companies' agents in 1868 or 1869. "You are giving others better rates than you are us," said Mr. Alexander, the representative of the firm. They did not attempt to deny it—they simply agreed to give him a rebate also. The arrangement was interesting. Mr. Alexander was to pay the open, or regular, rate on oil from the Oil Regions to Cleveland, which at the date was forty cents a barrel. At the end of each month he was to send to the railroad vouchers for the amount of oil shipped and paid for at forty cents, and was to get back from the railroad, in money, fifteen cents on each barrel. This concession applied only to oil brought from the wells. He was never able to get a rebate on oil shipped eastward. When he complained to the railroads he was told that if he would ship as large quantities as the Standard Oil Company he could have as good a rate.

Ship as large a quantity! It was a new principle in railroad policy. Were not the railroads public servants? Were they not bound, as common carriers, to carry ten barrels at the same rate per barrel as they did a hundred? If they were not, what was to become of the ten-barrel men? Could they live? Mr. Alexander remonstrated. The railroad agent was firm with Mr. Alexander. In all branches of business the heaviest buyer got the best rate; the railroad must regard this principle. It could not give him the same rate as Mr. Rockefeller unless he shipped as large amounts of oil, and he went back to his refinery knowing that he must do business with a handicap, nearly, if not quite, as great as his profit.

How had it happened that Rockefeller and his colleagues had secured this advantage so out of harmony with a railroad's obligation to the public? Nobody knew then. But ten years later the railroad man who granted them this privilege, and started them on the road by which, a few years later, they reached almost a complete monopoly of the oil business, stated the reasons for the discrimination in an affidavit which has never, to the writer's knowledge, been published. This man was General J. H. Devereux, who in 1868 succeeded Amasa Stone as vice-president of the Lake Shore Railroad. He came to this position at a moment when a lively contest was going on for the eastward oil traffic, and when the Pennsylvania Railroad, having the advantage, was claiming what General Devereux called a "patent right on the transportation of oil." The cheap rates which the Pennsylvania was giving, the wild speculations in both refined and crude, to which the officials of the Erie—Fiske and Gould—were lending aid, combined with the fact that a number of big and finely equipped refineries were going up in the Oil Regions, frightened the Cleveland refiners. Unless something was done, they told General Devereux, Cleveland would be destroyed as a refining center. Something was done—the Lake Shore ran its road still nearer to the heart of the Oil Regions, and began to give Rockefeller, Andrews, & Flagler rebates on their crude oil. General Devereux's reason for making special rates to this firm and to no other, was that while all the other refiners expressed the fear that the advantages of refining on the Creek close to the oil supply were such that they might ultimately all have to move from Cleveland to the Oil Regions, Rockefeller and his associates promised to fight it out in Cleveland if the Lake Shore would handle their oil as cheaply as the Pennsylvania could. Why the railroad should not have quieted the fears of the other firms by the same assurance as it gave the Standard, General Devereux did not explain. This was the beginning. Two years later, in 1870, the Lake Shore made a broader contract with the Standard. The road had been carrying little oil eastward for the firm for some time. The rates they offered were not low enough, and the Standard firm was shipping principally by water; but this method was slow, and the way, for a portion of this year, was closed. Soon after the Standard Oil Company was formed, in 1870, Mr. Flagler, representing the firm, proposed that if General Devereux would give them a special through rate they would ship sixty carloads a day. The rate asked was considerably lower than the regular open rates, but the advantage of having a regular amount shipped daily was so great that the railroad company concluded that their profit would be greater than by serving all alike. It was evidently merely a question of which method paid better. The question of the railroad's duty as a public carrier was not considered. The Standard's arrangement with General Devereux, in 1870, gave them steady transportation the year round to the seaboard, at a rate cheaper than anybody else could get. It was equivalent to renting a railroad for their private use. Every Cleveland refiner was put out of the race by the arrangement. The refining business was so prosperous at the time the arrangement was made that suspicion was not at first aroused, but in a year's time the effect became apparent. Firms which had been making $10,000 to $20,000 a year found themselves making little or nothing. But why? That they did not see. The oil business in Cleveland was growing prodigiously. By 1870 the city had become the largest refining center in the United States, taking 2,000,000 barrels of crude oil from the region—one-third of the entire output of the Oil Regions. Instead of being destroyed by the competition of refineries built close to the wells, it was growing under the competition, but in spite of this growth only one firm—the Standard Oil Company—was making much money. This was puzzling and disheartening.

It would seem as if the one man in Cleveland who ought to have been satisfied with the situation in 1870 was Mr. Rockefeller. His organization, from his buyers on the Creek to his exporter in New York, was well-nigh perfect. His control of a railroad from the wells to the seaboard gave him an advantage nobody else had the daring and the persuasive power to get. It was clear that in time he must control the entire Cleveland trade. But Mr. Rockefeller was far from satisfied. He was a brooding, cautious, secretive man, seeing all the possible danger as well as all the possible opportunities in things, and he studied, as a player at chess, all the possible combinations which might imperil his supremacy. These twenty-five Cleveland rivals of his—how could he at once and forever put them out of the game? He and his partners had somehow conceived a great idea—the advantages of combination.

What might they not do, if they could buy out and absorb the big refineries now competing with them in Cleveland? The possibilities of the idea grew as they discussed it. Finally they began tentatively to sound some of their rivals. But there were other rivals than these at home. There were the Creek refiners! They were there at the mouth of the wells.

What might not this geographical advantage do in time? The Oil Regions, in the first years of oil production, had been an unfit place for refining because of its lack of connections with the outside world; now, however, the railroads were in, and refining was going on there on an increasing scale; the capacity of the region had indeed risen to nearly 10,000 barrels a day—equal to that of New York, exceeding that of Pittsburgh by nearly 4,000 barrels, and almost equaling that of Cleveland. The men of the oil country loudly declared that they meant to refine for the world. They boasted of an oil kingdom which eventually should handle the entire business and compel Cleveland and Pittsburgh either to abandon their works or bring them to the oil country. In this boastful ambition they were encouraged by the Pennsylvania

Railroad, which naturally handled the largest percentage of the oil. How long could the Standard Oil Company stand against this competition?

There was another interest as deeply concerned as Mr. Rockefeller in preserving Cleveland's supremacy as a refining center, and this was the New York Central Railroad system. Let the bulk of refining be done in the Oil Regions, and that road was in danger of losing a profitable branch of business. For its own sake it must continue to support Cleveland—by which it meant the Standard Oil Company. The chief representative of the interest of the Central system in Cleveland was Peter H. Watson. Mr. Watson was an able patent lawyer, who served under the strenuous Stanton as an Assistant Secretary of War, and served well. After the war he had been made general freight agent of the Lake Shore and Michigan Southern Railroad, and later president of the branch of that road which ran into the Oil Regions. He had oil interests principally at Franklin, Pennsylvania, and was well known to all oil men. He was a business intimate of Mr. Rockefeller and a warm friend of Horace Clarke, the son-in-law of W. K. Vanderbilt, at that time president of the Lake Shore and Michigan Southern Railroad.

Two other towns shared Cleveland's fear of the rise of the Oil Regions as a refining center, and they were Pittsburgh and Philadelphia, and Mr. Rockefeller and Mr. Watson found in certain refiners of these places a strong sympathy with any plan which looked to holding the region in check. But while the menace in their geographical positions was the first ground of sympathy between these gentlemen, something more than local troubles occupied them. This was the condition of the refining business as a whole. It was unsatisfactory in many particulars. First, it was overdone. There was at that time a refining capacity of three barrels to every one produced, and this capacity was widely scattered. The result was, every now and then, ruinous underselling in order to keep or to secure a market. The export business was not what these gentlemen thought it ought to be. Oil had risen to fourth place in the exports of the United States in the twelve years since its discovery, and every year larger quantities were consumed abroad, but it was crude oil, not refined, which the foreigners were beginning to demand; that is, they had found they could import crude, refine it at home, and sell it cheaper than they could buy American refined. France, to encourage her home refineries, had even put a tax on American refined. Competition between the railroads was so keen that nobody could be sure what freight rates his neighbor was getting, and whether he might not any day secure a special advantage in transportation which would enable him to undersell. Then the speculation in crude oil caused wide variation in the cost of their product, as well as serious fluctuation in the refined market. In short, the business had all the evils of a young, vigorous growth. Its possibilities were still undefined, its future a mere guess. Time was bound to cure the evils in it, but the refiners were impatient of waiting.

In the fall of 1871, while Mr. Rockefeller and his friends were occupied with all these questions, certain Pennsylvania refiners, it is not too certain who, brought to them a remarkable scheme, the gist of which was to bring together secretly a large enough body of refiners and shippers to compel all the railroads handling oil to give to the company formed special rebates on its oil, and drawbacks on that of others. If they could get such rates, it was evident that those outside of their combination could not compete with them long, and that they would become eventually the only refiners. They could then limit their output to actual demand, and so keep up prices. This done, they could easily persuade the railroads to transport no crude for exportation, so that the foreigners would be forced to buy American refined. They believed that the price of oil thus exported could easily be advanced 50 per cent. The control of the refining interests would also enable them to fix their own price on crude. As they would be the only buyers and sellers, the speculative character of the business would be done away with. In short, the scheme they worked out put the entire oil business in their hands. It looked as simple to put into operation as it was dazzling in its results. Mr. Flagler has sworn that neither he nor Mr. Rockefeller believed in this scheme. But when they found that their friend, Peter H. Watson and various Philadelphia and Pittsburgh parties, who felt as they did about the oil business, believed in it, they went in and began at once to work up a company—secretly. It was evident that a scheme which aimed at concentrating in the hands of one company the business now operated by scores, and which proposed to effect this consolidation through a practice of the railroads which was forbidden by their charters, although freely indulged in, and which was regarded as the greatest commercial scandal of the day, must be worked with fine discretion if it ever were to be effective.

The first thing was to get a charter—quietly. At a meeting held in Philadelphia late in the fall of 1871, a friend of one of the gentlemen interested mentioned to him that a certain estate then in liquidation had a charter for sale which gave its owners the right to carry on any kind of business in any country and in any way; that it could be bought for what it would cost to get a charter under the general laws of the state, and it would be a favor to the heirs to buy it. The opportunity was promptly taken. The name of the charter bought was the "Southern [usually written South] Improvement Company." For a beginning it was as good a name as another, since it said nothing.

With this charter in hand Mr. Rockefeller and Mr. Watson and their associates began to seek converts. In order that their great scheme might not be injured by premature public discussion, they asked of each person whom they approached a pledge of secrecy. Two forms of the pledges required before anything was revealed were published later. The first of these, which appeared in the *New York Tribune*, read as follows:

"I, A. B., do faithfully promise upon my honor and faith as a gentleman, that I will keep secret all transactions which I may have with the corporation known as the South Improvement Company; that, should I fail to complete any bargains with the said company, all the preliminary conversations shall be kept strictly private; and, finally, that I will not disclose the price for which I dispose of my product, or any other facts which may in any way bring to light the internal workings or organization of the company. All this I do freely promise."

A second, published in a history of the "Southern Improvement Company," ran:

"The undersigned pledge their solemn words of honor that they will not communicate to anyone without permission of (name of director of Southern Improvement Company) any information that he may convey to them, or any of them, in relation to the Southern Improvement Company."

That they met with encouragement is evident from the fact that, when the corporators came together on January 2, 1872, in Philadelphia, for the

first time under their charter, and transferred the company to the stockholders, they represented in one way or another a large part of the refining interest of the country. At this meeting 1,100 shares of the stock of the company,
which was divided into 2,000 shares of $100 each, were subscribed for, and
20 per cent of their value paid in. Just who took stock at this meeting the
writer has not been able to discover. At the same time, a discussion came up
as to what refiners were to be allowed to go into the new company. Each of
the men represented had friends whom he wanted taken care of, and after
considerable discussion it was decided to take in every refinery they could get
hold of. This decision was largely due to the railroad men. Mr. Watson had
seen them as soon as the plans for the company were formed, and they had all
agreed that if they gave rebates all refineries then existing must be taken in.

Very soon after this meeting of January 2 the rest of the stock of the South
Improvement Company was taken. The complete list of stock-holders, with
their holdings, was as follows:

William Frew, Philadelphia, Pa.	10	shares
W. P. Logan, Philadelphia, Pa. 10	"	"
John P. Logan, Philadelphia, Pa.	10	"
Chas. Lockhart, Pittsburgh, Pa.	10	"
Richard S. Waring, Pittsburgh, Pa.	10	"
W. G. Warden, Philadelphia, Pa.	475	"
O. F. Waring, Pittsburgh, Pa. 475	"	"
P. H. Watson, Ashtabula, Ohio	100	"
H. M. Flagler, Cleveland, Ohio	180	"
O. H. Payne, Cleveland, Ohio 180	"	"
Wm. Rockefeller, Cleveland, Ohio	180	"
J. A. Bostwick, New York, N.Y.	180	"
John D. Rockefeller, Cleveland, Ohio	180	"
[Total]	2,000	shares

Mr. Watson was elected president and Mr. Warden secretary of the new
association. It will be noticed that the largest individual holdings in the company were those of W. G. Warden, of Philadelphia, and O. F. Waring, of
Pittsburgh, each of whom had 475 shares. The company most heavily inter-

ested in the South Improvement Company was the Standard Oil Company of Cleveland, Messrs. J. D. Rockefeller, William Rockefeller, O. H. Payne, and H. M. Flagler, all stockholders of that company, each having 180 shares— 720 in the company.

The organization complete, there remained contracts to be made with the railroads. Three systems were interested: the Central, which, by its connection with the Lake Shore and Michigan Southern, ran directly into the Oil Regions; the Erie, allied with the Atlantic and Great Western, with a short line likewise tapping the heart of the region; and the Pennsylvania, with the connections known as the Allegheny Valley and Oil Creek Railroad. The persons to be won over were W. H. Vanderbilt, of the Central; W. H. Clarke, president of the Lake Shore and Michigan Southern; Jay Gould, of the Erie; General G. B. McClellan, president of the Atlantic and Great Western; and Tom Scott, of the Pennsylvania. There seems to have been little difficulty in persuading any of these persons to go into the scheme. It was, of course, a direct violation of their charters as public carriers, but such violations had been in practice for at least four years in the oil business, and for a longer period in other industries. Under pressure or persuasion all of these roads granted special rates. For years they had been fighting bitterly for the oil trade, often cutting rates to get a consignment, until there was no profit in it. They were glad enough to go into any arrangement which guaranteed each a sure percentage of the business and gave them a profit on it. This the South Improvement Company did. They seem not to have agreed to the contracts until the company assured them that all the refiners were going in. The contracts they made were not on condition, however, that all were included. Three months after they were signed Congress investigated the great scheme. The testimony of the secretary of the company on this point before the Congressional committee is worth reading:

Q. You say you made propositions to railroad companies, which they agreed to accept upon the condition that you could include all the refineries?
A. No, sir; I did not say that; I said that was the understanding when we discussed this matter with them; it was no proposition on our part; they discussed it, not in the form of a proposition that the refineries should be all taken in, but

it was the intention and resolution of the company from the first that should be the result; we never had any other purpose in the matter.

Q. In case you could take the refineries all in, the railroads proposed to give you a rebate upon their freight charges?

A. No, sir; it was not put in that form; we were to put the refineries all in upon the same terms; it was the understanding with the railroad companies that we were to have a rebate; there was no rebate given in consideration of our putting the companies all in, but we told them we would do it; the contract with the railroad companies was with us.

Q. But if you did form a company composed of the proprietors of all these refineries, you were to have a rebate upon your freight charges?

A. No; we were to have a rebate anyhow, but were to give all the refineries the privilege of coming in.

Q. You were to have the rebate whether they came in or not?

A. Yes, sir.

"What effect were these arrangements to have upon those who did not come into the combination?" asked the chairman.

"I do not think we ever took that question up," answered Mr. Warden.

A second objection to making a contract with the company came from Mr. Scott, of the Pennsylvania road. "You take no account here," Mr. Scott told the secretary, W. G. Warden, who discussed the matter at length with him, "of the oil producer—the man to whom the world owes the business. You can never succeed unless you take care of the producer." Mr. Warden objected strongly to forming a combination with them. "The interests of the producers were in one sense antagonistic to ours; one as the seller and the other as the buyer. We held in argument that the producers were abundantly able to take care of their own branch of the business if they took care of the quantity produced." So strongly did Mr. Scott argue, however, that finally the members of the South Improvement Company yielded, and a draft of an agreement, to be proposed to the producers, was drawn up in lead pencil; it was never presented. It seems to have been used principally to quiet Mr. Scott.

The work of persuasion went on swiftly. By the eighteenth of January the president of the Pennsylvania road, J. Edgar Thompson, had put his signature to the contract, and soon after Mr. Vanderbilt and Mr. Clarke signed for the Central system, and Jay Gould and General McClellan for the Erie. The contracts to which these gentlemen put their names fixed gross rates of freight from all common points, as the leading shipping points within the Oil Regions were called, to all the great refining and shipping centers—New York, Philadelphia, Baltimore, Pittsburgh and Cleveland. For example, the open rate on crude oil to New York was put at $2.56. On this price the South Improvement Company was allowed a rebate of $1.06 for its shipments; but it got not only this rebate, it was given in cash a like amount on each barrel of crude shipped by parties outside the combination.

The open rate from Cleveland to New York was $2.00, and 50 cents of this sum was turned over to the South Improvement Company, which at the same time received a rebate enabling it to ship for $1.50. Again an independent refiner in Cleveland paid 80 cents a barrel to get his crude from the Oil Regions to his works, and the railroad sent 40 cents of this money to the South Improvement Company. At the same time it cost the Cleveland refiner in the combination but 40 cents to get his crude oil. Like drawbacks and rebates were given for all points—Pittsburgh, Philadelphia, Boston and Baltimore.

An interesting provision in the contracts was that full waybills of all petroleum shipped over the roads should each day be sent to the South Improvement Company. This, of course, gave them knowledge of just who was doing business outside of their company—of how much business he was doing, and with whom he was doing it. Not only were they to have full knowledge of the business of all shippers—they were to have access to all books of the railroads.

The parties to the contracts agreed that if anybody appeared in the business offering an equal amount of transportation, and having equal facilities for doing business with the South Improvement Company, the railroads might give them equal advantages in drawbacks and rebates, but to make such a miscarriage of the scheme doubly improbable, each railroad was bound to cooperate as "far as it legally might to maintain the business of the South Improvement Company against injury by competition, and lower or raise the gross rates of transportation for such times and to such extent as might be necessary to overcome the competition. The rebates and drawbacks to be varied *pari passu* with the gross rates."

The reason given by the railroads in the contract for granting these extraordinary privileges was that the "magnitude and extent of the business and operations" purposed to be carried on by the South Improvement Company would greatly promote the interest of the railroads and make it desirable for them to encourage their undertaking. The evident advantages received by the railroad were a regular amount of freight—the Pennsylvania was to have 45 per cent of the eastbound shipping, the Erie and Central each 27 1/2 per cent, while westbound freight was to be divided equally between them—fixed rates, and freedom from the system of cutting which they had all found so harassing and disastrous.

It was on the second of January 1872 that the organization of the South Improvement Company was completed. The day before, the Standard Oil Company of Cleveland increased its capital from $1,000,000 to $2,500,000, "all the stockholders of the company being present and voting therefor." These stockholders were greater by five than in 1870, the names of O. B. Jennings, Benjamin Brewster, Truman P. Handy, Amasa Stone, and Stillman Witt having been added. The last three were officers and stockholders in one or more of the railroads centering in Cleveland. Three weeks after this increase of capital Mr. Rockefeller had the charter and contracts of the South Improvement Company in hand, and was ready to see what they would do in helping him carry out his idea of wholesale combination in Cleveland. There were at that time some twenty-six refineries in the town—some of them very large plants. All of them were feeling more or less the discouraging effects of the last three or four years of railroad discriminations in favor of the Standard Oil Company. To the owners of these refineries Mr. Rockefeller now went one by one and explained the South Improvement Company. "You see," he told them, "this scheme is bound to work. It means an absolute control by us of the oil business. There is no chance for anyone outside. But we are going to give everybody a chance to come in. You are to turn over your refinery to my appraisers, and I will give you Standard Oil Company stock or cash, as you prefer, for the value we put upon it. I advise you to take the stock. It will be for your good." Certain refiners objected. They did not want to sell. They did want to keep and manage their business. Mr. Rockefeller was regretful, but firm. It was useless to resist, he told the hesitating; they would certainly be crushed if they did not accept his offer, and he pointed out in detail, and with gentleness, how beneficent the scheme really was—preventing the Creek refiners from destroying Cleveland, keeping up the price of refined oil, destroying competition, and eliminating speculation.

The perfection of the scheme, the inevitableness of the result, the persuasiveness of its advocate, the promise of great profits were different reasons for leading many of the refiners to succumb at once. Some of them took stock—more took money.

A few of the refiners contested before surrendering. Among these was Robert Hanna, an uncle of Mark Hanna, of the firm of Hanna, Baslington & Co. Mr. Hanna had been refining oil since July 1869. According to his own sworn statement he had made money, fully 60 per cent on his investment the first year, and after that 30 per cent. Some time in February 1872 the Standard Oil Company asked an interview with him and his associates. They wanted to buy his works, they said. "But we don't want to sell," objected Mr. Hanna. "You can never make any more money, in my judgment," said Mr. Rockefeller. "You can't compete with the Standard. We have all the large refineries now. If you refuse to sell, it will end in your being crushed." Hanna and Baslington were not satisfied. They went to see Mr. Watson, president of the South Improvement Company, and an officer of the Lake Shore, and General Devereux, manager of the Lake Shore road. They were told that the Standard had special rates; that it was useless to try to compete with them. General Devereux explained to the gentlemen that the privileges granted the Standard were the legitimate and necessary advantage of the large shipper over the smaller, and that if Hanna, Baslington & Co. could give the road as large a quantity of oil as the Standard did, with the same regularity, they could have the same rate. General Devereux says they "recognized the propriety" of his excuse. They certainly recognized its authority. They say that they were satisfied they could no longer get rates to and from Cleveland which would enable them to live, and "reluctantly" sold out. It must have been reluctantly, for they had paid $75,000 for their works, and had made 30 per cent a year on an average on their investment, and the Standard appraiser allowed them $45,000. "Truly and really less than one-half of what they were absolutely worth, with a fair and honest competition in the lines of transportation," said Mr. Hanna, eight years later, in an affidavit.

Under the combined threat and persuasion of the Standard, armed with the South Improvement Company scheme, almost the entire independent oil interest of Cleveland collapsed in three months' time. Of the twenty-six refineries, at least twenty-one sold out. From a capacity of probably not over 1,500 barrels of crude a day, the Standard Oil Company rose in three months' time to one of 10,000 barrels. By this maneuver it became master of over one-fifth of the refining capacity of the United States. Its next individual competitor was Sloan & Fleming, of New York, whose capacity was 1,700 barrels. The Standard had a greater capacity than the entire Oil Creek Regions, greater than the combined New York refiners. The transaction by which it acquired this power was so stealthy that not even the best-informed newspapermen of Cleveland knew what went on. It had all been accomplished in accordance with one of Mr. Rockefeller's chief business principles—"Silence is golden."

While Mr. Rockefeller was working out the "good of the oil business" in Cleveland, his associates were busy at other points. A little more time and the great scheme would be an accomplished fact. And then there fell in its path two of those never-to-be-foreseen human elements which so often block great maneuvers. The first was born of a man's anger. The man had learned of the scheme. He wanted to go into it, but the directors were suspicious of him. He had been concerned in speculative enterprises and in dealings with the Erie road which had injured these directors in other days. They didn't want him to have any of the advantages of their great enterprise. When convinced that he could not share in the deal, he took his revenge by telling people in the Oil Regions what was going on. At first the Oil Regions refused to believe, but in a few days another slip born of human weakness came in to prove the rumor true. The schedule of rates agreed upon by the South Improvement Company and the railroads had been sent to the freight agent of the Lake Shore Railroad, but no order had been given to put them in force. The freight agent had a son on his death-bed. Distracted by his sorrow, he left his office in charge of subordinates, but neglected to tell them that the new schedules on his desk were a secret compact, whose effectiveness depended upon their being held until all was complete. On February 26 the subordinates, ignorant of the nature of the rates, put them in effect. The independent oil men heard with amazement that freight rates had been put up nearly 100 per cent. They needed no other proof of the truth of the rumors of conspiracy which were circulating. . . .

A Tariff-Made City

The city of Pittsburgh is the greatest monument in this country to the practice of High Protection. For fifty years it has been the stronghold of the doctrine. For fifty years it has reaped, as no other center in the United Sates, the benefits of prohibitive duties.

The town lies at the heart of a district in which is produced from one quarter to one half of all the various kinds of American iron and steel as well as a goodly proportion of all our tin, plate-glass, and machine shop products. All of these articles have for years had the American market practically to themselves. All of these articles have for years been exported and sold at less prices than the American consumer can buy them [sic]. All these industries have produced enormous fortunes. So many, so conspicuous are they that a recognized American type in Europe and the United States is the "Pittsburgh millionaire." Now it is certain the tariff produced the Pittsburgh millionaire, but that was not what the tariff was fixed for by the Congress of the United States. The tariff was laid to protect and to help the Pittsburgh workman. According to the protectionist argument Pittsburgh, as the bulwark and center of protected industries, should produce the happiest, most prosperous and best conditioned workmen in the United States. How is it?

There has just been published in the review known as *Charities and the Commons* one of the most significant pieces of investigation the country has seen. It is the result of a year or more of work on the part of a band of trained investigators commissioned by the Charities Publication Committee. It gives a blueprint of Pittsburgh: the place itself, the people, and their work. What does this blueprint show of the workingman under protection?

It shows him working *twelve* hours a day for SEVEN days in the week, and once in two weeks filling a "long turn" or a twenty-four-hour shift. It is not simply the exceptional man who overworks in this cruel fashion. The twelve-hour day is the extreme of an "altogether incredible amount of over-

From the *American Magazine* (May 1909): 99–100.

work by everybody," so the Survey declares. Can you make a man by these hours? Is it any wonder that those who lived and walked among these men preparing this Survey report their saying "Too tired to read—too tired to think—I work and eat and sleep." Any wonder that they report the God-fearing women crying out for the Old Country: "We might not have been able to live so well there, but oh man, we could have brought up the children in the fear o' God and in a land where men reverence the Sabbath." Any wonder that those men who have not the restraining influence of a family drown fatigue at night in saloons and brothels?

And what do they earn for their toil? In the tariff protected industries steel and iron, the greatest number receive a wage, says the report, "so low as to be inadequate to the maintenance of a normal American standard of living. Wages adjusted to the single man in the lodging house, not to the responsible head of a family." And this in industries where "to protect the working-man" this country has for years taxed itself millions upon millions of dollars. The estimated tariff profit in the steel trust alone in 1907 was $80,000,000. Who got the money? Go look at the steel palaces and chateaux in New York and Paris. Go ask the Pittsburgh millionaires who fill the glittering places of pleasure in the great cities of Europe and this country, who figure in divorce and murder trials, who are writing their names on foundations and bequests and institutions.

How does this "protected" workingman live? What kind of households are these "builded on steel?" The reporter of the situation summarizes them:

"Evil conditions were found to exist in every section of the city. Over the omni-present vaults, graceless privy sheds flouted one's sense of decency. Eyrie rookeries perched on the hillsides were swarming with men, women and children—entire families living in one room and accommodating boarders in a corner thereof. Cellar rooms were the abiding places of other families. In many houses water was a luxury to be obtained only through much effort of toiling steps and straining muscles. Courts and alleys fouled by bad drainage and piles of rubbish were playing grounds for rickety, pale-faced, grimy children. An enveloping cloud of smoke and dust through which light and air must filter made house-keeping a travesty in many neighborhoods; and every phase of the situation was intensified by the evil of overcrowding—of houses upon lots, of families into houses, of people into rooms."

Among the worst illustrations of these *typical* conditions are certain properties owned by the very corporations who are reaping wealth from the tariff products. These beneficiaries of the generosity of the American people, the gentlemen who when they see the taxation in their interest threatened hold up the laborer and his good as a reason for continuing it, what do *they* say when these conditions are pointed out to them:— *"We don't want to go into the housing business. We are manufacturers, not real estate dealers. We may be forced to build houses in certain new districts in order to attract and hold labor, but in an old, settled community let the laboring man take care of himself. We don't believe in paternalism."*

They have had no more interest in preserving the lives of the men who do the terrible toil necessary to their wealth than in giving them decent housing. For years the death rate from typhoid fever in Pittsburgh has been the highest of any city in the civilized world. Everybody knew it. Everybody knew why. There was no supply of pure drinking water. A filtration plant was needed. Did any Pittsburgh millionaire offer to build it—insist that the industries which called the vast army of labor to Pittsburgh should build it? No, they left a corrupted city government to fight over the appropriation for the work and scattered in endowments and in institutions in other cities and other states, many times the five millions needed in Pittsburgh to save the lives of the workmen. They hold up to world admiration their love of great material problems—they argue with the American people that their skill in solving these problems is a good and sufficient reason for continuing general taxation in their favor. But a problem which worked out would benefit nobody but the humble two-dollar-a-day man who sweats out his life in the heat of their profitable furnaces does not interest them. It might savor of paternalism!

Not even the child has touched them. The conditions under which the children of the poor are brought up in Pittsburgh are such that babies die like flies. Of those along the river, a settlement worker told Samuel Hopkins Adams, when he was working on health conditions for the Survey: *"Not one child in ten comes to us from the river-bottom section without a blood or skin disease, usually of long standing. Not one out of ten comes to us physically up to the normal for his or her age. Worse than that, few of them are up to the mental standard, and an increasing percentage are imbecile."*

As to the schools, here is what an authority says:

"The school buildings are in many cases crowded, dark, dirty, often of three stories and bad fire risks. The condition of the children in these schools good and bad, rich and poor, may be known by the large proportion having defective teeth, reduced hearing, imperfect vision. An excessively large number of them are mouth breathers, partially so because they are unable to breathe through their noses in the smoky air of Pittsburgh, and very considerable number are below the stature and the weight determined for the average child. In a large percentage, the defects of teeth, nose and throat bring them below the physical normal. These are the children that wear out in childhood."

Is it a wonder that this gentleman suggested:

"Ought not the Pittsburgh schools to be closed and the children repaired?"

The Pittsburgh Survey is the most awful arraignment of an American institution and its resulting class pronounced since the days of slavery. It puts upon the Pittsburgh millionaire the awful stamp of Greed, of Stupidity, and of heartless Pride. But what should we expect of him? He is the creature of a Special Privilege which for years he has not needed. He has fought for it because he fattened on it. He must have it for labor. But look at him and look at his laborer and believe him if you can.

Justice takes a terrible revenge on those who thrive by privilege. She blinds their eyes until they no longer see human misery. She dulls their hearts until they no longer beat with humanity. She benumbs their senses until they respond only to the narrow horizon of what they can individually possess, touch, feel. She makes, as she has in Pittsburgh, a generation of men and women who day by day can pass hundreds of tumbled down and filthy homes, in which the men and women who make their wealth live, and feel no shock; who can know that deadly fevers and diseases which are preventable are wiping out hundreds of those who do their tasks, and raise no hand. Little children may die or grow up stunted and evil within their sight and no penny of their wealth, no hour of their leisure is given them. Women pass hours of incessant toil and die, broken and unhonored within their sight, and they raise no hand. Wealth which comes by Privilege kills. The curse of Justice on those who will not recognize injustice is the sodden mind, the dulled vision, the unfeeling heart.

Fear of Efficiency

One of the most unpopular words in use today is the word efficiency. From having been something which we were inclined to call the American need, it has become the great American alarm. It has meant until recently doing a thing in a clean, competent fashion without unnecessary fuss or waste. It is coming to mean doing a thing in machine fashion and in disregard of all human factors. What has brought about this change in our notion of the word efficiency?

It has come out of an attempt to create in industrial life a science of efficiency. In the last twenty years there has been developed in the industry of this country a new type of management. From being more or less haphazard and personal, industrial management is now being harnessed to fixed principles. These principles have been worked out with mathematical exactness and their soundness is capable of proof. Many men have been interested in their development, but to one man above all others is due the credit of their present scientific form. That man is Frederick Winslow Taylor.

About thirty years ago Mr. Taylor found himself at the head of a shop which was not turning out nearly so much product as he was confident it ought. Gradually he worked out a plan for getting out of his machines and men all that there was in them. He did this by completely revolutionizing shop management. He instituted a system of handling tools and supplies so exact that each worker had put into his hands at the proper moment the thing he needed. It is safe to say that in many shops each worker gained upward of an hour a day by this reform. Mr. Taylor devised a planning system by which each man knew in advance exactly what work was waiting for him and his machine. Each operation in a job was routed so that it fitted into the operation which had preceded and the one which followed. That is, operations fol-

From *The Independent,* July 7, 1917. On June 1, 1914, the *Independent* took over the *Chautauquan* monthly and dedicated a section to Chautauqua news and articles. This article appeared in that section.

lowed in their proper sequence so that they flowed together finally instead of being scattered over a shop and time being lost in bringing them together.

Mr. Taylor studied each machine in his plant to know exactly how fast it ought to be run to give the maximum product. Not infrequently he found that time was being lost because machines were run too fast.

Each of these steps made it easier for a man to do his work and consequently made it possible for him to do more work. Time which he had lost because of delays and friction for which he was in no way responsible was now his.

It was after these matters had been settled that Mr. Taylor first turned his attention to the workman himself. He studied the way he was doing his task. Often he found that his productivity was lessened because of his position at the machine or of an awkward way of handling a tool. The easiest and the quickest way of performing each task was worked out. When this had been fixed the worker was instructed in the new method. The result inevitably was that the man turned out more work.

Under the old management it had been the habit whatever a man's product never to pay him more than the average daily wage. That is, he never had an incentive to turn out all that he could do. Mr. Taylor made it a rule of his system that a man's pay should increase with the amount of his product. He never allowed the rate per piece to be cut. The result was that the workmen under this new science of management earn from fifty to one hundred per cent more than formerly.

In spite of the fact that the intelligent application of these principles results in a large increase in product, in profits and in wages, there have been many people to decry them. Labor particularly has fought them. We have even had bills in Congress aimed at making it a crime for the Government to use in its plants the tools of the science of management. Why should there be this fear of industrial efficiency? Possibly fifty per cent of the reason lies in the natural human attitude toward anything that is new. Men fear this science because they are ignorant of what it really means and does and they do not take the trouble seriously to investigate. Here is the reason of much of labor's opposition to scientific management. Again men fear it because it demands a change and none of us like too well to give up or correct our ways of doing things. Scientific management cuts out ruthlessly all of the privileges which grow in a carelessly managed undertaking. It demands time, close attention, discipline, and the average worker or manager objects to this.

But these are only the human objections to anything new. The fear of efficiency in this country lies in something much more serious. It has been enormously increased in the last three years by the development of the Great War. The most conspicuous exhibit of efficiency with which the world is familiar is that of Germany. In Germany efficiency means fitting every man into a task which has been prescribed for him by a superior. In a country where militarism rules, men must do and be what the government orders. The system requires training for a special service. It leaves little room for spontaneous individual choice. That is, an individual is not supposed to know what he ought to do. That is the business of his government.

Whatever a man may lose by this method there is no question but he gains in the safety and orderliness of his life. Provisions are made for his old age, for sickness and unemployment. He may sacrifice for the government, but the government looks out for him. The man attains, too, almost invariably a high degree of productivity in the thing at which he is set. He is an efficient man in a efficient machine. Why should we Americans revolt at this way of handling men? Why should it seem monstrous and fearful to us?

The democratic ideal in which we have been brought up breaks at every point with the German system. We believe that unless men are allowed to find for themselves the thing which they can best do, that unless they are free to follow their inner call the best that they have to give to the world will be sacrificed. Instead of forcing a training on the man we invite him to experiment. Above all, we feel that not only the good of the man but the good of society demands that his initiative and spontaneity be preserved.

If the suppression of the individual and his natural bent is inherent in the science of efficiency, then for this country it is doomed. In spite of all our bungling, there is no conviction stronger than that the most precious thing there is in man is his native talent. Is the science of efficiency as developed in our industrial life hostile to the spirit of democracy and to this inner need of men to work out their natural bent? Does the Taylor system make no allowance for this human need? To argue the negative is utterly to misunderstand the meaning of this new science. Mr. Taylor himself loved to call it a science of making men and when properly applied that is exactly what it is.

One of the most terrible features of our present day industrial life is the amount of unskilled menial work that is thrown upon men and women. The Taylor system boldly asserts that there should be no such thing as unskilled work in the world. It says that every task that is necessary should be studied and the best way of doing it found and taught. Great bodies of men and women have had their work dignified in this country and have consequently been themselves elevated by the application of scientific management to work which hitherto has been despised.

Wherever scientific management is intelligently applied one of the tasks which it sets for itself is the encouragement of individual talent. Every device is employed to encourage workers of all grades to exercise their ingenuity by suggestions and by experiments. Scores of valuable improvements are being contributed annually to our industrial life today through the encouragement that this new system of management is giving to individuals to let themselves loose in their work to see what they can do in the way of improving things.

The deep seated fear that the science of efficiency is inherently in conflict with democracy is not justified by the intelligent application of the Taylor system. On the contrary this science has come as a sympathetic handmaid of democracy, showing her how she can help men to develop themselves along the line of their inner call. This system at every point gives the lie to the old contention that if things are to be done well in the world there must be dictators at every point.

Moreover, wherever there has been an attempt to apply the science of management autocratically, where a manager has not believed with Mr. Taylor that the best results of the system are possible only when you consider first the individual man and his good, there has been failure. The same thing has happened that we have seen happening with the German conception of military efficiency; in overlooking, even denying, the part that the human factor plays in the world, it in the long run defeats itself. A system of efficiency which makes no allowance for ethical and intellectual considerations whether that system be applied to an army or to a factory surely fails in the long run.

A Fine Place to Work

One of the first impressions of an observer who, free of preconceived notions, studies a reorganised modern workshop is that the operatives are getting an altogether unprecedented degree of social life. A little analysis shows that this is the outcome of the new shop activities and ambitions.

Groups of men and women are naturally sociable. Join the crowd that watches a parade and observe the good terms which quickly spread sometimes for miles up and down an avenue. The helter-skelter throng has established relations. They jeer and chatter and accommodate one another. They exchange opinions and experiences. The rudiments of a social and political organisation may easily develop in the course of an afternoon in the accidental group crowding the side of a city block.

Observe how quickly they catch the spirit of the spectacle. They are gaiety itself over a Mardi Gras pageant; but let the demonstration touch the serious and they answer as certainly. It was a New York crowd which gave to the first Woman's Peace Parade the response which carried it. It was a venture of the most doubtful outcome, sure to excite the indignation of some, the ridicule of others. Its only strength was its touching impotency. Yet throngs of men and women watched it in silent, sometimes tearful, respect. They knew they looked on a prayer, a hope of that-which-is-to-come. The amazing sympathy and understanding they gave those marching idealists promises as much for the cause of peace as anything this country has seen since the war [World War I] began.

The chief promise of groups lies in this natural sociability and understanding. The finest, freest collective work men do develops from it. The failure to recognise and encourage it in undertakings is unintelligent as well as unkind; it reacts disastrously, dulling initiative and hindering cooperation.

In spite of the obviousness of the value of this social spirit, industry has

Originally published as chapter 2 of Tarbell's *New Ideals in Business* (New York: Macmillan, 1917), 29–49.

been slow, even stupid, in utilising it. There are thousands of offices, shops and factories in this country where there is no more cohesion between the workers than between the nails in a keg. The force is held together by staves and hoops. Take them off and they scatter. The conditions under which they labour do not admit of acquaintanceship. The managers discourage it. They do not want visiting, planning, talking in their plants, they tell you. True, little cliques may form, two girls or men become friends, but for the most part the men and women work side by side, often for years, without any form of communication.

The modern employer is wiser. He recognises that the efficiency he must have to succeed—if he has no privilege to carry him roughshod over competition—depends upon the health, interest and cooperation of his working force. He learns that all of these forces thrive naturally in a group of people who find satisfaction in working side by side. They do this when they have common social interests. To foster these interests then becomes a business policy.

It is one which has made enormous strides in the last ten years particularly, though it would be neither fair nor illuminating to treat it as a discovery of this period. If we look for the root of the experiments to promote sociability among working people we shall probably find them in the one secular social institution that early piety and industry tolerated, that is, the annual picnic. The severest of Protestant sects have long admitted the human need of fun to the extent of one picnic a year. Rarely was there a factory in the old days that did not limber up sufficiently to arrange an annual outing for the whole establishment, including wives, babies and friends.

Reluctant as the factory manager may often have been to give the time and the money for the annual outing, it was a well-established opinion fifty and more years ago that they could not afford to do without it. In some mysterious way, at which many sneered but which none could deny, those outings oiled the human machine. Work went with less friction and more interest in the weeks of preparation and of "talking it over." It was, no doubt, a good thing.

There is no knowing just when a few of the more reflective employers began to see that the interest and spirit awakened by the annual outing was something to be preserved and given opportunities to grow. Nor is there any way of knowing who first appreciated the relation between a field for out-of-door sports and the health and sociability of the factory; he belongs, of course, to the period of the ten-hour day; when men worked twelve and fourteen there was neither the light nor the life to throw a ball. He came with the shorter day and he heads a great and growing succession.

The factory athletic field is coming to be almost as much a matter of course as the sanitary drinking fountains, and where you find the latter you are almost sure to find the former, or its substitute. Even in many cities where the factory is crowded for land, a corner often is squeezed out for out-of-door sports. I doubt if there is an athletic field in the United States which has as much use to the square inch as the girls at the Clothcraft shop in Cleveland give to a bit of enclosed land at the side of the factory. It is not larger than a city lot, but it teems with excitement during noon hours and after the shop closes at four-thirty.

Mr. Feiss will tell you, in explanation of the time he and his associates give to encouraging the use of this bit of land, "I can't afford to have people working in my shop who don't have fresh air and fun." It is the reason he gives for his early closing hours. "I can't afford to have people working after four-thirty in the afternoon. They aren't sufficiently fit next day."

The Steel Corporation is so convinced of the value of the ball field that it encourages its subsidiaries everywhere to provide them. Probably thousands of dollars are spent annually by the companies for their upkeep, though the general practice is for the men to meet this by an equal, or at least a substantial, contribution of their own. In all the new plants such as that at Gary the ball field is considered as necessary as a first-aid room.

That the corporation is right in the special encouragement it gives baseball is indisputable—what the game is doing for health and sociability in American industries cannot be estimated. It is a poor management indeed, these days, and a thoroughly soured force which does not support departmental nines. As proud a man as I ever saw was the usually unapproachable vice-president of a big factory who, playing on the office team at the annual picnic, had made a "home run." It was days before he ceased talking about it, and when the office would no longer listen he went to the floor and lived it over with Jimmie B., a weaver who, in spite of this heroic deed, had won the game for the operatives.

All over the land you can duplicate the amusing experience of the hero of

Philip Curtiss's story "The Ladder." He had applied in a big concern for work. There was no opening until he chanced on an employee who had known him in his baseball days. The acquaintance promptly passed his information on to the employment agent. That worthy as promptly reconsidered his decision.

"What did you tell him about me?" the hero asked.

"That you were the best second-baseman in the State."

There is many a factory where operators and operatives would consider this a sound reason for employing a man, and why not if it is considered a sound reason for admitting a boy to college?

The rivalry between the teams of different plants and factories is coming to be like that between towns and schools. One of the most exciting series of games—outside of those of the leagues, and the big colleges—of which I know, is that between the forty or more teams of miners in the Frick Coke Company in the Connellsville District of Pennsylvania. It is doubtful if there are ever more than two or three men on a team who speak the same tongue, but that seems not to interfere either with their efficiency or their enthusiasm.

In the fall of 1913 I visited the coke towns a few days after the finals had been played. There had been a general holiday. The five thousand spectators were made up of the miners, their wives and children and the officers of the company from the president down. It had been a great day, and everywhere I went I heard it discussed. The hero of the district was an Italian miner who had won the final victory for his nine. At that particular moment you could not have pried a man out of that company! Moreover, the company could have counted on every man's cooperation in any reasonable proposition.

While baseball is easily the favourite factory game, as befits its national position, there are many concerns in which the variety of sports equal that of any college or athletic club. I know of one Rochester factory in which they play baseball, lawn tennis, bowling on the green, volley ball, croquet, soccer ball and quoits. Last winter the bowling team won the championship of the Industrial League of the city of Rochester against teams from all the principal establishments in the town.

So thoroughly has the industrial athletic field demonstrated its usefulness that no intelligent employer of labour familiar with advanced practices thinks to-day of building a new shop or factory in town or country without some provision for an out-of-door field or an indoor equivalent. Take a modern factory like the new one of Brown and Bigelow near Saint Paul, Minnesota. In building, the concern provided for some twenty acres of open space around the light, airy, comfortable factory it put up. In this space all the sports which interest the force are carried on. The director of the service department of the plant tells me that all of these undertakings are managed by the employees themselves through a club to which everybody belongs by virtue of his position as a worker.

Once a year nominations are made for officers of the club, and all employees have a chance to ballot for their favourites. Besides the officers, a governing board is elected in an advising capacity. Several of the present members of the governing board are workers at bench or machine.

The officers run all the club affairs, including a benevolent association and a dining-room; they prepare for the annual picnic; out of their treasury they furnish balls and bats for the baseball teams; they pay for the use of the bowling alleys on which once a week during the winter twelve teams from as many departments compete for a loving cup presented by the firm and for individual prizes offered by the clubs; they pay for the tennis courts and skating rinks. Brown and Bigelow's cooperation in this consists of furnishing space, light, heat and steam. Every time an employee is tardy, a fine of ten cents is imposed, and this money is turned into the club funds.

These organisations give wonderful training in collective action. Indeed, they are for thousands of people the only chance they have ever had for free, conscious cooperation. It is actually exciting to watch men and women develop through these organisations, not only in health and good spirits but in what they have never suspected they possessed, the power of leadership. A man or woman who has always been shy, sulky, uncommunicative, an indifferent and unambitious worker, will blossom into a leader in sports or in "getting up things." There is an immediate change in his attitude toward his work.

An alert manager recognises at once that he has here the making of a foreman. His task is now to watch, give encouragement and instruction, and at the right moment advance his find. Nothing is more valuable to him, more essential, than such discoveries, if he is trying to manage his business scientifically. The large force of instructors and function bosses required in a shop under scientific management can come only out of the factory itself, to get the best results. The strength of the system lies largely in developing workers to do higher-grade work. But where there is no more sociability than in most shops it is a slow and sometimes most discouraging task to find this material. Factory clubs and amusements constantly bring it out. It is a precious thing for the business, but it is life and future for the worker.

As a rule the provisions for out-of-door sports are modest enough, though there are a few plants in the country which almost take one's breath away by their magnificence. The National Cash Register has gone furthest, probably. In addition to baseball diamonds, tennis courts, children's playgrounds and clubhouses near the factory, Mr. Patterson keeps up for his employees on the outskirts of Dayton and within easy reach by a five cent ride on streetcars one of the loveliest small parks in the country. It has been handled with rare intelligence and, an unusual thing in our parks, originality. Surprises await you at every turn in "Hills and Dales," as it is called—devotion to birds, devotion to flowers, an instinct for views and "glimpses." There is a handsome clubhouse run by the employees, a girls' club and, most attractive of all, several camps furnished with everything necessary for instant use for whomsoever may apply!

The United Shoe Machinery Company is another concern which has arranged lavish out-of-door life for its five thousand or more employees. Close to its Beverly, Massachusetts, plant it has three hundred acres of land, the Bass River running through them, where every conceivable land and water sport is encouraged.

Elaborate equipments like these lead those who are unfamiliar with the hundreds of small ventures over the country to believe that the work is merely a "frill" of Big Business, one of its advertising schemes for reconciling a hostile public. No doubt some skillful advertising has been done through these ambitious undertakings, but this is certain—unless they are used they make a concern ridiculous. Deserted, they prove that something is wrong with the motive in their establishment or the method of their management. When the fields and diamonds and courts and roads are thronged at noon and night, on holidays and Sundays, we may set it down as a real thing, whether elaborate or simple.

As far as results are concerned it doesn't much matter whether it is elaborate or simple. The spirit is the life of it, not the machine. Neither the National Cash Register nor the United Shoe Machinery Company could persuade or force their employees to use their courts and grounds and clubhouses as freely as they do if they were merely an advertising scheme. They are used because the primary reason for their existence is the health, efficiency, and social pleasure of the workers. They "pay" the firm, or they would not be supported by two as hard-headed concerns as these; but they "pay" the operatives even more.

Big Business has no monopoly of this class of work. It can absorb a great deal of money, but it needs almost none. Indeed, it depends for success on that which money cannot buy—sympathy, understanding, sound humanity and sound sense. Nor did Big Business discover the value of the social interests of its employees to its own stability and its efficiency; like almost everything else it possesses it took over what it found, and developed it on a large scale. Small business originated the work, and it is small business which gets the finest results, as a rule, both for itself and for its people.

What *are* the results? How do you know them? When the army of employees rush back to their machines after a noon hour of comfort and play, fresh, zestful, singing, when they come back Monday morning or after a holiday brown, interested, full of talk of matches lost or won, of excursions, picnics, adventures, the wise man knows he is reaping the reward of his investment. When men and women tell you with enthusiasm: "Gee, but this is a fine place to work!" you know they are reaping the benefits of his investment. But what they get is by no means bounded by the factory walls or ended with their period of service. They are being educated in two things most essential to themselves and to the community, two things in which most of us are weak. They are learning how to be sociable and how to play and to enjoy people. These are permanent possessions.

The great body of people in this country do not know the value nor the delight of play. They work hard and cheerfully as a rule through a long day, and depend on sleep and food and what they call "taking comfort"—that is, sitting around in a more or less somnolent state—to fit them for the next day. They have never learned to take regular exercise, to seek a stimulating change of ideas, to go out after the new. They are not curious, eager or adventurous in their off hours, though they may be all that when at work. Life is but a collection of habits. If the habit of seeking recreation and social life has never been acquired, the effort to do so is a burden to the flesh and a worry to the spirit. Industry is fixing the habit in thousands of men and women. One of the convincing proofs of this is the extent to which in many parts of the country operatives, either in groups or as individuals, are providing simple quarters within easy reach of their work which they can use at will. All those who travel much become familiar with them: gay little shacks grouped in pleasant groves, log cabins perched on mountainsides, tiny houseboats anchored along river banks, bungalows by the sea. They are multiplying amazingly, particularly through the Middle West. It is one of the pleasantest exhibits of our present world, a proof that pleasure and health, as well as the means to get them, are being more and more widely distributed in the land.

One thing leads to another in groups. If the start is made there is no end to the ramifications. The men of a factory who have come together over baseball in the summer want a bowling alley, a card-room, a reading-room for winter, and they often ask the management for it. This is the sound and sure beginning for the factory clubhouse, an institution which is doing as much for factory social life as the athletic field. There are many such clubhouses, which buzz from morning until night with activities of every kind; but let no one imagine that it was merely the building and machinery which caused spontaneous interest. Most of these have grown from very small beginnings.

Ten years ago a dinner was given by the new president of the commonwealth Steel Company of Granite City, Illinois, Mr. Clarence Howard, in the little frame building then used as a factory eating-room. At this gathering a club called the Commonwealth Fellowship was organised. It now has a thousand members. Its quarters have expanded into a handsome and commodious brick building and its activities take in every conceivable interest of the plant and the working force. If one wants proofs that the cultivation of good fellowship on the highest Christian lines is practical in a factory, he ought to study the cooperation the Commonwealth Steel Company gets in its undertakings.

Here is an example of a character so unusual that it called forth the hearty commendations of the International Moulders' Journal, though the plant is an open shop. It was desired to make certain changes in the foundry in the interests of efficiency and economy, and the company offered to share half of the time saved with the moulders. In the early winter the men were informed that the change had saved several hundred dollars and that their half was ready for them. How should it be distributed? Times had been dull in the plant and a number of men had been idle. The moulders knew that the company had set aside a fund to aid these men. Accordingly they asked that the money coming to them be applied to this fund. The company answered by turning over the entire sum.

The clubhouse or club-room has generally as its first and possibly most important service the furnishing of a place in which to lunch. The lunch-room serves an industry in much the same way that an athletic field does. The day will come, I believe, when the failure to furnish proper lunching places for a working force will be looked on as one of the most uneconomical practices of the innumerable number with which industry burdens itself. People who eat cold meals from the corner of their desks or machines do it at the expense of their afternoon efficiency. I never see this untidy, cheerless practice in operation that I do not feel like suggesting to the officers and directors of the concern tolerating it that they lunch for a week in the same place and from the same cold food, and then test their afternoon efficiency.

Moreover, it is a waste of an excellent social opportunity. There is no way in which men and women more quickly come together than over common meals. "You can't fuss with the fellow you eat with," said a man at the Commonwealth. If they run their own lunching place, electing officers and deciding on expenditures, as many do, so much the better. If the officers and superintendents share the lunch-room even occasionally, the effect is excellent. At the Commonwealth Steel plant the lunch-room is even doing something to unsettle one of the most fixed of American—not European—prejudices. There are several coloured men in the factory. The locality, the Egypt of Illinois, has always held the extreme Southern view of the social place of the negro. In arranging the lunch-room separate tables were provided for white and coloured; but I was told it was not infrequent for a white man deliberately to take a coloured man's table or invite him to his. A little thing, perhaps, but it shows the quality of the fellowship which pervades the place.

It is usual to turn the lunch-room into an amusement hall after the meal is over. I once lunched with the president of a big Rochester manufacturing concern in a room probably one hundred and fifty feet in length by fifty feet in width filled with small tables and served in cafeteria fashion. The sides of this room were practically of glass. From the great windows one looked out on eight acres of ground equally divided by this wing. Great trees, beautiful shrubs and a most perfect sward, tennis courts, bowling greens, flowers and vines made it as lovely a place as one could ask. These operatives lunch in a place as beautiful as any resident of this beautiful city.

There were probably three hundred men and women using the room the day that I lunched there; the excellent and abundant food was given them at cost; my lunch cost fifteen cents. It was no better or cheaper than that I have eaten in scores of lunch-rooms between the Mississippi and the Atlantic, the rooms varying in size from big halls like this, sometimes handsomely decorated, to little rooms in a mansard roof of a city building. The lunch over, the groups naturally turn to amusements. In this particular place some fell to playing cards or chess, others to talking, a few to reading, many to dancing, or listening to the music. On a pleasant day the whole company would have gone outside to games or to walk in the grounds.

The effect of all these varied free activities on men and women who are employed on machines, as such vast throngs are in these days, is blessed. It breaks the intolerable monotony. The monotony is one of the most dangerous and cruel features of modern manufacturing. It is probably the chief cause of the unstable payroll. The worker is so limited in his interests that his mind turns on his own condition and situation. The machine becomes his enemy. He cannot endure it. He breaks away, to repeat the experience in different factories. He becomes a floater. It is either that or settling into dull endurance. But give the operative something to think of, something related to his work, and the monotony and fatigue are relieved.

The wise woman who directs the social activities of the Pilgrim Laundry of Brooklyn said to me once that no girl could do two thousand collars a day if she didn't have something interesting to think of, something which concerned herself. She sees to it that there is always something pleasant planned for the girls to do. It is the thought of a play they are to give, a dance, an excursion that keeps their minds alive and happy while their fingers carry on the rapid work demanded of them.

"You don't know how changed life has been for me since Miss A——— came here and showed us how to organize clubs and things," a fine sober girl said to me in a white goods factory once. She had been pointed out as the editor of the factory paper, a lively little monthly full of the activities of the place, and had stopped her machine to answer my questions. "You see, now I can think of the paper and what I shall put into it while I do my work. Before, I had nothing to think of and I did get so tired every day."

"Do you do as much work?" I asked.

"More," she said, and pulled out the little account book to prove it. "It goes easier; all the girls say so, too."

The activities which grow up in these industrial groups are by no means limited to amusements and sports. They are frequently devoted to self-improvement. Sewing, domestic science, stenography, arithmetic, literature, technical branches related to the industry, spring up naturally as the force becomes acquainted. The benefit of this to the worker is no more bounded by his term in the factory than is the benefit that comes to him from out-of-door sports. Here again he has learned something about himself. He has found ways of enriching and enlivening his life, and the knowledge cannot be left behind if he leaves the factory. He is a better, happier, and more efficient citizen for his term of service there.

The factory profits from this improvement while he stays by it. He profits throughout his life.

There are of course multitudes of people to argue that all this is none of the employers' business, that people find what they want, that there are enough opportunities everywhere for pleasure and improvement if men and women have the energy to look for them.

Why establish playgrounds, ball grounds, parks, they ask, when every city does something of the kind and they are never fully used?

Generous and thoughtful as a city may be in scattering open spaces it cannot meet this particular need. The worker requires a space at hand where he can put in his short noon and evening leisure at play in factory uniform. No city can provide an open space for each factory. Grand Rapids, Michigan, comes as near to doing this as any town I have seen. It aims to give a playground within a half mile of every child, and it certainly has an open space within the same distance of almost every factory; but this is far from meeting the demand I am talking of. Rochester, New York, has a large and well-distributed system of parks, but there are several factories within the city limits which have provided athletic grounds. The Eastman Company has in its Kodak Park on the outskirts of the town a beautiful setting of turf and shrubs and vines for its great factories, and scattered throughout the space are tennis courts and ball fields.

The top floor of the factory lunch-room has been turned into an assembly hall which will accommodate many hundred people. I once attended a party there, given by a group of factory girls. There were literally hundreds of couples on the floor, among them many of the officers and directors of the plant. Their wives were with them. Mr. Eastman was present with a group of friends. This is the custom of the place. It was as merry and democratic a party as anyone could wish.

Many contend that factory amusements are a wasteful overlapping of the social activities of churches, settlements, municipalities. My own observation is that there is always more demand for healthful amusements than supply. There is a factory district in New York City of not over twenty blocks where there are ten thousand girls and women at work. Outside of the cheap dance halls, movies, and theatres there is not in this area provision for evening sports for over one thousand, if that.

Neither church, family, nor state is deprived of any opportunity or support by the social activities of the factory. They are all improved and stimulated by them. As for the established social centres, they will lose only when they are less inviting, less stimulating, If they are undemocratic—that is, absorbed by sets, as often happens—they will lose. If their activities smack of condescension, they will lose. If they are philanthropies, not encouraging pleasure for pleasure's sake but that they may teach something indirectly, they will lose. Otherwise, they will gain.

Leadership, kind, wise, inspired by the conviction that factory and shop under modern conditions furnish one of the finest opportunities in the world to develop people both as individuals and groups, is essential for the work. Such leadership has brought to more than one factory such a spirit of happiness that men and women again are singing at their work. There is no reason they should not.

The machine is an almost sentient thing. Its roar and clash and whir to him who has learned to know it has its own strange rhythm and song. The worker who has come to it in health and courage has no quarrel with his machine. Indeed, he often sings to it and with it.

One of the happiest things that I have seen in factories on which an intelligent scientific management had laid its always kind (if always firm) hand has been the singing of girls over their machines. But they cannot do it on the long day, on poor pay, or on hearts to which joy is a stranger. They will do it only when they have come to feel and to say, "My, but this is a fine place to work."

The Floyd Collinses
of Our Mines

If that pitiful Kentucky tragedy which dragged its hopeless way through seventeen days of the month of February will turn the minds of but a fraction of the hundreds of thousands of men and women, whose first thought in the morning, during those days, was of Floyd Collins' plight, why, then, the boy will not have perished in vain.

Floyd Collins was pinned down by a falling rock while exploring the narrow passages which run like spider legs from the caves below the surface in the sandy soil near Cave City, Kentucky.

Everything that men—and resourceful men—could do was done to extricate him, but the case was hopeless from the first. The shifting earth claimed its prey.

Floyd Collins died the victim of his love of adventure and discovery.

Every year over NINE HUNDRED bituminous coal miners are tombed in American mines as he was. Falling earth, rocks, timber, coal, trap them. They die victims of industry—part of the price we pay for warmth and flying wheels.

Nine hundred Floyd Collinses a year—nine thousand in ten years—and we treat the awful toll as a necessary incident to keeping the world running. Yet each one of these trapped miners died as Floyd Collins did—unless the engulfing earth is merciful and kills by a blow. "A lonely, black death" one who sat at the mouth of the pit through those seventeen days described it. "Entombed alive far down in the earth, with no human voice nor hand to comfort him, no human ear to hear his futile, frenzied cries—the rocks held him so jealously even in death that it meant death itself to take him from their clutches."

Can the death list of miners from their cause be cut down? Must we engulf nine hundred men yearly in taking out soft coal? We need not. A careful and scientific testing of the veins which are opened, followed by timbering

Undated [1925?] typescript, Pelletier Library, Allegheny College, Meadville, Pennsylvania.

adequate to the risk revealed—timbering which all careful and responsible mine owners use and which in some states the law requires and at least partly enforces, would cut the nine hundred in half.

Why do we not save these men then? Why? Careful testing, proper timbering cost money—take time—they interfere with quick, cheap production. "We'll risk it!"

But it is not a jealous earth, resenting man's interference that destroys all the Floyd Collinses of the mines. The nine hundred a year engulfed are but half of the lives spent yearly in the United States in getting out bituminous coal. For ten years, 1912–1922, the yearly average, so our best authority, the United States Bureau of Mines, reports, was 1,824—forty-three men out of every thousand employed. That is fully three times as many as they kill in Great Britain.

What is the matter with us that we endure this? Is it ignorance? Perish the thought! An American mine owner will resent the imputation with scorn. I have heard them myself. What Bulletin can tell him anything about mining! He knows; and moreover our United States Bureau of Mines is the best in the world—and there is nothing about mining it doesn't know and it is a nuisance in its insistence on safety devices.

There is only one answer then, for we certainly *do* kill three times as many per thousand as Great Britain does. If my mine owner friend is right and we know, it follows we don't practice what we know—that we take the chance in other things as well as in proper tunneling.

That is it—knowing but not doing is what is killing men in our mines at this awful rate. "Tardy adoption of safeguards, lagging years behind engineering knowledge of what can and ought to be done," declares John B. Andrews, the active head of the American Association for Labor Legislation, who has studied the methods of mining both in Europe and in this country, who cooperates with mine owners and mine bureaux, and whose only interest in the work is saving lives.

Take the matter of explosions—dangerous things at best, explosions—but you can't mine without them. They blast the rocks—open the veins; and some are less dangerous than others. That has been proved by scientific trials. Indeed, our Federal Bureau of Mines has worked out a table of what is called "permissible" explosions—those that properly handled are comparatively safe.

Do you think the mine owner confined himself to these "permissibles"? Not at all. Last year only about eighteen per cent of the explosions used were in the safe list. Nobody knows how many Floyd Collinses of the mine met "a lonely, black death" because a reckless overseer employed black powder—a thing which all those who have had mining experience say should rarely, if ever be used, and for which there are "permissible" substitutes recommended by the Bureau of Mines, and used with satisfactory results by those mine owners who do care and who not only systematically do everything they know to make things safe, but who are constantly searching [for] better methods, experimenting with new devices and materials.

Thank God it is men of their type that have proved beyond a doubt that there is a way of preventing one of the terrible, sweeping disasters that from time to time have desolated villages and shocked the land.

Explosions from coal dust killed more than four hundred men in American mines last year. At the Castle Gate mine 172 men were killed at one blast. When the community began to count the loss it found 868 widows and children to be cared for.

But explosions from coal dust are unnecessary; that is, there is now in existence a cheap method of prevention worked out by scientific experiment—a large part of which has been under the direction of our Bureau of Mines—successfully applied by law in Great Britain and France for some ten years, but only used in this country by perhaps fifty of our enlightened mine owners, and not by any means yet generally required by law. It took 172 lives and the making of 868 widows and orphans to bring Utah to require by law that the method be enforced there.

And what is it that will prevent these appalling catastrophes? The simplest of things. Everyone can understand the volumes of fine dust which must arise in mining coal. This dust "settles on everything," as a housewife says—over the walls and roofs and floors and cars; but let it be stirred—thrown into the air by the local explosions of the mine and it is easily ignited with results as awful as from the explosions of gas.

Miners have long studied the problem, tried water to "wet the dust down," but it was useless—even dangerous, some say. Finally they tried the medical dictum: "like *cures* like." Grinding rock with fine dust they blew it over the surfaces of the mine. Every layer of coal dust was overlaid by one of rock dust. Rock dust and coal dust mixed are non-explosive. Coal dust explosions, so it is claimed, have passed forever from the mining history of England. The law compels all mines to be regularly dusted with ground rock.

In the United States where we have helped prove that this method of treating the dangerous dust is effective, we allowed four hundred Floyd Collinses of the mines to be killed last year because we did not use our knowledge.

There are enlightened American mine owners who are using the rock dusting process—there are states like Utah adopting it—but in a matter of this kind, uniformity is essential—all states must act.

If at any moment of those seventeen days that young Floyd Collins lay pinned down by rock in his Kentucky cave, legislation could have saved him, can we doubt we would have had it? An extra session, if necessary!

Rock dusting legislation enacted *now* in every state which counts coal mining in its industries will save from a wretched death in the next twelve months literally hundreds of the Floyd Collinses of our mines.

Part III

Home and Career for Women

Introduction

The articles in this section are the ones that most likely reflect Tarbell's own feelings about the roles and experience of women in the workplace and the home. Her treatment of these topics is complicated; Tarbell could express contradictory views. On the one hand, Tarbell demands concern for and equal treatment of women in the workplace, and this stance suggests that she views work and career as perfectly appropriate for women. On the other hand, she makes it abundantly clear that, in her opinion, the God-given functions of women are to bear and care for children and to educate them—especially daughters—in the ways of home and hearth. As Tarbell writes in "The Business of Being a Woman," "The central fact of the woman's life—Nature's reason for her—is the child, his bearing and rearing. There is no escape from the divine order that her life must be built around this constraint, duty, or privilege, as she may please to consider it." She addresses the procreative act itself, if obliquely, saying that the girl "finally faces the most perilous and beautiful of experiences with little more than the ideas which have come to her from the confidences of evil-minded servants, inquisitive and imaginative playmates, or the gossip she hears in her mother's society."

Tarbell did try to counter some sexist notions, and in so doing she enunciated her notion of a complementary equality between the sexes: "The theory that the man who raises corn does a more important piece of work than the woman who makes it into bread is absurd." But Tarbell also distances herself from the feminists when she continues, "The theory that she does something more difficult and less interesting is equally absurd." "The Business of Being a Woman" features dense language and wide-ranging discussion as it suggests the "right" place for women—in the household. But the subtext reveals much about Tarbell herself, as a single, childless woman who forcefully tells women that they *should* do what she does not do.

The two 1887 articles here reprinted from *The Chautauquan*, "Women as Inventors" and "Women in Journalism," were written early in Tarbell's career, when she seems to have been more comfortable dealing with facts and figures than relying on her own interpretations of life and society. Even so, these two pieces suggest some of the themes that characterize Tarbell's later writing.

For instance, Tarbell's somewhat prickly, oft-repeated claims that in the workplace women are as capable as men apparently lay behind the piece on women inventors. *The Chautauquan* earlier had carried an article claiming that women had been granted only 334 patents, most of them for articles of household use, and Tarbell set out to disprove that argument. She does so irrefutably, citing patent office records of 1,935 inventions and demolishing the claim that most women's inventions have to do with the household.

In her piece on "Women in Journalism," Tarbell names some of the prominent American women in the profession and cites the requirements for membership in it. She asserts that this field is wide open to women, so long as they equal men in talent: "Any woman who can do as strong and finished work as a man will find a position." Other characteristics cited by Tarbell seem to be drawn from her own personality, as if she considered herself a model woman journalist: flexibility, ability to tolerate drudgery and follow directions, industriousness, good health, a broad knowledge base, a crisp writing style, accuracy, self-control, and, finally, ability to grow in the profession. Even these attributes are not always enough, however. The woman in journalism still must graduate from the "finishing school" of actual work experience. Apart from identifying fields in which women journalists might excel (society, philanthropy, moral reform), Tarbell painted journalism as a field in which women and men functioned as equals.

The undated piece "Inequality of Pay for Women" in industry was a memo for a talk and as such is a bit disorganized and hard to follow, especially at its end. To back up Tarbell's plea for fair pay, it makes good use of facts supplied by an authoritative source: "Justice demands that if she gives equal service she should have equal pay."

The author feels that the principal reason women do not get equal pay is that they do not stay on the job as long as men do. That they do not is primarily because they elect the "far more important task" of child bearing and rearing: "Women are not cut out by nature and not expected by society, to give themselves to offices and factories. They have a far more important task on hand and in justice to that task, it is not possible for the great body of women to give their eight or ten hours a day."

Another component of woman's natural role is that of talker, Tarbell argues in "The Talkative Woman." She refers not to serious talk, such as the writer herself might engage in, but rather to chatter intended as a means of teaching children to talk. Tarbell seems at once both to belittle and aggrandize this incessant talking of women, as she notes "how infinitely more valuable to the world is the chatter of women than all the books they ever wrote or orations they ever delivered."

In describing a woman called to the bedside of an ailing daughter, Tarbell writes, "She came, full of dread and anguish. Without a sign of what was in her heart, she established herself by the bed, chattering for hours of things at home: the amusing sayings of the new Scotch cook, the tricks of the last puppy, the gaieties of the neighborhood. Chatter? Yes, God-sent chatter."

In this piece it is hard to tell just what is in Tarbell's heart. Tarbell strikes the reader as the sort of person who would never "chatter." Yet here she seems to praise that activity, to the point of being contemptuous of women who try to learn substantial things to fuel their conversations. In praising women's superficial chatter, Tarbell suggests that attempts by women to educate themselves, to free themselves from the routines of house and children, are inappropriate, somehow subverting the natural order of things. It is difficult to reconcile these comments with Tarbell's own reality as a professional woman—childless, well-educated, and anything but "chatty."

The typescript "Women as Bosses" finds Tarbell in a shoe factory, describing in detail a woman, "Jane," who oversees a section of the factory. Proving that women are fully capable of functioning efficiently in a domain usually left to men, to Tarbell this "forelady" is a real hero: "When disgruntled feminists tell me women are being kept back from the top round of industry by masculine intolerance and jealousy, I remember Jane."

The piece ends with Tarbell showing uncharacteristically equal support of career and of family for women. But she does caution that the choice between career and marriage is a difficult one indeed: "If, having a definite call to a career, she does choose marriage, let her be certain the day will come that she will be conscious of undevelopment; equally, if, with the definite call of a talent, she deafens her ears to marriage, there will come sooner or later the consciousness of limitation."

The Business of
Being a Woman

RESPECT for the Creator of this world is basic among all civilized people. The longer one lives, the more thoroughly one realizes the soundness of this respect. The earth and its works *are* good. Most human conceptions are marred by strange inconsistencies. The man who praises the works of the Creator as all wise not infrequently treats His arrangement for carrying on the race as if it were unfit to be spoken of in polite society. Nowhere does the modern God-fearing man come nearer to sacrilege than in his attitude toward the divine plan for renewing life.

A strange mixture of sincerity and hypocrisy, self-flagellation and lust, aspiration and superstition, has gone into the making of this attitude. With the development of it we have nothing to do here. What does concern us is the effect of this profanity on the Business of Being a Woman.

The central fact of the woman's life—Nature's reason for her—is the child, his bearing and rearing. There is no escape from the divine order that her life must be built around this constraint, duty, or privilege, as she may please to consider it. But from the beginning to the end of life she is never permitted to treat it naturally and frankly. As a child accepting all that opens to her as a matter of course, she is steered away from it as if it were something evil. Her first essays at evasion and spying often come to her in connection with facts which are sacred and beautiful and which she is perfectly willing to accept as such if they were treated intelligently and reverently. If she could be kept from all knowledge of the procession of new life except as Nature reveals it to her, there would be reason in her treatment. But this is impossible. From babyhood she breathes the atmosphere of unnatural prejudices and misconceptions which envelop the fact.

Throughout her girlhood the atmosphere grows thicker. She finally faces the most perilous and beautiful of experiences with little more than the ideas

Originally published as chapter 3 of Tarbell's *The Business of Being a Woman* (New York: Macmillan, 1912, rpt. 1925), 53–83, reprinted by permission.

which have come to her from the confidences of evil-minded servants, inquisitive and imaginative playmates, or the gossip she overhears in her mother's society. Every other matter of her life, serious and commonplace, has received careful attention, but here she has been obliged to feel her way and, worst of abominations, to feel it with an inner fear that she ought not to know or seek to know.

If there were no other reason for the modern woman's revolt against marriage, the usual attitude toward its central facts would be sufficient. The idea that celibacy for woman is "the aristocracy of the future" is soundly based if the Business of Being a Woman rests on a mystery so questionable that it cannot be frankly and truthfully explained by a girl's mother at the moment her interest and curiosity seeks satisfaction. That she gets on as well as she does, results, of course, from the essential soundness of the girl's nature, the armor of modesty, right instinct, and reverence with which she is endowed.

The direst result of ignorance or of distorted ideas of this tremendous matter of carrying on human life is that it leaves the girl unconscious of the supreme importance of her mate. So heedlessly and ignorantly is our mating done to-day that the huge machinery of Church and State and the tremendous power of public opinion combined have been insufficient to preserve to the institution of marriage anything like the stability it once had, or that it is desirable that it should have, if its full possibilities are to be realized. The immorality and inhumanity of compelling the obviously mismated to live together, grow on society. Divorce and separation are more and more tolerated. Yet little is done to prevent the hasty and ill-considered mating which is at the source of the trouble.

Rarely has a girl a sound and informed sense to guide her in accepting her companion. The corollary of this bad proposition is that she has no sufficient idea of the seriousness of her undertaking. She starts out as if on a life-long joyous holiday, primarily devised for her personal happiness. And what is happiness in her mind? Certainly it is not a good to be conquered—a state of mind wrested from life by tackling and mastering its varied experiences, the *end*, not the beginning, of a great journey. Too often it is that of the modern Uneasy Woman—the attainment of something *outside* of herself. She visualizes it, as possessions, as ease, a "good time," opportunities for self-culture, the exclusive devotion of the mate to her. Rarely does she understand that happiness in her undertaking depends upon the wisdom and sense with which she conquers a succession of hard places—calling for readjustment of her ideas and sacrifice of her desires. All this she must discover for herself. She is like a voyager who starts out on a great sea with no other chart than a sailor's yarns, no other compass than curiosity.

The budget of axioms she brings to her guidance she has picked up helter-skelter. They are the crumbs gathered from the table of the Uneasy Woman, or worse, of the pharisaical and satisfied woman, from good and bad books, from newspaper exploitations of divorce and scandal, from sly gossip with girls whose budget of marital wisdom is as higgledy-piggledy as her own.

And a pathetically trivial budget it is:

"He must tell her everything." "He must always pick up what she drops." "He must dress for dinner." "He must remember her birthday." That is, she begins her adventure with a set of hard-and-fast rules, and nothing in this life causes more mischief than the effort to force upon another one's own rules!

That marriage gives the finest opportunity that life affords for practicing, not rules, but principles, she has never been taught. Flexibility, adaptation, fair-mindedness, the habit of supplementing the weakness of the one by the strength of the other, all the fine things upon which the beauty, durability, and growth of human relations depend, these are what decide the future of her marriage. These she misses while she insists on her rules; and ruin is often the end. Study the causes back of divorces and separations, the brutal criminal causes aside, and one finds that usually they begin in trivial things— an irritating habit or an offensive opinion persisted in on the one side and not endured philosophically on the other; a petty selfishness indulged on the one side and not accepted humorously on the other—that is, the marriage is made or unmade by small, not great, things.

It is a lack of any serious consideration of the nature of the undertaking she is going into which permits her at the start to accept a false notion of her economic position. She agrees that she is being "supported"; she consents to accept what is given her; she even consents to ask for money. Men and society at large take her at her own valuation. Loose thinking by those who seek to influence public opinion has aggravated the trouble. They start with the idea that she is a parasite—does not pay her way. "Men hunt, fish, keep the cattle, or raise corn," says a popular writer, "for women to eat the game, the fish, the meat, and the corn." The inference is that the men alone render useful service. But neither man nor woman eats of these things until the woman has prepared them. The theory that the man who raises corn does a more important piece of work than the woman who makes it into bread is absurd. The theory that she does something more difficult and less interesting is equally absurd.

The practice of handing over the pay envelope at the end of the week to the woman, so common among laboring people, is a recognition of her equal economic function. It is a recognition that the venture of the two is common and that its success depends as much on the care and intelligence with which she spends the money as it does on the energy and steadiness with which he earns it. Whenever one or the other fails, trouble begins. The failure to understand this business side of the marriage relation almost inevitably produces humiliation and irritation. So serious has the strain become because of this false start that various devices have been suggested to repair it—Mr. Wells' "Paid Motherhood" is one; weekly wages as for a servant is another. Both notions encourage the primary mistake that the woman has not an equal economic place with the man in the marriage.

Marriage is a business as well as a sentimental partnership. But a business partnership brings grave practical responsibilities, and this, under our present system, the girl is rarely trained to face. She becomes a partner in an undertaking where her function is spending. The probability is she does not know a credit from a debit, has to learn to make out a check correctly, and has no conscience about the fundamental matter of living within the allowance which can be set aside for the family expenses. When this is true of her, she at once puts herself into the rank of an incompetent—she becomes an economic dependent. She has laid the foundation for becoming an Uneasy Woman.

It is common enough to hear women arguing that this close grappling with household economy is narrowing, not worthy of them. Why keeping track of the cost of eggs and butter and calculating how much your income will allow you to buy is any more narrowing than keeping track of the cost and quality of cotton or wool or iron and calculating how much a mill requires, it is hard to see. It is the same kind of a problem. Moreover, it has the added interest of being always an independent *personal* problem. Most men work under the deadening effect of impersonal routine. They do that which others have planned and for results in which they have no permanent share.

But the woman argues that her task has no relation to the state. Her failure to see that relation costs this country heavily. Her concern is with retail prices. If she does her work intelligently, she follows and studies every fluctuation of price in standards. She also knows whether she is receiving the proper quality and quantity; and yet so poorly have women discharged these obligations that dealers for years have been able to manipulate prices practically to please themselves, and as for quality and quantity we have the scandal of American woolen goods, of food adulteration, of false weights and measures. No one of these things could have come about in this country if woman had taken her business as a consumer with anything like the seriousness with which man takes his as a producer.

Her ignorance in handling the products of industry has helped the monopolistically inclined trust enormously. I can remember the day when the Beef Trust invaded a certain Middle Western town. The war on the old-time butchers of the village was open. "Buy of us," was the order, "or we'll fill the storage house so full that the legs of the steers will hang out of the windows, and we'll give away the meat." The women of the town had a prosperous club which might have resisted the tyranny which the members all deplored, but the club was busy that winter with the study of the Greek drama! They deplored the tyranny, but they bought the cut-rate meat—the old butchers fought to a finish, and the housekeepers are now paying higher prices for poorer meat and railing at the impotency of man in breaking up the Beef Trust!

If two years ago when the question of a higher duty on hosiery was before Congress any woman or club of women had come forward with carefully tabulated experiments, showing exactly the changes which have gone on of late years in the shape, color, and wearing quality of the 15-, 25-, and 50-cent stockings, the stockings of the poor, she would have rendered a genuine economic service. The women held mass meetings and prepared petitions instead, using on the one side the information the shopkeepers furnished, on the other that which the stocking manufacturers furnished. Agitation based upon anything but personal knowledge is not a public service. It may be easily a grave public danger. The facts needed for fixing the hosiery duty the women should have furnished, for they buy the stockings.

If the Uneasy American Woman were really fulfilling her economic functions to-day, she would never allow a short pound of butter, a yard of adulterated woolen goods, to come into her home. She would never buy a ready-made garment which did not bear the label of the Consumer's League. She would recognize that she is a guardian of quality, honesty, and humanity in industry.

A persistent misconception of the nature and the possibilities of this practical side of the Business of Being a Woman runs through all present-day discussions of the changes in household economy. The woman no longer has a chance to pay her way, we are told, because it is really cheaper to buy bread than to bake it, to buy jam than to put it up. Of course, this is a part of the vicious notion that a woman only makes an economic return by the manual labor she does. The Uneasy Woman takes up the point and complains that she has nothing to do. But this release from certain kinds of labor once necessary, merely puts upon her the obligation to apply the ingenuity and imagination necessary to make her business meet the changes of an ever changing world. Because the conditions under which a household must be run now are not what they were fifty years ago is no proof that the woman no longer has here an important field of labor. There is more to the practical side of her business than preparing food for the family! It means, for one thing, the directing of its wants. The success of a household lies largely in its power of selection. To-day selection has given way to accumulation. The family becomes too often an incorporated company for getting things—with frightful results. The woman holds the only strong strategic position from which to war on this tendency, as well as on the habits of wastefulness which are making our national life increasingly hard and ugly. She is so positioned that she can cultivate and enforce simplicity and thrift, the two habits which make most for elegance and for satisfaction in the material things of life.

Whenever a woman does master this economic side of her business in a manner worthy of its importance, she establishes the most effective school for teaching thrift, quality, management, selection—all the factors in the economic problem. Such scientific household management is the rarest kind of a training school. And here we touch the most vital part in the Woman's Business—that of education.

Every home is perforce a good or bad educational center. It does its work in spite of every effort to shirk or supplement it. No teacher can entirely undo what it does, be that good or bad. The natural joyous opening of a child's mind depends on its first intimate relations. These are, as a rule, with the mother. It is the mother who "takes an interest," who oftenest decides whether the new mind shall open frankly and fearlessly. How she does her work, depends less upon her ability to answer questions than her effort not to discourage them; less upon her ability to lead authoritatively into great fields than her efforts to push the child ahead into those which attract him. To be responsive to his interests is the woman's greatest contribution to the child's development.

I remember a call once made on me by two little girls when our time was spent in an excited discussion of the parts of speech. They were living facts to them, as real as if their discovery had been printed that morning for the first time in the newspaper. I was interested to find who it was that had been able to keep their minds so naturally alive. I found that it came from the family habit of treating with respect whatever each child turned up. Nothing was slurred over as if it had no relation to life—not even the parts of speech! They were not asked or forced to load themselves up with baggage in which they soon discovered their parents had no interest. Everything was treated as if it had a permanent place in the scheme to which they were being introduced. It is only in some such relation that the natural bent of most children can flower, that they can come early to themselves. Where this warming, nourishing intimacy is wanting, where the child is turned over to schools to be put through the mass drill which numbers make imperative—it is impossible for the most intelligent teacher to do a great deal to help the child to his own. What the Uneasy Woman forgets is that no two children born were ever alike, and no two children who grow to manhood and womanhood will ever live the same life. The effort to make one child like another, to make him what his parents want, not what he is born to be, is one of the most cruel and wasteful in society. It is the woman's business to prevent this.

The Uneasy Woman tells you that this close attention to the child is too confining, too narrowing. "I will pity Mrs. Jones for the hugeness of her task," says Chesterton; "I will never pity her for its smallness." A woman never lived who did all she might have done to open the mind of her child for its great adventure. It is an exhaustless [sic] task. The woman who sees it knows she has need of all the education the college can give, all the experience and culture she can gather. She knows that the fuller her individual life, the broader her interests, the better for the child. She should be a person in his eyes. The real service of the "higher education," the freedom to take a part in whatever interests or stimulates her—lies in the fact that it fits her intellectually to be a companion worthy of a child. She should know that unless she does this thing for him he goes forth with his mind still in swaddling clothes, with the chances that it will not be released until relentless life tears off the bands.

The progress of society depends upon getting out of men and women an increasing amount of the powers with which they are born and which bad surroundings at the start blunt or stupefy. This is what all systems of education try to do, but the result of all systems of education depends upon the material that comes to the educator. Opening the mind of the child, that is the delicate task the state asks of the mother, and the quality of the future state depends upon the way she discharges this part of her business.

I think it is historically correct to say that the reason for the sudden and revolutionary change in the education of American women, which began with the nineteenth century and continued through it, was the realization that if we were to make real democrats, we must begin with the child, and if we began with the child, we must begin with the mother!

Everybody saw that unless the child learned by example and precept the great principles of liberty, equality, and fraternity, he was going to remain what by nature we all are, imperious, demanding, and self-seeking. The whole scheme must fail if his education failed. It is not too much to say that the success of the Declaration of Independence and the Constitution depended, in the minds of certain early Democrats, upon the woman. The doctrines of these great instruments would be worked out according to the way she played her part. Her serious responsibility came in the fact that her work was one that nobody could take off her hands. This responsibility required a preparation entirely different from that which had been hers. She must be given education and liberty. The woman saw this, and the story of her efforts to secure both, that she might meet the requirements, is one of the noblest in history.

There was no doubt, then, as to the value of the tasks, no question as to their being worthy national obligations. It was a question of fitting herself for them.

But what has happened? In the process of preparing herself to discharge more adequately her task as a woman in a republic, her respect for the task has been weakened. In this process, which we call emancipation, she has in a sense lost sight of the purposes of emancipation. Interested in acquiring new tools, she has come to believe the tools more important than the thing for which she was to use them. She has found out that with education and freedom, pursuits of all sorts are open to her, and by following these pursuits she can preserve her personal liberty, avoid the grave responsibility, the almost inevitable sorrows and anxieties, which belong to family life. She can choose her friends and change them. She can travel and gratify her tastes, satisfy her personal ambitions. The snare has been too great; the beauty and joy of free individual life have dulled the sober sense of national obligation. The result is that she is frequently failing to discharge satisfactorily some of the most imperative demands the nation makes upon her.

Take as an illustration the moral training of the child. The most essential obligation in a Woman's Business is establishing her household on a sound moral basis. If a child is anchored to basic principles, it is because his home is built on them. If he understands integrity as a man, it is usually because a woman has done her work well. If she has not done it well, it is probable that he will be a disturbance and a menace when he is turned over to society. Sending defective steel to a gunmaker is no more certain to result in unsafe guns than turning out boys who are shifty and tricky is to result in a corrupt and unhappy community.

Appalled by the seriousness of the task, or lured from it by the joys of liberty and education, the woman has too generally shifted it to other shoulders—shoulders which were waiting to help her work out the problem, but which could never be a substitute. She has turned over the child to the teacher, secular and religious, and fancied that he might be made a man of integrity by an elaborate system of teaching in a mass. Has this shifting of responsibility no relation to the general lowering of our commercial and political morality?

For years we have been bombarded with evidence of an appalling indifference to the moral quality of our commercial and political transactions. It is not too much to say that the revelations of corruption in our American cities, the use of town councils, State legislatures, and even of the Federal Government in the interests of private business, have discredited the democratic system throughout the world. It has given more material for those of other lands who despise democracy to sneer at us than anything that has yet happened in this land. And *this has come about under the regime of the emancipated woman.* Is she in no way responsible for it? If she had kept the early ideals of the woman's part in democracy as clearly before her eyes as she has kept some of her personal wants and needs, could there have been so disastrous a condition? Would she be the Uneasy Woman she is if she had kept faith with the ideals that forced her emancipation?—if she had not substituted for them dreams of personal ambition, happiness, and freedom!

The failure to fulfill your function in the scheme under which you live always produces unrest. Content of mind is usually in proportion to the service one renders in an undertaking he believes worthwhile. If our Uneasy Woman could grasp the full meaning of her place in this democracy, a place so essential that democracy must be overthrown unless she rises to it—a part which man is not equipped to play and which he ought not to be asked to play—would she not cease to apologize for herself, cease to look with envy on man's occupations? Would she not rise to her part and we not have at last the "new woman" of whom we have talked so long?

Learning, business careers, political and industrial activities—none of these things is more than incidental in the national task of woman. Her great task is to prepare the citizen. The citizen is not prepared by a training in practical politics. Something more fundamental is required. The meaning of honor and of the sanctity of one's word, the understanding of the principles of democracy and of the society in which we live, the love of humanity, and the desire to serve—these are what make a good citizen. The tools for preparing herself to give this training are in the woman's hands. It calls for education, and the nation has provided it. It calls for freedom of movement and expression, and she has them. It calls for ability to organize, to discuss problems, to work for whatever changes are essential. She is developing this ability. It may be that it calls for the vote. I do not myself see this, but it is certain that she will have the vote as soon as not a majority, but an approximate half, not of men—but of women—feel the need of it.

What she has partially at least lost sight of is that education, freedom, organization, agitation, the suffrage, are but tools to an end. What she now needs is to formulate that end so nobly and clearly that the most ignorant woman may understand it. The failure to do this is leading her deeper and deeper into fruitless unrest. It is also dulling her sense of the necessity of keeping her business abreast with the times. At one particular and vital point this shows painfully, and that is her slowness in socializing her home.

Women as Inventors

Since 1871 the wonderful Model Hall in the Patent Office at Washington has been in charge of Mr. R. C. Gill. This gentleman, fitted for the position both by his mechanical skill and his enthusiasm, works with rare devotion among the thousands of devices in the department. In classifying and arranging models scientifically, he exercises care and judgment. In connection with his position Mr. Gill has done not a little special work. One piece in particular, which is still in manuscript and whose statements have never been made public, is of much value. It is "the *first* and *only* record of female inventors who have obtained letters patent from the United States for their inventions." The record is complete up to December 14, 1886.

Mr. Gill gave all his leisure time for three years to the compilation of this record, with no other object in view than that women burdened by self-support might know what others had accomplished in inventions, and possibly be stimulated to efforts which would save them from overwork and poverty. Certainly he deserves kindly and hearty recognition for the service he has rendered.

But what does the record show? Three things worth knowing and believing: that women have invented a large number of useful articles; that these patents are not confined to "clothes and kitchen" devices as the skeptical masculine mind avers; that invention is a field in which woman has large possibilities.

Popular opinion contradicts all these statements. In a late issue of this magazine, one of our noblest and best informed advocates for more work and better wages for women, Mary Lowe Dickinson, wrote: "In the field of invention, woman has hardly entered upon her privileges; for only three hundred thirty-four patents have as yet been issued to women. Out of twenty-two thousand issued last year, only ninety were to female inventors; and most of these are for articles of household use."

From *The Chautauquan* 7 (Mar. 1887): 355–57.

Mrs. Dickinson does not make careless statements. She undoubtedly has as authority the most trustworthy figures yet published. But until Mr. Gill compiled his record not even the half-truth was known. What are the facts? Up to December 14, 1886, there had been granted to women by the United States, letters patent for one thousand nine hundred thirty-five inventions, almost six times the number usually quoted.

The first of these patents is dated 1809 and was granted Mary Kies for a method of weaving straw with silk or thread. In 1821, '22, '25, '28, '31, '34, and '41, patents were taken out, one for each year. They were for "hats and bonnets," "stove feet," "manufacture of moccasins," "whitening of leghorn straw," a "globe for teaching geography," a "method of manufacturing textile fabric from the external fibers of milkweed," and a "corset." A narrow range? True, and a small number; but quite as broad as woman's range at that period, and the number compares very favorably with her opportunities.

In the '50's, thirteen patents were granted; in the '60's the number increases to two hundred sixteen; in '76 there were one hundred thirty-six granted; and in '86, up to December 14, there had been one hundred sixty-nine. With a few exceptions the patentees have been residents of the United States. Twenty-two in all have been granted foreigners, including some important articles. The first of this class was to Mary Bayles of England, for a paper wrapper for needles. One of the most valuable patents recently granted is to a lady of Berlin, Germany, for a pocket sewing machine. Before letters patent were taken out in this country she had received them from five European countries.

Bare numbers are thus sufficient to show that the field of invention is one to which the feminine mind has turned and quite as largely as to most other fields formerly held exclusively by men. Compare the whole number of women physicians, lawyers, or editors with the whole number men in the same profession, and the proportion will be scarcely if any larger than is the proportion of patents taken out in the United States by women, to the number granted men.

The "clothes and kitchen" argument is interesting, but scarcely as forcible as it is ordinarily accounted. For if it be true, that women have patented more devices for wardrobe and household uses than in all other fields combined—it is no disparagement to her ability. An invention is an invention whether it be for house-work or mill-work, and the kind of mental quality it requires is the same. It is only reasonable to expect that ingenuity will be exercised proportionately to opportunity. If the number of inventions in any single class belong to the industries which occupy the most of the time and thought of the majority of women, the result is what might be expected.

By actual count, one-sixth of all her inventions have been granted for articles of dress. They include numerous varieties of corsets, straps and bands, dress elevators, shields, glove-fasteners, leggings, clasps of all kinds—all the important devices which do so much toward making a woman's dress compact, comfortable, and economical. Some of these articles have been great successes, and have brought the inventors comfortable fortunes.

The proportion of patents for household contrivances is still larger. The favorite articles seem to be dish-washers, sad-iron cleaners, sewing-machine attachments, churns, and cooking utensils. Many of the patents suggest pictures at once pathetic and comical. Who cannot fancy the desperation into which that woman was driven who patented a "preparation for kindling fires"? And what must have been her experience who devised a "paste for razor-strops"? The monotony of three daily installments of soiled dishes, the annoyance of sticky irons, the wear and tear of poor machine attachments, the maddening up-and-down movements of the old-fashioned churn, the awkwardness of early stove apparatus, have necessitated these inventions. What better field for woman to exercise her ingenuity?

Any article that will lighten and brighten the housewife's grind is a national blessing. The household inventions have not only always been the most needed, most profitable, and most important; they still remain so. The multiplicity of the demands of modern life calls for more scientific methods, less muscle and drudgery, more brains and skill in the kitchen. Invention must accomplish this, and who so well fitted by experience for the work as women?

Of course where an invention for household use is simple, practical, and reasonable in price, it sells. Mrs. Hannah V. Shaw, of Lawrenceburg, Indiana, is likely to make a fortune out of a dust-pan which she has patented. Such contrivances mean to the housekeeper just what a successful improvement in farming implements means to the farmer, easier and cheaper work, and so must succeed.

But how about other classes of inventions? Mr. Gill's record shows that there is no branch of industry in which woman has operated and not left proof of her mechanical skill. One of the handsomest models of the Patent Office is of a sub-marine telescope patented in 1845 by Sarah Mather. This is the first patent granted by the United States for a sub-marine telescope. Fire-escapes appear frequently on the list; one of them is a particularly ingenious contrivance for turning a bed-spring into an escape. From the dangers of water as well, they have contrived devices sufficiently practical to receive patents. In 1870 Sarah Saul patented a "life-preserver skirt"; a life-boat and life-raft are in the list, most appropriately, for there are Ida Lewises to manage them. Boot and shoe making has been improved not a little by the inventions of women.

Some good results are shown in mechanical devices. Conspicuous among the number is a machine for driving barrel hoops, a steam generator, a baling press, a steam and fume box, an automatic floor for elevator-shafts, a rail for street railways, an electric illuminating apparatus, a railway car safety apparatus, packing for piston rods, car coupling, electric battery, locomotive wheels, materials for packing journals and bearings, machine for drilling gun stocks, a stock car, an apparatus for destroying vegetation on railways, another for removing snow from the tracks, a non-inductive electric cable, an apparatus for raising sunken vessels, a dredging machine, a method of constructing screw propellers, locomotive and other chimneys, a railway tie, a covering for the slot of elevated railways, besides many more of a similar nature.

Some of these contrivances are very ingenious. For example, take Miss Montgomery's improvement in locomotive wheels. The invention consists in substituting a curved corrugated beam to the periphery of the wheel instead of the usual fellies of wood or other material, as in the iron wheels of locomotives, and in applying a tire of iron or steel with ribs or tongues fitting into the grooves formed by the curved corrugated beam. To give a certain elasticity to the wheel, where this may be desirable, a sheet of india-rubber is introduced.

An interesting contrivance has been patented by Miss Mary Walton of New York, for deadening the sound on elevated railways. Everyone familiar with elevated railways has been annoyed by the deafening noise. Her invention consists in certain combinations of the rail, the longitudinal guards, and the cross-ties with flooring and partitions, thus forming enclosures for bedding the rails in sand or like materials, which smothers the noise, and when the sand is covered with asphalt the enclosed parts are protected from the weather.

The list is sufficient to show that in mechanical work where women have never had opportunity for exercising ingenuity, and for which all training has been denied them, there has been a very respectable amount accomplished. Where anything has been done it has been due, of course, to some accidental opportunity. Society has been quite too proper up to this point to encourage women in becoming mechanics. A woman who possessed a mechanical bent, encountered skepticism and discouragement. Her friends were troubled if, when a child, she preferred a hammer to a doll; as she grew older, she was scolded if she made kites instead of patch-work; and at a later age she was in danger of hearing herself called unmaidenly if she showed a talent for the carpenter's bench rather than the piano.

The experience of Miss Margaret Knight of Boston, who in 1871, patented a valuable machine for making paper bags is to the point. Miss Knight once described to a friend her early experience as a mechanic: "As a child, I never cared for things that girls usually do; dolls never possessed any charms for me. I couldn't see the sense of coddling bits of porcelain with senseless faces; the only things I wanted were a jack-knife, a gimlet, and pieces of wood. My friends were horrified. I was called a tomboy, but that made very little impression on me. I sighed sometimes because I was not like the other girls, but wisely concluded that I couldn't help it, and sought further consolation from my tools. I was always making things for my brothers. Did they want anything in the line of playthings, they always said "Mattie will make them for us." I was famous for my kites, and my sleds were the envy and admiration of all the boys in town. I'm not surprised at what I've done. I'm only sorry I couldn't have had as good a chance as a boy, and have been put to my trade regularly."

When Miss Knight desired to manufacture a few of her machines, she met from workmen, constant skepticism of her ability to superintend the work. It was only her persistence and the skill which they could not but respect, which finally won her recognition. But how silly the popular sentiment which prevented her having "as good a chance as a boy"!

The United States contains a goodly number of women farmers, and the thought bestowed on the business has resulted in not a few useful contrivances; notably a grain elevator, several varieties of fences, one of them a flood-fence, a grain and cockle separator, a grain and malt drier, a reaping and mowing machine, a mode of protecting fruit trees from curculio, several improvements for harness, wagons, and carriages, and a cotton-picker. In dairy work there is an excellent array including *cow-milkers*, milk-strainers, detachable spouts for milk pails, butter-tubs, churns, and the like.

That favorite outdoor employment, bee-keeping, has taxed her ingenuity not a little. Among the results are bee-hives, a machine for manufacturing honey-comb foundations, and a bee-feeding device.

The sick-room has received a large number of contributions. There have been patents granted for as many as twenty medical compounds, or patent medicines, not including those for salves and ointments. The contrivances for hospitals include varieties of beds for the sick, medical spoons, a table and head-rest for invalids, several varieties of supports, beside many queer contrivances, ingenious, and, perhaps, useful.

In art industries some work has been done. Perhaps the invention which attracts the most attention is that by the distinguished sculptor, Harriet Hosmer. It is a method of making artificial marble, patented in 1879 while Miss Hosmer was in Italy. Two years later a Miss Watts of Maryland also took out a patent for artificial marble. Several contrivances have been invented for firing china. Other inventions connected with art work are for teaching drawing, for painting on velvet in oil colors, coloring photographs, and similar work.

Two classes of invention in which we might reasonably expect much, have very little; that is, toys and school-room contrivances. Not a score of patents all told, have been issued to women for toys. We cannot conclude that women have never exercised their skill in making playthings, for there is scarcely a house that cannot show some peculiar and ingenious home-made toy. The true state of the case is, women have never patented what they have devised. The toys include nothing particularly striking unless it be one "for the production of *loud explosions.*" Whatever could have induced a *woman* to patent such an arrangement is not clear. "Loud explosions" are about the last thing needed in play rooms.

Among educational devices are numerous slates, several sets of locks, a tablet for teaching penmanship, a scholar's companion, a game of fractions, appliances for setting writing copy, a book cover, and globes; an array in no wise equal to the large amount of work women do in the school-room. The most interesting device in this list bears the name of the charming and helpful writer, Mrs. A. D. T. Whitney. Letters patent were granted her in 1882 for the invention of a set of alphabet blocks. Of these blocks Mrs. Whitney writes: "The invention is a set of blocks from a half-inch cube to the same four inches in extension. . . . The child builds the letters, thus learning them from construction instead of the unconscious and difficult analysis which he is obliged to use in mastering the characters as presented in the whole. . . . The invention has lain almost idle, for want of any channel or agency through which it might have been thoroughly introduced. It has been warmly welcomed and approved by parents and teachers who have tested it. I am too busy in other ways to follow it up with any expenditures of time and money, but it is there—to remain until called for."

It must not be inferred from the above statements that one invention is the limit of a woman's power. Many women have made a business of inventing and putting their goods on the market. Eliza Alexander of New York, has taken out patents for a sewing-machine, for several braiding attachments for machines, and for lawn tennis apparatus. In '63 and '64 Clarissa Britain of Michigan, received letters patent for seven different articles, including a floor-warmer, ambulance, boiler, combined boiler and dinner-pail, and lamp burner; variety enough to prove her ingenuity at least. Helen Blanchard of Massachusetts, has received eleven different patents. Maria Beasley of Pennsylvania, has patented a variety of articles, among them the machine for driving hoops on barrels and the steam generator already mentioned. The list might be extended indefinitely. It is sufficiently long to prove the point.

This record, in every particular so much more creditable than popular opinion admits, is by no means the only proof of the inventive genius of the feminine mind. One familiar with the daily life of the large number of women in this country in "moderate circumstances" must have observed how large a part of their comforts, adornments, and advantages, they owe to their ingenuity. It is inventive genius, nothing else, that enables a woman to carry a gown down from herself though a family of daughters and at last bring it out as a part of the lining of a bed-quilt or the cover of a chair-cushion. It is inventive genius which will make half the furniture of a room out of dry goods boxes and cretonne with an enviable result. The coziest sitting rooms, the neatest wardrobes, the prettiest Christmas presents, are due to the inventive faculty of women.

In many other departments of work this faculty is conspicuous. Women who are connected with large establishments frequently make suggestions and improvements, which are worth large sums to the business. It is the habit to speak of these women as "handy," or "full of ideas." Such women are inventors; their work, inventions.

There are good reasons why the list is not more extensive. If a woman does contrive a useful article it is ordinarily for her own convenience; she is satisfied in meeting her own wants, or doing something "original." Her ingenuity usually has no higher ambition. Her life is so circumscribed that she does not see the advantages to herself and {her} family of a patent on her device. Or it may be ignorance about securing patents, doubt abut her model, the expense to be incurred, the skeptical remarks of friends or the demands of her daily life, {that} prevent her taking measures to appropriate to herself the financial advantage there may be in the invention.

Another cause for few patents is that all training in handling tools is withheld from girls. As a bright woman of my acquaintance, herself a partner and joint manager in a large paper-mill, recently remarked, "Girls are so entirely and totally ignorant of practical mechanics that it is about as astonishing a feat for them to originate any invention as it would have been for Noah to have invented a steam-engine for his ark." When they do possess mechanical skill it has been "picked up." It cannot be urged against them that they have no deftness. Every model they have put on the shelves of the Patent Office proves their skill. Many a housewife is her own carpenter, locksmith, and tinner. If she can learn to split her own kindling wood she can learn to handle a saw and hammer.

After a patent has been secured, a work must follow from which many women shrink. It is putting the article on the market. When one has influential friends they may assist her; when she has money it is not difficult to secure competent persons to manage her business; if she has neither, her tact, business skill, and courage must serve her.

A private letter from Madam Foy of Connecticut, who has had a long experience in pushing her own inventions, gives several practical hints on this point. She writes: "In the first place, an invention should meet a recognized want. An article that does this, and is practical, will commend itself to the good sense of the people, and can be easily introduced into market. A few nicely made samples, assigned to the right parties, will soon be disposed of, and in a short time they will be in demand and selling on their merits. In construction, an article should be so simple that designing persons (and their name is legion) will not be able to make an article which will meet the same want, at less expense, and thus undersell the original inventor. Much of the success of the business built up on my inventions, is due to a strict adherence to the above described principles."

A notable case of a woman pushing an invention successfully has been given to the public recently in Madam Coston's "A Signal Success," a book in which the author tells the story of how the famous Coston signals, the invention of her husband who died before their usefulness was fully demonstrated, were introduced to the various governments which have since adopted them. Madam Coston's perseverance, energy, and tact were unfailing in the enterprise, and her reward has been abundant.

There is at present a healthier tone in society than ever before in regard to the kind of employments a woman may pursue. The world sensibly says, Do whatever you can do well. How, not what, shall decide your fitness. A woman who has inventive skill may easily find a place in which to exercise it. As opportunities for industrial education increase, there will be little opposition to girls who desire to learn the use of tools. No improvement which a woman can originate will be slighted because it comes from the hand of a woman. It only remains for her to take full possession of a field in which there is abundant opportunity for her to win great successes and do great good.

Women in Journalism

A complete list of the representative women of the day would include the names of a large number of journalists. There would be Mary Booth of *Harper's Bazaar,* Mary Mapes Dodge of *St. Nicholas,* Ella Farnum Pratt of *Wide Awake,* Lucy Stone and Alice Stone Blackwell of *The Woman's Journal,* Jeannette Gilder of *The Critic,* Kate Upson Clark of *Good Cheer,* Estelle M. Hatch ("Jean Kincaid") of the Boston *Globe,* Sallie Joy White of the *Boston Advertiser,* Margaret E. Sangster of the New York *Christian Intelligencer,* Rebecca Harding Davis of *The Inquirer,* Jennie June of *Demorest's Monthly,* Ellen Hutchinson of the *New York Tribune*, and scores more of honored names, made familiar by connection with leading periodicals.

If an estimate of the relative number of women finding employment in different channels was made, the various branches of journalism, departmental, reportorial, and editorial, would be found to contain a respectable percentage of the whole.

The paragraph column of the newspaper, especially of papers which devote attention to the woman question, contains an increasing number of attractive items concerning women in journalism.

Ambitious women cannot but be fascinated by the facts revealed. If money, independence, and social position are within the reach of one woman, why not of another? The *raison d'être* of the present article is to give a tentative answer to this question.

There is, perhaps, no profession whose requirements are less understood by women than that of journalism. There are few editors, who have not learned from the applications for positions which their mails contain, how crude an idea the average woman has of the work. Her usual plea for fitness is that she "was considered a good essay writer when in school," testing herself by the popular notion that a good journalist is one who is able to say bright things, make rhymes, and write essays. Now "essay-writing," however admirable, will not make a journalist.

From *The Chautauquan* 7 (Apr. 1887): 393–95.

Journalism is an organization for turning out periodical reading matter; and whether the particular product be a country newspaper, a city daily, or a monthly magazine, it requires a complicated, many-sided labor to produce it. Writing is but one of the many parts of the business. Before anything can be written, the policy of the periodical must be considered, the relative importance of different subjects, decided, and materials, collected. After the actual writing, comes the necessary editing which decides whether the communication is on the line of the paper, is properly written, is too long or short, and is prepared for the printer. A process of proofreading and making-up follows the editing. Each one of these operations is quite as legitimate journalism as the writing, and quite as necessary.

The woman who would become a journalist must fit into the organization wherever she is needed. She may be asked to read articles and prepare them for the printer, to condense a paper of five thousand words into one thousand without omitting a point or weakening an argument, read proof, hold copy for the proof-reader, write advertising circulars, review books, write obituaries, report events, write headlines, answer questions, look after the exchanges, make clippings, compile articles, write editorials, or do a hundred other things. If she earns a permanent place she must do some one of these things better than any other available person, and before she rises to an editorial position, she ought to know how to do them all, and what is more, know when others are doing them right.

Journalism is by no means purely literary work, nor is it without its disadvantages. The halo which surrounds it is largely fictitious. Every department of the work has more or less drudgery connected with it; the editor-in-chief knows what he wants and does not want, often in direct opposition to personal tastes; the hurry of the work particularly on daily and weekly papers is a heavy strain; the associations in reportorial positions are not always pleasant; advancement is often slow, as even a person well-fitted for the work is a long time obtaining thorough command of his resources.

The disadvantages peculiar to women are not many. A greater liberality of ideas as a rule characterizes journalists than other professional men, and the question of ability is usually the only one raised. There are certain kinds of reporting [such] as police and morgue news impossible to a woman; but it is a kind of news which advancing civilization makes more and more unpopular.

From a somewhat extended correspondence on this point, I find that, as a rule, the women who have been active in journalism find its disadvantages to be those incident to the profession and not those arising from sex. Mrs. Marion V. Dudley, formerly of the *Milwaukee Sentinel,* and now president of the Wisconsin Author's Club, gives as her opinion of its disadvantages "necessary haste, monotony, and often superficiality." Mrs. A. S. Duniway, formerly of the *New North West,* of Portland, Oregon, says, "You have no time to correct your blunders until after the world has seen them, and then it is too late; your best friends will often misconstrue your motives, and your worst enemies will assail you in publications that they are cautious to keep out of your reach till to is too late to checkmate their movements. The salaries paid to journalists are fickle; sometimes a writer makes a lucky hit, but with the vast majority, it will always be simple drudgery, as illy paid as other labor."

Lucy Stone finds the greatest disadvantages that one is "all the time tempted to lower his standard to catch the popular breeze and go with the current and become as cheap and as poor as it may be"—a temptation to which she, of all journalists, has never yielded. Miss C. J. Bartlett, formerly the editor of the *Oshkosh Daily Times* and at present pastor of All Souls' Unitarian Church of Sioux Falls, [South] Dakota, gives as her verdict, "not being what is called 'a good all round man,'" but adds, "a woman who understands her business and does not presume on her womanhood is almost always treated with courtesy."

The advantages, however, more than counterbalance this enumeration. If one has proved herself capable, work can nearly always be obtained with ease. A successful journalist must progress in ideas, in information, in capacity for work; this fact makes the calling particularly desirable. The constant change of view and subjects keeps the mind from falling into "ruts," though this advantage is offset by the danger of superficiality. Journalism offers large opportunities for doing good, for influencing public opinion, and for purifying the atmosphere of the times. Socially a woman journalist of education and refinement holds large power. With her more than with any other class of women lies the power to establish the *salon* as an American social institution. In not a few cases women journalists have accomplished something of this kind. Mary Clemmer's home on Capitol Hill, in Washington, was in her time, a center for the meeting of many rare men and women. Miss Booth's Saturday evenings have become a social feature of literary life in New York. Harriet Prescott Spofford says of these gatherings: "If there is such a thing in this country as a *salon,* it is to be found here, where every Saturday night may be met an assemblage of the beauty, wit, and wisdom, resident or transient, in the city." The present administration in Washington [that of Grover Cleveland] has done not a little to further the social position of women journalists by the kindly recognition it has given them.

Capital is essential for the would-be journalist. This capital consists in qualities rather than acquisitions. No "School of Journalism" can hope to furnish them. The first of these qualities is the power to work continuously until a task is done. "The two blades to the editorial scissors are thrift and industry," said Samuel Bowles, and the habits of all successful journalists confirm his statement. Mary Booth sits in the editorial offices of *Harper's Bazaar* from nine in the morning until four in the afternoon, taking only a light lunch at her desk. She says: "Editorial work, like woman's work, is never done and the planning of which it very largely consists goes on day and night without interruption." For nineteen years she has followed this plan, taking only brief vacations. Mrs. Fran Leslie, who is editor-in-chief and publisher of all the various periodicals bearing that familiar name, looks after the business and the editing of her large establishment, reading all the proofs, and approving every make-up. The ability to work continuously twelve months out of the year is the price of success in journalism. It is not a spurt for a week or month and then an "easy time" but a strong steady pull day in and day out.

The power to work makes health essential. Indeed, no ambitious woman should go into journalism without this qualification. While she may do the work of a department, she cannot carry the responsibility of higher positions without the steady nerve and the fire which health alone makes possible. Enthusiasm she must have, not over her hobby alone, but over things in general, a power to interest herself in anything; in the working of a patent medicine "ad," the report of a dairymen's meeting, or the latest development in the European war situation.

General information such as the college or a broad and thoughtful course of reading supplies, is indispensable. There is really no information that will not come in play, and the more special knowledge the better. Moral, social, and political science and history are of the first importance; then large familiarity with the men, the customs, the industries, and the opinions of the day; languages are splendid tools; so is a general knowledge of the church, science, art, music and the drama.

The value of a good English style to a journalist cannot be overestimated. A style clear, vigorous, crisp, nervy, is to a certain extent a natural gift, but if it is not natural, clearness, at least, may be cultivated, and a long way toward vigor is never saying a foolish or unnecessary thing. Mrs. Esther T. Housh of *The Women's Magazine* says on this point, "Culture will show, like birth. If a journalist can have both she has an heritage. The gift of saying sharp truths in smooth words may be natural, but it can be acquired."

No matter how brilliant a paragrapher, or leader-writer one is, if his statements are not accurate, if his logic is shaky, he cannot succeed. A slip in a fact, or a conclusion, is even more striking if it occurs in a brilliant sentence. This need of care pervades every department of the work. The reporter who calls John J. Smith, John S. Smith, will find himself in the traditional "hot water"; and he who presents a "make-up put together with a pitch-fork" is very liable before the edition is run to conclude with the disgusted small boy that "life is not what it is cracked up to be."

Self-control is an excellent journalistic weapon. The woman who presents a carefully prepared report of what seems to her a very important event and sees the editorial "blue" go crashing through her fine touches, or who is confronted by some vexatious oversight in her proof-reading or copy-handling, feels like crying. But tears are *not* a part of the journalistic capital. An editor with a daily, a weekly, or a magazine form on his hands has no leisure for "feelings." It is useless to tell him as dear old Burton does that "a woman in tears is no more to be minded than a goose getting its feet wet," he cannot see it in that light. Control over personal tastes is quite as essential as control over feelings. When a woman enters journalism she must not put forward her femininity to such an extent as to demand that the habits of an office be changed on her account; nor can she presume on her womanhood. "I can't keep track of my lady clerks," said the head of a government department to me in Washington, "a few of them make themselves so *much more numerous* than the same number of men." A churlish thing to say, perhaps, but the worst of it is, that not infrequently such a remark is true; and when it is true, it is fatal to the genuine success of women whether they be in government employ, or in journalism.

One more quality—it is the power of growing. Apply this test before entering journalism. Can you thrive under drudgery? This is the test of success. Ella Farnum Pratt charmingly says, "Good editors are born, not made; they get their food and sun, dew, bracing wind, and baptismal rain, from all sources and *grow right along* no matter where they stand. Transplanted, their daily experience yields special food. They will thrive, too, upon the delightful day-long drudgeries of their work. Be sure of this last test in deciding upon your 'born editor.'"

As a supplement to this extended list of qualifications read the following opinions of successful women journalists, and remember that the points they make are in no sense theoretical, but are convictions arising from actual experience. Lucy Stone says, "Unflagging interest in a subject, general information, wide-awake interest in current events"; Mrs. Dudley, "Patience, common sense, good judgment, quick perceptions, and action"; Miss Bartlett, "A nose for news, the ability to appreciate what the public will be interested in, the ability to put what you have to say in a brief, terse, but conclusive way"; Lilian Whiting of the Boston *Traveller,* "Health, temperamental ability, keeping touch with literature and life, fairmindedness."

But if a woman knows she can work, has good health, can arouse an interest in anything, is well-informed, of good judgment, and has a "stiff upper lip" she must still learn journalism by actually doing it. There is but one "finishing school"—experience. Jennie June began her career with dramatic notices written to relieve her husband. Jeannette Gilder's first experience was on the Newark *Daily Morning Register.* She wanted experience and stayed by the paper through some stormy weather in order to get it. Her subsequent success proves her wisdom.

A woman who has spent half her life in journalism in the West, and is now editing a magazine in New York, says: "The women who succeed in journalism, or any other profession or business, are those possessed of brains and energy enough to 'make a way,' if there is none already prepared for them."

Mary Clemmer declares that "comparatively few appreciate the value of the discipline of trained faculties that may come through doing faithfully and well, the drudgery, so to speak, of intellectual work," and adds, "I once entered into a written contract to write a column per day on any subject I was instructed to write on, for three years in advance, and at the end of that three years I had not for a single day failed of filling my task, which included everything from book reviews, comments on the Government, public men and affairs, to a common advertisement paragraph. You see that I did not miss the apprenticeship of literary work." During the last year of this contract she received a salary of five thousand dollars; a practical proof of the value of "drudgery."

There are notable exceptions, of course, to the rule of apprenticeship. Mrs. Mary Mapes Dodge after a successful career as an author became associate editor of the *Hearth and Home*, and it was from that position that she was called to take charge of *St. Nicholas*. Miss Booth stepped at once from literary work into the editorship of *Harper's Bazaar*. Ella Farnum Pratt started in the editorial chair of *Wide Awake*. But these are rare cases. Where a woman is known to have unusual critical and literary ability she may be given a high position, but it is exceptional. Inexperience is a dangerous thing.

The woman who aims at becoming a journalist must be satisfied with any respectable opening. Of one thing, however, she may be sure; her advancement will be as rapid as her ability, willingness, and adaptability are great. A woman who shows that she can turn her hand to anything in an office is too rare a bird to be kept long in the background.

While almost every variety of journalistic work is suitable for women, there are several departments pre-eminently so. The household column is growing in favor, and only a woman can edit such a department with skill. This variety of journalism has introduced several successful editors to the public. Kate Upson Clark, now of *Good Cheer,* first made her reputation by her wise, bright, and sympathetic editing of the "Helping Hand" in the *Philadelphia Press.* Mrs. Louisa Knapp, now editor of the *Ladies Home Journal* at a salary of five thousand dollars per year, did her first editorial work on the household department of the *Tribune and Farmer.*

There are many kinds of reportorial work in which women excel; the social field is eminently hers. She has the light, bright touch combined with the good taste which makes the social column so fascinating and so inoffensive.

Philanthropy and moral reform are pre-eminently woman's professions, and the aid she may give through the press is incalculable. The work of Helen Campbell for the *New York Tribune* in her "Prisoners of Poverty," those thrilling pictures of the life of the poor of New York City, is a type of work which sooner or later the press must espouse, and will do best through women. It is the duty of the one-half of the world to find out how the other half is living, and no means can be more effective and far-reaching than that which Mrs. Campbell is using.

In a recent article Thomas Wentworth Higginson wrote: "I am told by editors that you may almost count on the fingers of one hand, the women in America to whom you can assign a subject for a magazine paper, requiring scholarly effort and labor, and have the work well done. This is the gap that needs to be filled by literary women at present. The supply of second grade fiction—and by this is meant all fiction inferior in grade to George Eliot's—is now tolerably well secured. But the demand for general literary work of a solid and thoughtful nature, demanding both a scholarship and a trained power of expression—this is never very supplied among men, and is, with few exceptions, unsupplied among American women."

While the work here referred to is properly literary work, it is of a nature that is easily done in connection with purely journalistic work. Where a member of a staff can write careful and scholarly papers of the nature Mr. Higginson refers to, he becomes exceedingly valuable. The increased number of women who are receiving college education and looking toward journalism for work will do well to consider Mr. Higginson's suggestion.

The conclusion from this brief review of the profession and the qualifications it demands is inevitable. It is a field wide open to women. The standard it raises is high, but the opportunity is a great as her ability. Any woman who can do as strong and finished work as a man will find a position.

Inequality of Pay
for Women in Industry

A variety of problems constantly [is encountered] in industry when we come
to the value of services. There is the question of the discrepancy between the
salaries of men and women. In the last forty years there has been a constant
increase in industrial and business life of women employees. They are doing
now scores and scores of tasks formerly done only by men. The increase of
automatic operations in the factory, the increase of salesmen in shops, the increase of clerical work, also the increase in the devices which are employed to
save time and secure efficiency, keep things up to date and also keep full and
satisfactory records, have called in great numbers of women, but rarely in any
of these occupations do you find that the salary of the man and woman is the
same for the same work. That excellent organization, the National Industrial
Conference Board, recently published a report on the investigation into clerical salaries in the United States and it has some interesting data on the discrepancy between earnings of men and women in this field where there are
such numerous numbers of women.

For the sake of comparison this report divides the wages paid for clerical
work into two classes, the highest and the lowest, an arbitrary condition of
course. This report finds clerical positions can be divided into twenty different classes, that there are different grades of clerks, chief clerks, senior clerks,
junior clerks. There is a head bookkeeper. There are classes of stenographers
and typists. There are filing clerks, mailing clerks, switchboard operators—
twenty kinds in all in a modern, well-equipped office. For the purpose of
classes this Board divides these office workers into two classes, the highest
and the lowest paid. You take the highest paid group and you find that in
almost every case the men are drawing larger salaries than women, that while

Undated [1930s?] typescript, labeled "Memo for Atlantic City Talk," Tarbell Papers Collection, Pelletier Library, Allegheny College, Meadville, Pennsylvania. This is a very rough
draft and at some points lacks coherency. Nonetheless, Tarbell's concern over equal pay
for equal work comes through clearly.

there are women in this highest paid group, there are very many more men. There will be one woman chief clerk for six men; one woman head book-keeper to eleven men; one woman cashier to fourteen men. But when you drop down into the lowest paid group you find the women far outrun the men, that is, take it in an office of the lowest paid group and you will find 69 women chief clerks to nine men. You will find 52 order clerks [are women] to 35 of the men. Take it by and large in office employment as in factory employment the great body of women occupied have to be satisfied with the low wage while men take the high. Many women complain bitterly. They claim that they are doing the same work and therefore they should get the same pay. They will tell you in Wall Street that there is now and then a woman who will command a salary not only equal to, but far outstrip that of a man, but these cases are rare. The general opinion seems to be that, comparing the two in office employment, the woman has less initiative, she is more afraid of responsibility, she is less regular and also there is less hope of her staying on in the business.

As I see it, there is more in this last reason than in any other, unless it may be the lack in initiative. Women are not cut out by nature and not expected by society, to give themselves to offices and factories. They have a far more important task on hand [the bearing and rearing of children] and in justice to that task, it is not possible for the great body of women to give their eight or ten hours a day to a regular employment. Moreover, the great body of these women do not want to do this. They feel no call for that, while they feel a very strong and imperative call to the work cut out for them by nature and society. Employment for the great mass of them is a stop-gap, a tide over. Nevertheless it is true that larger and larger numbers of young women are looking on life differently from what women once did. The whole attitude toward the home as an institution is changed with the changes in the productive life of the nation. The tasks for the women are not what they once were, the responsibilities are not what they once were. She has not been able to develop the educational, spiritual, intellectual and superior social side of her task in such a way as to employ all her time. She prefers to work, frequently prefers to work if she is married and it is the women who come in as a steady factory, not merely working a short period, with no expectation of staying on, that suffers for the transients. It affects the whole position of women in industry. Here is where we need a measuring stick. Justice demands that if she gives equal service she should have equal pay and also if she is more or less . . . she should suffer for that. It is one of the complicated and difficult problems of adjusting the pay to service, something that must be done if we are going to have peace in industrial life.

One great difficulty in making these adjustments has been in the past and is to a lesser degree true today, the unwillingness of the employing class to consider the workers' point of view. They offer so much and the workers can take it or not, no discussion. This has led to numerous abuses in seasonal and poorly organized factories. There is going on now in New York City and has been for many weeks, a strike of the paper box worker. Paper boxes are made in great quantities in New York City. In fact, under unsanitary conditions and the wages paid are the lowest. A Union of the girls has attempted to elevate the industry, but they could get no sympathy or cooperation from the manufacturers and the result is a painful industrial war, not the less painful because it is unimportant. The necessity of some form or organization which will permit the workers to negotiate the present grievances is absolutely essential from their point of view and any enlightened employer with an eye to the stability and progress of his business, knows that he must have some way to enlist, encourage and develop workers. There are various forms of organization which more or less satisfy these needs of the two sides. There is the Union. There is the old fashioned organization of industry, where foreman and superintendents are supposed to go as liaison officers between the rank and file of the managers, listen to complaints, carry instructions, presenting the case of the worker to the officer higher up, they are his representative as well as the representative of the management. Then there is the system of employers representation. Here your representation comes from the management. Then there is the more recent employer representation, a varied form of organization in which representatives of both sides sit together in regular sessions and consider the problems to come to a decision and both sides abide by the decisions. Now, all these forms are working well in industries where there has been patience and good will. In the early days, when employers refused consideration of workers' conditions, the Union was the only method. It was, as I have said, a military body, but as time has gone, it has been more of a negotiating body and less military. Still, its primary appeal is to force. [*Rather awkwardly, the manuscript ends here. It is virtually certain that Tarbell revised it and provided a conclusion before delivering her talk.*]

The Talkative Woman

TALKATIVENESS is a hallmark of femininity. A silent woman may be admirable, but she stirs uneasiness. She is like a moon in eclipse, mysterious and fascinating, but not for daily life. The new woman bent on making over the sex is contemptuous of talkativeness. To allow the simple interests of daily life to run unconsciously and merrily off the tongue does not harmonize with the strenuous career she has planned for womankind. Not that she would shut her mouth. Far from it. She would make her a conversationalist, not a talker. There is the same distinction between the two that there is between the agriculturist and the farmer. There is the same term of life, for while the agriculturist is an experiment for a day, the farmer goes on forever.

For a habit which persists through the ages, in the face of censure and ridicule, as woman's talkativeness has, there is a reason. Generally it lies in the depths of life, where critics do not always explore. May it not be that woman's persisting habit of chattering has its reason?

One morning I found myself sidetracked in a Pullman sleeper. The train stood in a lovely wooded spot where birds sang and early flowers bloomed. The car was perfectly silent until there came in from breakfast a late pair—a young mother and a child possibly two years old.

Scarcely were they seated when the chattering began. It was the subject matter of it which quickly caught my ear. "Wobin, wobin," shouted the child suddenly, "see, see!" "Yes," the mother said, "Robin, Robin what?" "Wobin wed-best," promptly said the youngster. "Sing, wobin, sing," he ordered. "What's that?" asked the mother, pointing to a bluebird swinging gayly [*sic*] on a limb near the car. "Gosbick," he replied hesitatingly. "No, bluebird"— and so it went on, an excited watching and chattering over the birds that filled the trees.

How a child so young could have learned to distinguish form and color

Originally published as chapter 4 of Tarbell's *The Ways of Woman* (New York: Macmillan, 1915), 63–78.

in birds as this one had, how it had acquired so lively and genuine an interest in them, excited my curiosity to such a point that I sought an interview.

"Is he as young as he looks, and how did you do it?" was the burden of my questions.

"Twenty months," the mother said, "and as to how it started, it was my chattering to him as I tried to amuse him with a picture book of birds. When I saw he was trying to speak the names, that he caught the colors and forms, I led him on. Last winter I took him to the Natural History Museum, and found he was able to distinguish several of the birds in the cases. So we've gone on. He knows a few notes. He's learning many words, but of course what I prize is the habit of observation and of comparison he's acquiring. He is really becoming quite an attentive child."

I did not find in my brief talks with the woman whether or not she had ever studied psychology. It did not matter, she was doing better, for she was discovering the stuff from which that science is made. She had found that in the education of children, interest is at the bottom of learning, and that interest comes from going over and over all the various features of the thing— letting one lead to another. Perhaps she knew already [William] James's rule for cultivating attention: *"The conditio sine qua non* of sustained attention to a given topic of thought is that we should roll it over and over incessantly and consider different aspects and relations of it in turn." Perhaps she knew that James had declared that "an education which should improve this faculty" [that of "sustained attention"] "would be the education par excellence."

But, as I say, she had something better—something that many who learn the laws and rules never know—she had discovered the truth on which the laws are framed.

In this little experience is wrapped up the chief reason why talkativeness has persisted among woman. One of their chief obligations has always been teaching the child to talk. It could only be done by incessant repetition, going over and over the names of things until his ear caught the sound, his tongue framed it. It is not difficult to sustain the thesis that if it were not for the chattering of women, the child would never learn to talk. It has been done with grace and wit by one of the most brilliant French contemporary writers, Remy de Gourmont. He even goes so far as to declare that this chattering of women is a more important literary service than the writing of poems or philosophies.

There is no one, probably, that will deny that the first words a child attempts to speak are mere imitations of sounds—that they mean no more to him than sounds do to a parrot. When he begins to imitate there is always, or should be, a woman beside him, repeating, smiling, encouraging him. The play goes on, month in and month out. With infinite patience she chatters to him until consciousness is aroused. Then rapidly his education goes on, as it was doing in the case of my pair in the sleeper: Words are attached to objects; facts about objects are perceived; their form, their color, their odor, their relations to the little learner. The words for all these perceptions are slowly gathered in. Then the child learns to compare, to distinguish values, to remember not merely the sounds he learns but the meanings of those sounds. His mind is opened to the world, and through a woman's chattering!

"When he leaves her hands at six or seven," says M. de Gourmont, "he is a man, that is, he talks, which is what makes a man." "The great intellectual work of woman," he goes on, "is teaching language. The grammarians claim that they do it, which is absurd. Children know how to talk before they go to school. They already use all the forms of the verb; all the shades of syntax, easily and correctly. The schoolmaster teaches them that a certain form which they use is the imperfect of the subjunctive, but that is not teaching them language. Language is a function, grammar is the analysis of that function. It is as useless to know grammar in order to speak a language as it is to understand physiology in order to breathe with the lungs or walk with the legs. This power of language the child gets from the woman. It is to her honor that later he will use it as a poet, novelist, philosopher or moralist, or, to use Nietzsche's strong phrase, as a 'creator of values.'"

Take this view of it—and who shall or can dispute its truth?—and how infinitely more valuable to the world is the chatter of women than all the books they ever wrote or orations they ever delivered. It is of that fundamental order of things, without which cultivation, even civilization, could not go on.

But feminine talkativeness plays another role almost as important as this of teacher and preserver of human speech. It is that of entertainer and consoler. There is none other so universal, and on the whole so sure of its mark— storytelling, song-singing, sports and dancing combined have not done more in the world to break the dismal strain of fatigue, of pain, of discouragement than the gay talk of women. Here is what I mean, picked up in a hospital: A young woman was facing a dangerous operation and revolting bitterly against the situation. Her mother was sent for. She came, full of dread and anguish. Without a sign of what was in her own heart, she established herself by the bed, chattering for hours of things at home: the amusing sayings of the new Scotch cook, the tricks of the last puppy, the gayeties of the neighborhood. Chatter? Yes, God-sent chatter, based on a profound, if instinctive, sense of the human heart and its needs; it broke the revolt. This sort of service is part of the daily life of women. The old are warmed and enlivened by it; the discouraged forget themselves in it; the strenuous relax under its influence. It is one of the great consoling forces of society. It makes the daily hardships and efforts of millions of people endurable, not for any knowledge it shows, not for brilliance or wisdom or importance, but purely as a natural expression of the devotion, the sympathy, the affection that the chatterer feels for another.

But it is so idle, so silly, this chatter! Nothing is idle or silly which is born of an unselfish impulse to amuse, to arouse, or console another. Talk becomes silly only when it is selfish, vain, pretentious. No matter what the subject, it is tedious and uninteresting when it springs from one of these roots. There never yet was a satirist so cruel that he found material in the talk of a woman directed to teaching her child to speak, to the amusing of a worn-out husband, the consoling of a suffering friend. Their efforts become beautiful and sacred because of their intent. One sees only that, and thinks not at all of the things said.

It is not these women who have made talkativeness a reproach. It is those who are contemptuous of such common services, those who consider no talk worthwhile unless the subject matter is what they call "intellectual"—that is, as a rule, outside of the matter of which they know much, or in which they have more than the superficial interest they feel in anything which for the moment commands society's attention. The satirist never had fairer game than the woman who, convinced that conversation depends for quality on subjects, sets out deliberately to gather up facts and ideas in order that she may talk about them. It has become an activity, this of feeding for talk. There are teachers who weekly tell women what has gone on in the world, in order that these women may appear to be familiar with current events. There are other teachers who make digest of books and articles for them to speak of, others who tell them what to think of new music, new movements, new plays. They use their conscientiously gleaned information with confidence and fluency, convinced that they are elevating society.

There is plenty of material in our American cities and towns to justify Don Marquis in his lively conversations of Hermione and her "Little Group of Advanced Thinkers." These serious young women feel themselves "forced to take up many things to keep abreast of modern thought." They find it hard work, but reflect that it is a duty they "owe the race, . . . which makes the sacrifice easier." They feel it important to understand the French Revolution—the Caillaux trial led them to this conclusion! "So," says Hermione, "we took it up one evening and studied it thoroughly." Heredity they heard of, and to understand it spent an evening on sea urchins—at least Hermione thinks it is heredity—in connection with which they studied the sea urchin, "though it may have been in connection with biology—or—or—"

Possibly Hermione is less trying than the young woman who talks without ever having taken up any subject seriously for even one evening. It depends upon which of the two you are listening to. But all this is not saying that the woman who uses her tongue for another's benefit has no need of intellectual equipment. There is nobody needs it more. But she must have the real thing, not the superficial—she cannot teach her child or console her friend with faked interests, themes hastily picked up between luncheon and tea time from the lips of a purveyor of facts. She must know and feel and delight in what she talks about. Her purposes are so deep in the heart of things they cannot be reached by light plummets. The more she really knows and sees and appreciates, the better she can do her work. All the education and cultivation she can get is none too much for one who leads a little child to consciousness, who lifts the heavy burdens of life from the shoulders of friends or mate.

It is as natural for the normal woman to talk as for the bird to sing. It is the spontaneous expression and giving of herself. It is this naturalness which gives to her talkativeness its perennial charm as well as its incalculable value in the scheme of things. The woman in the human group is much like the

Monarch in Pierre Mille's delightful tale of that name. "Why do people call me the Monarch? Why am I loved? Why always happy? Because," he explains, "I always have time to talk. Without me the people around here would be bored to death. I go and come, laugh and sing, I cost nothing but a glass of wine, and a bit of supper. What do I give? I give *myself*."

The woman gives herself.

Women as Bosses

The Superintendent had invited us to lunch with him in the new factory cafeteria, after our round of the shops—"us" being the company nurse, the employment manager and myself. It was easy to see as he gave the invitation that he was swelling with pride over what he had to show!

And well he might. It had taken twenty years of patience and cunning to persuade his Board of Directors that decent lunching quarters were as essential in a factory as decent sanitation and lighting and it had taken almost as long to convert his working force to accept and use them. But at last he has won. He had a right to swagger a bit.

I remembered his first attempt—a few feet of floor space stolen from a noisy crowded ship, partitioned off for a rest room for the scores of girls he employed. It had been a sad makeshift in reality—rough tables, backless benches, knocked together by the factory carpenter—gas jet for heating water. But the girls had made it habitable with paint and posies and curtains at the one window. I don't know that I ever enjoyed factory hospitality more than drinking tea with the girls in that room, listening to their frank comments on the ways of their bosses, as well as their plans for decorating the corner set aside for them.

The men in the ship had jeered at first but later a few of the more domestic ones had complained of favoritism. Nothing could have pleased the Superintendent more. He let them complain—let the demand grow and then finally stole another bit of space for them. Not all the men used it. Scores pretended at least to prefer to eat "cold victuals" on their work benches in bad weather, outside propped against the factory wall on sunny days. But the irreconcilables dwindled—even became demanding—asking for hot water tanks, electric plates, dishes! It had ended in their being as interested in their crowded corner as the girls themselves.

Undated [1920s?] manuscript, Tarbell Papers Collection, Pelletier Library, Allegheny College, Meadville, Pennsylvania.

But this morning I knew I was not to take my lunch in either of these makeshifts. The Superintendent had won and when a new factory had been put up a few months before my visit, a great hall over the assembly room, where they put together the multitudinous wheels and cogs and shafts and screws I had seen made on my rounds, had been set aside as a cafeteria and amusement hall. It has been equipped with the latest and most elaborate conveniences of a modern restaurant, shining nickel coffee, tea and hot water urns, electric range, and plates, aluminum pots and pans, dish washing and potato-paring machines, drying racks—a multitude of ingenious contrivances to save labor and quicken service. The great room this kitchen served was filled, not crowded, with porcelain topped tables, seats for six hundred, and at the moment the Superintendent entered six hundred faces lifted and turned to survey his party!

We filed behind a glittering brass rail gathering up as we went the usual cafeteria outfit—one nickel tray, knife, fork and spoon, paper napkin, glass of water, and thus equipped chose from the menu, which we had already studied in the lobby where it was posted, with prices. I still remember my lunch, it was so good and cheap! A macaroni salad, cream and egg sauce on lettuce, a large ball of cottage cheese with a seasoning of onion, bread and butter, buttermilk and canned peaches for desert—twenty-six cents.

I am afraid I showed shameless curiosity about what the six hundred were eating and how much they were spending. Few I found were spending as much as I. They prided themselves on their economy. Not a few brought a large part of their lunch from home, using the table and buying only a bowl of soup or milk. They clung to their dinner pails and possibly the home cooking. Others had dropped the dinner pail entirely, contending the factory lunch was cheaper. Chief in this class were single men and men whose wives worked in shops or factories, in other parts of the town. Not a few of these latter joined their men for lunch in the cafeteria. These little midday reunions were nearly always gay—there was joking and laughter. It was like breaking the work hours with a picnic.

We talked of all these things—went over the development of the factory cafeteria as we had each seen it—talked so long that finally we were alone in the big room and had come around to the subject that at the moment I was most curious about—a forewoman we had met in our morning's survey, supervising a department where men, seasoned skilled workmen as well as women, were employed.

What kind of boss did she make? Did the men accept her? Why was she there instead of a man? I had been told a hundred times by factory Superintendents that men resented a woman boss. How had this woman succeeded? What about women in industry, anyway? How high could they go?

The Superintendent was grizzled and his jaws were square but the lines of his forehead ran across not up and down and around his eyes were numbers of friendly wrinkles. He was seasoned—forty years in iron and steel—first a moulder, then the head of a gang, from a gang to a room, from a room to a big shop, and now the head of the plant. What he knew—he knew—he had learned it by wrestling with men and things as they are. "Humph," he said, "How high—high as they will. Take Miss C. there (Miss C. was the factory nurse) she could fill my place as well as I do." The nurse gasped, and I eyed her with wonder and awe—"With my experience," he added. "There's the whole question with women in industry—experience. There are some of them that will fill any place there is—given their head—others that will if there is some man behind who sees what's in 'em. Something they don't know and don't want to believe maybe. I've had 'em like that.

"That forewoman that surprises you so didn't have to be pushed ahead. She has worked up like a man does, like I did—always had her eye on the job ahead and got it. When the last vacancy came she was worth more than any man in the place. They knew that. If she hadn't been they would have driven her out. Now they are proud of her—do anything for her.

"If you had looked about more you wouldn't be so surprised to see a woman bossing men in a factory. There are hundreds in the country and there are going to be more, and if they can run a room they can run a plant—run the company. There are women who complain because women are not getting a chance in industry, and there are men who claim she couldn't do the work if you gave them a chance. If they knew more about industry they wouldn't say that—they're behind the times!

"Take my sister, Jane, head of a room in a shoe factory. She settled the question for me. No use arguing when you have a woman like Jane. It's with the women as bosses as it is with some of the machines you've been seeing this morning, as it is with the factory restaurant—plenty to say they won't work—plenty to refuse to see that they are working, but that don't change the fact, does it? You can't stop that forewoman out there. Directors came on a visit a while ago. There was a banker among them. He was shocked when he saw her. 'It's a bad precedent,' he said. 'First thing we know some woman will want to be on the Board.' I shouldn't wonder—why not? If they grow to it. That's what my sister Jane did and I grew to Jane. She's been a liberal education on the woman question to me. I know now there are women who can fill any place a man can if they are willing to work for experience. It isn't passing laws, or agitating as some seem to think, that makes a boss out of a woman—it's work and patience and common sense—willingness to climb like a man. That's what settles woman's place in a factory. You better go talk to Jane."

It was my first and only meeting in the industrial world with a man of first class ability, in a position of importance, who was willing to tell a woman subordinate that she could fill his shoes—with experience—or to assure a group of women visiting that industry was an open field to them if they were willing to follow the same path that men were obliged to follow. And of course at my first chance I did go to see Jane—the woman who had been my superintendent's "liberal education on the woman question."

The great stitching room which she ruled was not difficult to find in the shoe factory, but you had to look for her in what seemed to an outsider a headless confusion of machines and hampers and human beings whirling about in a clatter of meaningless noises. I was to stay long enough in this room to discover that what looked to me like confusion resolved itself to those who knew into a practical and well ordered handling of the work of the room.

Jane's room stitched "heavies." That is, it put together the parts which make the upper of heavy leather shoes. These parts came and went by the thousands in the hampers which crowded the aisles, every part properly tagged and numbered and traceable on the instant to Jack or Jim who had cut it, to Bill or Mary who had stitched it. Instead of confusion it was controlled order.

As for the noises which bewildered me, I was to learn that they, too, had their meanings—that together they make for ears habituated to them a harsh symphony. Let one suddenly cease—break—rise to a shriek, and Jane would jump to attention. I have seen her dart across the room to a machine gone wrong as I have seen an experienced chauffeur suddenly stop his car and go to exploring its mysterious insides.

I found her finally in the throng, putting her O.K. on a load of finished work—a woman of fifty-odd years—large-faced, strong handed, upright, neat and severely plain in dress. Her heavy gray hair, permanently waved, was turned over a large pompadour, at the moment rakishly shifted to one side. I was to learn that when the work was particularly heavy—so heavy that Jane had to keep her capacity house—some 400 men and women—on their toes, her pompadour always worked to the right, though on dull days it stayed properly on top of her head. This was such a day—1050 dozens of "heavies" were to be received, sewed, inspected, tagged and turned over by 5 P.M. No wonder the aisles were crowded with hampers, and that Jane's pompadour lost its balance!

And yet she showed no sign of hurry when I presented my credentials and asked for a talk. A word to an assistant and she led the way to her little office. "I expect you can't hear out there," she said, with the amused tolerance I often have noticed in people who live with machinery and part of whose industrial creed is, "Get used to whatever is." "I'm used to it but I must say it rests me to get a little quiet."

A girl knocked—"Can I go home?"

"Yes," said Jane, curtly—no questions—just, "Yes."

"You've been here a long time," I said, "How in the world do you handle it?" For to me her job—those 400 people—those 12,000 "heavies"—seemed a distracting task. And she was the perfection of leisure.

"Thirty-six years," said Jane. "I was 16 when I took my first job in a shoe factory—errand girl. Mother wanted to make a dressmaker out of me—always hated to sew—liked to move around. I knew I wanted to stay as soon as I got in—I liked machines and that's more than most women do. A machine in a factory seems to scare them—no interest—but I had. I made up my mind I was going to be a shoe worker—go the limit."

"Go the limit? What do you mean?"

"Why, be head of a room. I saw I could right off. I went at it systematically. Whenever I had the chance I took a new machine. Lots of girls are kept back because they won't try a new machine—afraid they won't earn so much for two or three weeks—don't look ahead. We've got 30 or 40 operations out there, and there isn't one I haven't worked on. The foreman soon saw he could use me when somebody dropped out for a day and was always putting me at odd jobs. I suppose he thought I was good natured, didn't know I was looking ahead to filling his place. Every now and then he put me on the floor, looking after work. It went on that way for three years and then he broke down, had to have a vacation. There wasn't a man in the room who knew as much as I did about the work, and so they put me in his place."

"Did the men object?"

"Men object? Never. They knew me. They had been used to seeing me help the foreman—they had come to me for instruction. It was natural I should be there. I had more trouble with the girls. Girls never trust a woman boss as they do a man. They are brought up with the notion that women don't understand machinery—seem to think they can't, when all's the matter [is that] they haven't had experience with it. Then of course it's more interesting for them to work under a man, I understand that. I've heard a new girl say more than once, 'What does she'—meaning me—'know about machines? That's a man's business.' Fact is, she wanted to have a man to go to. Once they were used to me, saw I knew my business and wouldn't stand nonsense, they were my friends.

"Well, that foreman broke down three times in about three years, and I was always asked to take his place. Then when it was sure he couldn't come back—never be well again, the big boss said I better keep the room. That was 30 years ago. Of course it was small then—only about 50."

There was a knock. A girl appeared, "Can I go home?"

"No," said Jane, curtly. No questions—just "No." The girl went out.

"Now, will you please tell me why you said, 'Yes' before and 'No' now? Perhaps it's none of my business, but if I am to understand why you are forelady I must understand how you handle and hold your force, as they tell me you do. They tell me there are men out there who have been under you 30 years."

"Twenty-five," said Jane, flushing with pleasure. "Call me Mother. Some of 'em say they wouldn't work for anybody else in the world.

"About those girls? Simple enough. Katie has a sick baby home—she's a good steady old hand—wouldn't lose an hour's work if she could help it, but she's worried and when a girl's worried it's best to ease up on her. Make her go on, and she'll be turning out bad work—breaks her down. No, I won't have a girl worried any more than I can help. As for Susan, she's new and she's lazy. I'm trying to break her in to steady habits, but she takes advantage. She saw Katie go, didn't know why, thought I was easy today, because I had company. Ain't ever easy like she thinks," she added grimly. "I wouldn't be doing my duty to her if I was.

"You've got to understand men and boys and women and know something about how they were brought up and how they're living to keep a force. And no two are alike. That's what a lot of people who never handled anybody—not even themselves—don't understand when they work up nice ideas of how you should run a factory. I keep these folks together by coming in when I see something ails them and helping 'em out if I can."

"How are you going to make a good worker out of a careless girl?"

"As many ways as there are careless girls—all need different treatment. Sometimes they need to be shamed and sometimes encouraged. Sometimes they need to talk about their mothers who are shiftless, of their fathers who drink, and sometimes about their boyfriend who is losing interest or their husband who's flirting with some other woman, or a baby that's coming. You must sense that something's wrong like you do a sound in the machinery that don't belong.

"Makes all the difference in the world if you can get ahead of a trouble you see coming. Got a case tonight that sort of bothers me—don't quite know what to do. Woman out there married to one of the best men in the factory— a crack machinist. She would work and I told him he better let her. She'd never learned to keep house. Now she's taken to flirting with a new hand— everybody in the room onto it—nobody saying anything. Gossip's one thing I *won't* have—they all know it. But I can just feel them watching to see if I have noticed how she makes eyes at that fellow and how she manages to meet him mornings and walk out with him at night. Me? Onto it? Been my chief business for 30 years to be onto things like that.

"What folks want most is to be happy, and work alone isn't what makes them happy. It's love and homes and children and religion and fun and health—they'll work for these things. So I try to see they get the thing they want at the time they want it. Sometimes it's a wife or a husband, and sometimes it's a bank account—sometimes a radio set and sometimes a new set of teeth. All depends on age and condition. But seeing what they've got to have I sort of suggest how they can get it. That's how I build up *my* force—keep 'em—develop 'em, for of course you're not doing a first class job if you just keep enough people together to turn out the work. You must see what's in people and bring it out. Why, I've had girls—and men, too, for that matter—who just fought getting ahead. There's a forelady across the street, of whom I'm right proud—sweet woman—came to me when she was 15. Smart as they make 'em and pretty and good. She liked machines and understood 'em but she only wanted her own—didn't want to touch another; but she liked to accommodate, so every now and then I shifted her—just to help me out, I told her. Sweet to see how she'd learn a new one and how quick she'd get up speed. 'Twan't long before she'd earn as much on a half-dozen machines as on her own, and then I worked her in on the floor—a day or two at a time when one of my assistants needed to get off. But she hated responsibility—cried when I asked her to come on for good.

"I shamed her out of that. 'How would you like it if I told the big boss—that's what we call the superintendent—when he asked if you weren't fit to be a forelady's assistant—"Yes, but she's too lazy."'"

"She came on—never had a better helper. Now she has a room of her own over at Black's. But she never forgets me. Every now and then she comes over and asks my advice."

"Jane," I said, "you're a great psychologist."

She looked puzzled. "I hear people talking about psychology at the foremen's meetings, but I don't understand it very well. I ain't educated. All I know about is my folks."

I hung around Jane and her room for several days, gathering from workers and outsiders bits of her industrial history and piecing them together. I found that Jane had grown step by step to her understanding of folks as she had to her mastery of shoe-making. At one time or another she had been guilty of all the faults that are charged against women as bosses. There are numbers that are familiar.

They are uncertain in temper, "easy" today, harsh tomorrow; they have their favorites; they are harder on girls than men; they are unsympathetic with the troubles of those they do not like; they are emotional, scolding and crying in crises. Jane at one time or another, I concluded from the gossip I picked up from oldtimers, had been guilty of all these faults. There were several early episodes that might easily have ended her career if she had not been of what she called the "learning kind" if she had not unerringly sensed her own weaknesses and had not overcome them. It made her wise in dealing with her "folks," and the knowledge the workers had of her conquest of herself gave them peculiar respect for her and influence with them. "She don't talk bunk to us," one man told me. "She knows."

There was one phase of Jane career that puzzled me. Why wasn't she the superintendent of the factory—the owner for that matter! As far as knowledge of shoe making and business sense were concerned, she was equal to all her supervisors. I finally asked.

"Jane, you told me when you came in you were determined to 'go the limit'—why didn't you? Why aren't you superintendent of this place—you fit for it?"

"Sure, I could do it," she said with easy confidence, "but forelady is my limit. Your limit is what you want most. This is what I want—not more authority—not more money. I'm well fixed. What I want is folks in my work, I want to be next to them. I wouldn't be if I were superintendent. I love my people. Honest to goodness, I couldn't live without them. But they don't know it, and I wouldn't have them."

When disgruntled feminists tell me women are being kept back from the top round of industry by masculine intolerance and jealousy I remember Jane—and her kind, for while I've never known another so great a forewoman I've known many of her kind, and most of them had stopped satisfied where they were. They'd found what they most needed—people to work with—to boss—to love!

But this is not saying there are no women who take the higher rungs of the industrial ladder—step from the head of a room to the head of a business again and again, their own business. There are hundreds of them. Properly and naturally the greatest number have made their way to the top in the two fields of industry which women have dominated from time immemorial—food and clothing. We have cooked meals and stitched the seams from the cave on, adapting our methods to the changes in the ways of doing things which man's restless inventive and organizing nature has forced upon us. Today thousands of women are making fortunes large and small in this country by inventing, preparing and providing foods—foods of every description, sold in every conceivable way—by mail, over the counter, in tea rooms, restaurants, hotels. A special talent for candy, or cake making, for preserving or picking, for cooking and serving, used intelligently, is as sound a base for a good business as a woman, ambitious for independence, can have. Not that it is a simple matter to establish a profitable candy or pickle or cake factory—even on a most unusual product. It requires the same kind of qualities that it does to put an automobile or a radio set in the market and persuade a multitude that they can't live without it. Hundreds of ambitious women are finding ways, however, to overcome the difficulty and to establish firmly on small or large scale, their food creations, and thousands more are succeeding in the none less difficult task of running tea rooms and hotels.

Almost every town and city in the country can—and does—boast these days of the pluck, endurance and good judgment of some daughter who has built up a tidy fortune by making or handling food. New York City's favorite story of this nature at this writing is of a woman who has just found herself—thirty-eight years old, with an invalid husband, and three children and $38. Her husband had been a coffee broker, a coffee broker who would never sell roasted coffee, though she, the wife, had always believed there was money in it. Forced to act, she followed her judgment; bought, roasted and packed coffee which she sold by correspondence. She struggled along with her roasting and packing and letter writing until eight years ago, when she decided to open a little coffee shop in the Grand Central Station, and to give away hot waffles of her own making with every purchase! She literally struck it rich. The call for waffles was so great that she was soon obliged to enlarge her quarters. Within eighteen months she had doubled her space twice and she has been going on doubling and doubling until now, after twenty years, she signs a million dollar lease. In 1926 she did business of two million dollars.

After foods, garment making is the business where the largest number of women are finding independence, particularly making clothes for women. This latter branch is an industry in itself turning out a product yearly worth over a billion dollars and employing some 200,000 workers—two-thirds of which easily are women.

The headquarters of the manufacturers of women's garments is in New

York City where the leading firms are gathered in one quarter known as the Garment Center—every woman ought to visit it. It is the most revolutionary piece of factory centralization in this country, if not the world. The abuses under which garments of all kinds have been made in American cities and towns, are fresh in mind. Twenty, even fifteen years ago—the conditions prevailing outraged the public and led to fast and furious legislation.

My judgment is that most women, if they had the sympathy and understanding of the group in which they found themselves, would venture without hesitation to drive the tow horses, and that the reason that so few do adventure is the lack of this sympathy and understanding. I am thoroughly convinced, too, that the life of the country will be enriched by women carrying on, along with marriage, any career towards which they may be inclined.

This is certain; a woman ought not to ask herself, and she ought not to be asked to choose between a career and marriage. If, having a definite call to a career, she chooses marriage, let her be certain the day will come that she will be conscious of undevelopment; equally, if, with the definite call of a talent, she deafens her ears for marriage, there will come sooner or later the consciousness of limitation.

Part IV

Tarbell Reacts to Her Times

Introduction

Ida Tarbell was unusually well situated to observe her world and write about it. She toured and lived in Europe early in her career and crisscrossed the United States on fact-finding and speaking tours. Particularly on the *American Magazine*, she worked alongside some of the best journalists of her time. Even before that, in her earliest years, she was motivated by a powerful work ethic instilled by her family and by her first experiences in journalism.

This section of the book samples Tarbell's more general, popular writing in mass-circulation magazines and elsewhere. The first article, a historic one for her, is the first piece under her name published in *The Chautauquan*. Most of the remaining work is from the 1930s, when Tarbell was in her mid- and late seventies, slowing but still productive.

What this section demonstrates is Tarbell's knack for looking at the world in ways that are at once highly personal and highly professional. This capacity can be seen especially well in the four selections "Work," "My Religion," "If Not Prohibition—What?" and "Is Our Generosity Wearing Thin?" Three of these were written in the 1930s; "My Religion" is undated but probably of the same vintage. The commentary in these four pieces is direct, pointed, grounded in fact, and illustrated with clear examples, as Tarbell's best writing always is. The theme throughout is individual and collective responsibility. Tarbell, as an industrious, almost ascetic worker, judged others in terms of her own work and personal habits. These essays reflect that stance, particularly the view that people are responsible for themselves and for their fellows.

"The Arts and Industries of Cincinnati" was the first substantial piece printed in *The Chautauquan* under Tarbell's by-line. It is a lengthy examination of Cincinnati, its industries, its art, and its women. At times the prose is turgid, but the piece shows Tarbell's thoroughness and is similar in character to other material in the magazine at the time. There is even a touch of humor, probably unintentional, as Tarbell discusses the biggest industry, pork packing, and then moves to the city's heavy industry and its production of pig iron.

The article on the value of "Work"—the pleasure that comes from it, its virtual necessity in an individual's life—uses examples from nature to suggest that, to people, work is like the unchanging forces of nature. The stars and planets move predictably, eclipses are always on time, Tarbell points out. She recalls that Margaret Fuller Ossoli once announced that she accepted the universe. "She better," responded Ralph Waldo Emerson. Says Tarbell, "We better, or the first thing we know the world will spew us out of its mouth as the universe does a revolting star."

With "My Religion," too, Tarbell takes an almost academic approach, examining the subject in a style that is analytical but at the same time deeply moving: "It is not in theologies, creeds, ceremonies that we find the most vital and profound expression of religion—it is in the kind of man the religion makes. A man's tolerance, sympathy, charity—a man's relation to other human beings, reflects the depth and genuineness of his spiritual communion."

Tarbell's treatise on religion omits any mention of the major denominations of her time, an interesting gap given that the Methodist church played such an important role in her early family life. The criticisms of organized religion implicit and explicit in this essay express one of Tarbell's key themes—that individuals bear heavy responsibility for their own actions and beliefs. The essay closes with a sentence that reinforces Tarbell's notion that people act on their own and struggle in their relationships: "It comes from the striving in solitude and silence to enter into a fuller understanding of the divine."

Addressing two important issues, the articles "If Not Prohibition—What?" and "Is Our Generosity Wearing Thin?" seem to have been written almost reluctantly, with some agonizing. Prohibition was, of course, one of the most controversial topics of her day, and Tarbell took the view that the Eighteenth Amendment banning consumption of alcoholic beverages (1919–33) had not been effective. The piece included here exemplifies particularly well how fairness and balance—even in dealing with measures she opposed—pervade Tarbell's writing. She personally opposed drinking alcohol, but analysis of the facts led her to believe that Prohibition should be ended. Tarbell reasoned that, in a democracy, individuals need to be able to make their own choices, "however wantonly they may at times abuse the power of choice." The theme of individual responsibility comes through clearly.

The article on generosity examines the collective responsibility of communities to support their weak, downtrodden, and otherwise needy citizens. At one time, Tarbell writes, Americans saw clearly the need to support community improvement activities and to assist persons suffering on account of illness, accident, or bad luck. But the infusion of federal relief funds, together with bureaucrats to administer them, diminished local communities' impetus to help. Further, the availability of federal relief money made increasing numbers of people dependent on this money. Assessing American giving habits, Tarbell argues that to lose the "fundamental obligation" of taking care of one's neighbor would spell a national disaster.

The remaining pieces in this section, with the exception of the last, are among the lightest and most cheerful that Tarbell wrote. In "Flying—A Dream Come True," she sounds almost giddy over her first flight in an airplane. Even so, the description is thorough and incisive. Tarbell was not one to use many exclamation points, but this article contains several. "There was no sound except the purr of the engine over our heads. You have no idea how wonderful that purring was! I think I should grow to love it."

"The Economic Test," part of a *New Yorker* section called "Onward and Upward with the Arts," and the untitled, undated typescript we named "On Old Age: Script for a Radio Address" form a pair. The former was published in the *New Yorker* and describes Tarbell's experience making a paid radio address. "On Old Age" is the text of the radio address itself, setting forth the author's views of old age and its impact on the ability to work. As might be expected, Tarbell's view is that age should be no impediment to productive effort; she enlivens this piece with well-seasoned amusement.

The article on the radio address dwells on the professionalism of the radio broadcasters she observed. Her high regard for professionalism, by now, comes as no surprise: "There was nothing of the amateur about this gathering. I have always been impressed with the difference in tempo, the sparkle, which distinguishes those working on a real job from those on a made job."

The *New Yorker* article "Man-Afraid-of-the-Cars" is an odd little piece, a commentary on fear of the unknown that mixes one of Tarbell's earliest and strongest recollections with a contemporary experience. It is a bit of criticism of the rich and their unwillingness to confront the unknown. This work contains one of Tarbell's few remarks on her unmarried state. She had seen the parting of what she thought were two young lovers "and felt a little sorry for myself that the day had gone when I could sob so heartily on anybody's shoulder."

The undated "Road Town: A Vision" is a haunting, unusually (for Tarbell) passionate piece. It is a detailed account of a mysterious pale-faced man, whose vision for "Road Town" was to relieve the summer suffering of tens of thousands of sweltering low-income New Yorkers. The man, a zealot, was so moved by the misery of New York's poor that he formulated a plan for using the wide-open spaces of Long Island to provide housing and bring them relief.

The utopian plan was never carried out, but Tarbell saw the value in it: "There is nothing impossible in 'Road Town,' nothing but man's inertia and money's cowardice and the lack of vision in good people who want as much as my inventor to see those whom he calls 'my people' free from the terrible curse of summer heat in a city like New York."

The Arts and Industries of Cincinnati

The choice of the site for the city of Cincinnati was a stroke of genius. Five hundred miles by river windings from the meeting of the waters of the Ohio with those of the Mississippi lies a plateau some twelve miles in circumference. Lofty hills from whose summits the track of the Ohio can be traced afar shut it in. The river divides the plain into two nearly equal parts. Here in 1779, on the north bank of the Ohio, the village was first laid out.

Since that day when the population, as the early records say, counted "eleven families and twenty-four bachelors," the plateau has been overrun, the hillsides appropriated, and far up and down the river and over the hills the people have spread until the Queen City numbers three hundred thousand inhabitants and ranks eighth in size among the cities of the United States.

Cincinnati has more distinctive traits, however, than size. The Teutonic element in the population is important in estimating the city's character. Fully one-third of the people are Germans. So thickly are they settled in a certain portion that it is popularly known as "Over the Rhine." It is common for the signs to be painted in both English and German, as in the Zoological Garden, where the familiar "Keep Off the Grass" is repeated, *"Das Gras nicht zubetreten."* To the influence of this German element can be easily traced the pronounced musical and artistic tastes of the city.

Cincinnati has won national recognition as a musical and dramatic city. The annual May festival, the opera and dramatic festivals, the magnificent Music Hall, the College of Music, and the fifty thousand dollar endowment for open air concerts, given by the Hon. William S. Groesbeck, are the expression of a ripe popular taste for good music.

The artistic bent is equally strong; an art school of seventeen years experience, an art museum, and unusual skill in applied art, places her first among the cities active in the western art movement.

From *The Chautauquan* 7 (Dec. 1886): 160–62.

The enormous growth in less than a hundred years of life has resulted in large wealth. Great fortunes have come into the hands of many individuals and often in the oddest ways. The origin of one vast estate of the city is said to be two copper whiskey stills given a young lawyer for defending a horse thief—his first case; these stills he traded for thirty-three acres of woodland; before he died this land was worth two million dollars.

This wealth is productive; it circulates. The manufacturing interests are large. In 1870, Cincinnati was made a port of entry and in the first year fifty-two million dollars worth of imported goods was withdrawn from the custom house. Four million dollars have recently been devoted to improving the public streets. Money has been put freely into public works. When Music Hall was built, the first subscription was one hundred eighty-five thousand dollars from Mr. Reuben R. Springer; Mr. Charles W. West gave one hundred fifty thousand dollars in 1880 to the Art Museum. The first endowment of the Art School was seventy-five thousand dollars from Mr. David Sinton. Where a public want or taste has been expressed it has speedily found money for gratification.

Cincinnati takes the lead among American cities for instituting and carrying out movements of general public interest. All its tendencies are animated by a spirit of enterprise intensely American. Its musical and dramatic festivals, its art exhibitions, and industrial expositions are the expression of this spirit. The last enterprise in particular displays her resources.

The city can justly be called the founder of the American expositions. In 1828 the mother of the novelist, Anthony Trollope, came from England to take notes on America and Americans; for three years she lived in Cincinnati. Madame Trollope went back to England and wrote a horrifying description of American manners and customs, but she had left a germ behind her that quite compensated for the abuse. While a resident in Cincinnati she built a curious structure known as "Madame Trollope's folly" and started in it a bazaar. In ten years this bazaar became the Ohio Mechanics' Institute. Eighteen of these institutes had been held when the war turned hands and heads and hearts from local to national issues. The war over, the old enterprise revived and in 1869 a grand exposition of textile fabrics was held. The demand for an annual display of the industrial wealth of the city soon became general, and in 1871 the First Cincinnati Industrial Exposition was instituted; the thirteenth of these annual affairs closed October 9 of the present year.

The decision to make a permanent institution of the Cincinnati exposition led to the erection of a building for its accommodation. The musical interests of the city at the same time demanded a hall. The two were combined. Music Hall was built, and on either side, wings were added, three stories in height, to give additional space for exhibits; the cost of the building was a half million dollars.

These expositions have attracted general attention and exerted wide influence. Cincinnati's success was made a strong argument for undertaking the Philadelphia Centennial and the former city furnished the director, General A. T. Goshorn, to the national exposition. Other cities have quite generally followed her example. During September and October of the present year, St. Louis held her third annual exposition. In August Mrs. President Cleveland in the Adirondacks touched the [telegraph] key that opened the exposition in Milwaukee. Pittsburgh, Louisville, Chicago have all adopted Cincinnati's idea.

The exposition recently closed was in the main a home affair. No premiums were offered. This arrangement kept out those who cared to enter only to secure medals for advertising capital. There were few foreign wares. The corn castle and pumpkin pagoda, the Clydesdale and Percheron, the Jersey cow and Poland pig were all wanting.

First in point of value came:

The Industries

In 1885, Cincinnati had within her limits five thousand seven hundred thirty-eight manufactories. It was a trial, to temperance people, to find beer-bottling the first exhibit in Power Hall at the recent exposition; and really horrifying to discover that the only sign outside the exposition building was for the same beverage, two enormous hogsheads, with gaudy paintings thrice life-size on their heads, but the brewing and bottling of beer is a leading industry of the city, and the managers of the business, notorious for their worldly wisdom, succeeded in securing the best position in the hall for their display.

The largest industry is pork-packing with its attendant branches of lard, candle, soap and oil making. Cincinnati was formerly the largest pork packing center in the country, but Chicago has wrested this honor from her hands. There are aesthetical reasons for not representing this business in public beyond a display of candles, soap, and oil.

The situation of Cincinnati on the Ohio, and within easy distance of the coal mines of western Pennsylvania and Ohio, naturally makes it an iron center. Blast furnaces turn out quantities of pig iron, and a variety of machinery and forged articles attest the extent of the city's iron interests.

Furniture is a fourth specialty; and the skill in which her art students are showing in wood carving, leads to the hope that a distinctive style of furniture may at no distant day add to both the industrial and the art reputation of the city.

Each industry is represented in one or another form. Here is a saw-mill that sends from its teeth a board fifty-four inches wide. An annex accommodates a variety of brick-making machines. The rough clay thrown into the hopper comes out a perfect brick ready for baking. Immense circular saws are exhibited in one department. Here an improved fan keeps a ball bobbing or streamers flying over the current of air it produces. Wonderful lathes cut out an endless variety of nick-nacks [sic]—spool-holders and stocking-darners, ungraceful but useful accompaniments of the sewing table.

A flour mill stately as a monument and intricate as a labyrinth, stands in comical contrast to the baby affair of one hundred years ago. A steady rap, rap, rap calls attention to a perfected contrivance for reducing gold ore. Magnificent machines for working in iron and brass ply their wheels in obedience to the masterful touch of the Corliss engine. A section is devoted to the mysteries of incandescent lights, a particularly interesting display to Cincinnatians who still wander in the dim glare of gas-light. A glittering beauty of a fire engine holds a leading position in the exhibits of the exposition. A fitting fact—for it is to Cincinnati that the honor of making the first practical application of steam to the fire engine is due, and to her may be traced the beginning of the modern fire department.

Great machines have a dignity and meaning most impressive. They palpitate with power; controlled they are beneficent giants; in loose they are demons of misrule. Standing at the entrance to this long hall filled with machines for almost every conceivable purpose, for conquering fire, for turning out breadstuffs, turning iron and brass and steel into use and beauty, putting thought into print, dragging great weights, creating light— manufacturing rises to new dignity in the mind.

But the display has its funny side. Inventors do not always make dignified articles, and the ponderous, awe-inspiring machines alternate with button fasteners, ear-trumpets, roller organs, egg beaters, carpet sweepers, flour sifters, ice-cream freezers, clothes tongs, an endless array of ingenious and useful articles, but not calculated to awaken enthusiasm. One interesting feature is the style in which many of these displays are made. Works of art are wrought out in paint brushes with the help of an occasional scrubbing or whitewash brush; pagodas are made of pine needle pillows; pyramids of beer bottles; and infinite architectural abilities are demonstrated to lie in canned goods and patent medicine flasks.

Striking displays of floral work show the prosperity of the florists' trade. Several times during the exposition, Flower Day brought in wonderful designs wrought from rare and beautiful buds and blossoms. Nature and art were exhausted for subjects. There was an aster bust of George Washington in a wig of tuberoses; a dahlia alligator, life size; a god of love working woe with a Marechal Neil shaft; a chariot drawn by carnation butterflies; a fierce goat with a boat of immortelles. There were a stork and a watch, a summerhouse, a frog as big as a turkey, a locomotive, crosses, crowns, urns, pedestals, all in flowers, an amazing collection of ingenious and usually beautiful objects.

The ninety thousand employees of the manufactories of Cincinnati are placed in a city offering the best advantages to their children, their sick and their infirm.

Schools and Beneficent Institutions

are numerous. The public schools have attained a national reputation for thoroughness and success. At the Philadelphia Centennial and at the expositions of Paris, Berlin, Vienna, and New Orleans the highest honors have been given the Cincinnati schools. The first attention is given to the usual curriculum; the first specialty is drawing. At the recent exposition the walls of the rooms containing the educational exhibits were lined with creditable work in drawing from the various schools. In the matter of apparatus and furniture the best is chosen. The virtues of the school furnishings were made doubly impressive by the presence of a set of much worn school furniture of the log-school-house period. Since 1882, Arbor Day has been observed in the Cincinnati schools—another sign of progress. Manual training has not been introduced, though the question is agitating. Wisely the educational department contained displays of what had been done at other places in this line. Exhibits of work were made by the Toledo Manual Training School and the Hebrew Technical Institute of New York City. The latter school made one of the most suggestive exhibits of the Children's Industrial Exhibition held last spring in New York.

A visitor to the exposition had an opportunity of studying in a rather peculiar way, the Cincinnati institutions of mercy. It was by the occasional presence of more or less of the inmates. One day thirty or forty members of the Old Men's and Widow's Home were present; again a large delegation from an orphan asylum; the House of Refuge was represented; and, most astonishing of all, was a visit from one hundred thirty-two of the inmates of the Longview Insane Asylum. The delight of the visitors and the care of the attendants were the best possible comment on the institutions.

Art

The history of the art movement in Cincinnati is most gratifying. The present status could not, however, be fairly studied in the recent exposition. The works exhibited had been brought from abroad, and the majority were catalogued "for sale," giving a trade air to the collection, not inspiring to the art lover. There were many good things in the collection: a Titian, a Madonna by A. Caracci, a landscape from Turner, an exquisite ivory bust of Rembrandt, and a considerable number of pleasing pictures from well-known artists of the day. The art museum and school made no display, preferring that visitors should go to them.

Within the past six years over a million dollars has been given to art in the city. Three hundred thousand dollars was raised in thirty days in 1880, to build the art museum. The building still incomplete stands in Eden Park on the hill above the city. In style it is Romanesque, the walls of blue granite, with a roof of red Akron slate. The interior is finely arranged, the arched entrance in particular being impressive. The collections are not large. They include a display of textile fabrics, the Elkington reproductions of metal work, the Hellingford arms and armor, a fine display of art pottery, nine hundred or more drawings from Lessing, and a well-selected gallery in oil. The latter includes many copies of the old masters, a large number of German pictures, and a few from American artists.

The art school is building near the museum; when complete it will furnish the best arranged accommodations of any school in America. At present there are over four hundred pupils with working rooms in the city. The teachers hope to hold the annual exhibition in the new building in the spring.

In several particulars the art movement in Cincinnati offers a worthy example. It has sought the best models, fostered originality, and encouraged practical applications of skill. Wood carving is one branch in which particular advancement has been made. The great organ in Music Hall offers the most conspicuous application of this art to be seen in the city. When it was proposed to build the organ, the leaders in wood carving offered to carve the screen. It was a labor of love and stands [as] a perpetual inspiration to beautiful work and generous public spirit.

In the application of art to pottery even more has been accomplished. For several years the Kezonta ware of Cincinnati has been favorably shown. The ware does not aim at originality, Barbertine and Royal Worcester shapes and decorations being copied mainly. The Rookwood Potteries, a later enterprise, are doing work of distinctive character. Their shapes are not new, but the glazes and decorations are original. The ware has won more than a local reputation and leads to the hope that it may result in an American pottery as distinctive and as beautiful as are any of the wares of Europe. A third art pottery had a display this year in the exposition, the Avon, but its work was largely in imitation of the Rookwood designs.

The discussion of the art of Cincinnati leads naturally to a word about

Woman's Work

Last year at the New Orleans exposition the most suggestive contribution to the Woman's Department was the wood carving and pottery from the women of the Ohio Valley.

The present museum was first agitated by the women's Art Museum Association. The Woman's Pottery Club first suggested the use of the Ohio clays. The Rookwood Potteries are the thought of a woman, Mrs. Maria Longworth Nichols, and her energy and generous gifts have made them what they are. The art school is largely composed of young women working in brass, wood, and clay, as well as in oil and black-and-white.

In the expositions, women have always taken a leading part. At the Thirteenth, the decorative art department was entirely under the charge of Mrs. Senator Hardacre, a former Cincinnati newspaper correspondent. The commissioners sent this lady to Boston, New York, Baltimore, Washington, and other cities in search of novelties. The result was entirely satisfactory. There were antique furniture, endless varieties of "specimens," and curios in abundance. The painted placque [sic], the drawn-work tidy, the plush wonder, and the ubiquitous crazy quilt, as is usual, monopolized much space. One quilt even surpassed in novelty, the masterpiece of the New Orleans Exposition; while the Southern Fair boasted a mosaic of one hundred thousand five hundred eighty-four pieces, Cincinnati displayed the *first* of all crazy quilts. Fertile, the mother of American expositions, of the steam fire-engine and of the crazy quilt!

The New York Woman's Exchange had a large display in this department. The Cincinnati Exchange did not exhibit, though at their rooms a variety of fancy articles and fine needle work is shown quite equal to that from the larger city. This exchange, gives more attention to the sale of pies, cakes, and canned fruits than to fancy work, and finds more money in this trade.

A sensible exposition enterprise was undertaken by a woman's society of Covington, Ky. The members provided daily lectures on the science of cooking, in connection with an exhibit of a model kitchen.

An interesting and novel bit of woman's work was discovered in the fruit display of the Snider Preserve Co. This company is preparing fruit which both in flavor and appearance rivals the expensive imported fruits. Catsup, chow-

chow, and salad dressing come from the same factory. The latter are prepared entirely from the formulas of Mrs. Snider and are winning their way to European as well as American tables. She is now experimenting in canned chicken salad from which experienced caterers declare she will make a fortune if successful. To bring the process of preserving to perfection, Mrs. Snider went to Europe to study the methods in use in the factories there.

The variety of enterprises which occupies Cincinnati has created broad sympathies and active interest among the people. One feature of the exposition showed this feeling in a very entertaining way. The commissioners brought on as an attraction for the closing days, the Japanese Village. This village is a collection of seventeen Japanese shops equipped with native workmen. It was brought to this country last year by Mr. Fred Deakin, an American who for seven years has done business in Japan. His commercial relations with the government were such that he succeeded in securing the community for exhibition in the United States on the promise that he would return the forty or more Japs, dead or alive, at the expiration of the tour. The village contains screen makers, barbers, carpenters, clay modelers, jewelers, porcelain decorators, lacquer workers, tailors and so on, giving an excellent idea of the industries and methods of the Japanese.

Artisans of every kind showed great interest in the work of the village, making intelligent comparisons of methods. At the Rookwood Potteries, the potter at his wheel took time to ask as we watched him:—

"Have you seen the Jap clay modeler at the Expo? Do you see how differently I work from him?"

The city is interested not only in its money-making but in developing resources and in improving methods. The result is a people at once thrifty and of broad and elevated tastes. Morally, Cincinnati has a lot to learn. Its foreign population has made it a beer-drinker and Sabbath-breaker. The number of beer gardens and saloons scattered about the streets is appalling. Work in the factories and shops stops on Sunday, but to all appearance it is only to give time for frolic. The theaters, gardens, and museums are open all day. The result is not, however, so serious as might be anticipated. There are multitudes of pleasure-seekers abroad, but few carousers.

Strong forces are at work creating a higher moral tone. The leading Christian denominations have strong congregations, and connected with many of them are mission churches and schools. Accompanying the great charities of the city are vigorous organizations for moral reformatory work. This thorough, constant, and advanced effort to Christianize the city, combined with the healthful and elevating tastes of the mass of the people is sure to raise speedily the moral standard of Cincinnati.

Flying—A Dream Come True

Members of The American Magazine family will be interested in the news that Ida M. Tarbell recently made a trip in a flying machine. She went purely for pleasure, with no idea of writing a word about her experiences. But when the adventure was over she dictated a personal letter to a friend, describing her trip. Following are extracts from the letter.

I THINK you know that I have always believed that some day we should fly. I cannot remember the time when I did not believe this. I think it dates back to the success of my first kite. You perhaps do not remember, but I knew Professor Langley in the years that he was making his famous experiments on the Potomac. I shall never forget how he took me once to a big room in the Smithsonian Institution to show me the first heavier-than-air machine that actually worked. It has always been one of my griefs that he never lived to see people really going through the air. There is no doubt that his experiments contributed enormously to what we are doing now. And yet he died bitter in heart because people did not recognize the value of what he knew he had demonstrated. Then a number of years ago I was at Baddeck on Cape Breton Island, where I watched Alexander Graham Bell experimenting with kites and planes. While I have not doubted for a moment for years that men would fly, it is only recently that I have had it firmly fixed in my mind that some day I was going to fly. And the way that came about was this:

A few months ago Henry Woodhouse, the enthusiastic editor of "Flying," wrote me a note apropos of something I had happened to say to an interviewer about my faith in the future of aviation. He begged me to take a flight, to justify what I had said. I told him yes; but every one of a half dozen aviators that he chose, promptly fell and broke their necks, and finally I concluded that as I did not purpose to break mine I had better give it up. Last Monday, however, he called me on the telephone and told me he had a safe

From *The American Magazine* (Nov. 1913): 65–66.

man and a safe machine, and would I come? I returned a prompt yes, only to weaken later when I realized that I had not caught the name of either the man or machine. However, when I learned in a note from Mr. Woodhouse confirming our arrangements that the aviator was young McCurdy, whom I had known as a boy experimenting with Mr. Bell at Baddeck over his kites, and the machine was a Curtiss flying boat [which takes off into the air from its position floating in the water and after flying lands back in water], where I did not have to sit on a cobweb but had a firm board beneath my feet, I concluded to go ahead. I went down yesterday afternoon with a party to Port Washington. In the bottom of my heart I expected that I would want to run away when I saw the machine. To keep me from doing so I really counted on the fact that I probably would be too vain to flunk before strangers; but it was curious how different it all was!

Mr. McCurdy was just taking out a pupil (a Captain in the English army). The machine was drawn up on a runway [out of the water]. It was the innocent-looking little affair that the illustrated papers have made so familiar—quite like her name, the Babette. She had a little slipper-like body with two seats just back of the steering wheel, and here McCurdy and his pupil seated themselves. The assistants pushed her off and turned her around. So far it was much like the launching of any small boat. Then McCurdy stood to start the engine, and the cry went up to those of us who were standing close to the water, "Get back, get back." I did not know why, but of course started back—not quick enough, however, to prevent the terrific wind the propeller raised from twisting my skirt and tearing off my hat. It was the first hint had that the dainty little contrivance had a terrific force in her. She was demonstrating that, however, for before I could right my disheveled garments she had made a long run over the water, splashing and sputtering, had risen, and was soaring down the bay. She went and came in a circuit of six miles four or five times, and as I watched her I became not more fearful of going up but more fearful that I might not get a chance, for there were half a dozen people about crazy to try it.

When the Babette was again on the runway they told me that I might go. There were no more preparations than for an auto ride. I took off my hat and put on a little silk hood such as I use for a long trip in a machine, borrowed a pair of goggles, and stepped into the slipper. They pushed her off, turned her around, and in a moment we were racing over the water. I forgot to mention that they put me into a cork jacket, saying that of course nothing would happen but that it was a wise precaution, in case we did land in the water!

Although we must have started off at fifty miles an hour, the spray was only a few drops on my glasses. We made a circle of perhaps a quarter of a mile and then I was conscious that we were above the water. I did not know when we came out, and looked over the side of the boat to see if I was right. The surprise of it seemed to stun me. Not that I lost consciousness, but I was literally lost in the amazement at the suddenness and ease of it. In the twinkle of an eye, without knowing when or how it happened, without the least sense of motion after leaving the water, I found myself a mile or more from the starting point, one hundred and fifty or two hundred feet in the air, the water, the bluffs, houses, boats slipping swiftly by far below.

It was the breaking in of these facts that seemed to bring me back to myself. My senses reasserted themselves and I became conscious that we must be flying very fast, though the motion was so gentle that it was no motion. There was no sound except the purr of the engines over our heads. You have no idea how wonderful that purring was! I think I should grow to love it. There was no sense of the impact of the air, although we were going at the rate of eighty-five miles an hour, no pressure on the face. There was none of the jar that you have even on the best railroad track, even at the highest speed. There was no vibration perceptible, such as wear my nerves so much even in the best of cars. You sailed and did not know that you moved. I suppose there is no word to describe what I was experiencing but—flying.

Our first lap was three miles and we must have made it in a minute and a half. McCurdy had warned me not to be frightened when we turned, because the machine would dip heavily; "I will nudge you so you will know what it means," he said. But I knew he was turning, I felt the tilt, but I had absolutely no sense of nervousness. The only thing I did was to put out my hand on the edge of the boat, a trick of mine in any sudden motion, even in a carriage. The moving of my hand seemed to release the tension at which I was holding my body. I began to think, which I had not done before, "Here I am in the air, flying. I am not afraid, I can move about." Just then we passed over a great sail boat with one man in it. To prove that I could move, to show

McCurdy that I was not paralyzed, as he might well have believed if his attention had not been riveted on his business, I tried a feeble little wave with my hand—an act of pure bravado. You cannot imagine the joy that I had in seeing the man wave back! Then we passed a steam yacht where the people all crowded to the rail to look up at us, and I waved this time freely—enthusiastically!

In about four minutes we had made the six miles and were back at our starting point, making a great turn through the air. All our party were standing at the wharf waving to us. I couldn't get my handkerchief in time, but I could use my hands, and did. We made the second turn with the same wonderful tilt. By the time we started on our second round my senses had reasserted themselves sufficiently for me to turn right and left, to look at the aviator, who sat as rigid as a piece of the machinery, to look at the hills, to look over the boats, to wave my hand again and again. Then the whole thing begun to go to my head and I wanted to laugh and shout. The sense of exhilaration is one that I have never known before. You seem to have gotten as far above all physical fears as you are above the earth, and you have a curious sense of being part of the whole thing.

Before he started I had said to Mr. McCurdy, "Tell me what I must not touch, because if I lose my nerve I do not want to embarrass you by seizing anything or making any false move." He pointed out to me the only thing that I better not touch, and said, "You can make no false moves. You can even stand if you want to." If we had started on our third round I know that I should have attempted to stand up. But I did not have quite enough time for that. I was a little too interested in what he was doing with the machine. For he suddenly dove down from perhaps two hundred feet toward a boat with three men in it, who were watching us. He came down so suddenly that the men ducked into the bottom of the boat. Then we rose again and came down only a short distance from the landing place. I did not know when the boat struck the water except for a little spray that dashed into my face. We went straight to the landing place, making it perfectly, a much more exact and easy landing than I ever saw any kind of water-craft make.

Of course, everybody was down to meet us and I do not know how long I sat in the boat not realizing that I must get out, so overwhelmed was I with the wonder of the thing—that I had not been afraid, that it all was so natural, that the thing was so easy, so supremely superior to any other motion that I had ever experienced. I do not know anything to describe it, only to tell you that it gave the same sensation that you get in seeing a great bird lying on the air, as they do sometimes, without any apparent motion of the wings.

One of the gentlemen in the party said to me when I was back on land, "Hold out your arm, Miss Tarbell." I did it without thinking. He said, "I want to see if it is shaking," and I was very much set up to find that neither hand shook at all. I was the more satisfied with this because once when I was called up in a hotel which was on fire and was told to come at once, I remember that I gathered up hastily a few things and started out, congratulating myself that I was so cool. As I passed through a room I saw a fan of mine that I was fond of and reached out to get it. My hand trembled so that I could scarcely get my fingers about it.

As a matter of fact, this trip of mine, to those who are familiar with aviation, is the most commonplace kind of thing, not worth a long letter like this. What I have never realized, and I suppose most people do not realize, is that there are 115,000 people flying every week, that there are 7,000 licensed aviators and at least 10,000 not licensed now in the world, that there are four great manufacturing establishments in this country—the Curtiss, that makes the flying boats that I was in yesterday; the Wrights in Dayton, Ohio; the Benoist in St. Louis; and the Burgess concern, that I think is in Massachusetts, who are so busy that it is impossible to get an order filled by them for some months. Flying is an accomplished thing. You will fly one of these days, I shall fly again—I hope. Possibly before we die we may both be traveling back and forth to business from country to city in an aeroplane!

If Not Prohibition—What?

Having come slowly to the reluctant conclusion that intemperance in this country after ten years of prohibition is more sinister and corrupting than before the Eighteenth Amendment was adopted, I feel that, as a citizen, I am not free to evade the straight question the *Woman's Journal* is putting to several of its contributors—the question, "If not prohibition—what?"

Any answer I can make will be hesitating. I see no straight way out of our present predicament. I am convinced, however, that something must be done. Enforcement at its best will never be more than partial. The evils of prohibition are of an insidious nature. They will increase, rather than decrease with time. Yet any drastic change is bound, so far as I can see, to produce for some time new confusion, new abuses, irritated and violent dissatisfaction.

Under prohibition a great and powerful traffic outside of the law has been established, taking the place of the legalized and badly regulated traffic of old days. To destroy this liquor piracy, supported as it is by strong political, social and economic influences, will be a task from which any Government might shrink. Certainly our Government, unable as it is to end, even seriously to cripple, the present traffic, will find it a baffling and difficult task to replace it with a system which it can hope to control, as will be imperative, of course, if the amendment is repealed, even if the Volstead Act is modified. My mind shrinks from the difficulties that we must face when we attempt really to grapple with the evils which prohibition has brought upon us.

Conscious as I am of these difficulties, I would prefer that the country go back to 1918 in its handling of liquor, rather than to remain where it now is. I have several reasons for this. The foremost is, that I believe the principle of prohibition is immoral—it denies a man's freedom to choose in a matter which is his own business. I believe that law and its organized agencies for enforcement can never be as successful in developing temperance and self-control in people as education and appeals to self-respect. Law and its agen-

From *The Woman's Journal* (June 1930): 5–7, 47, 48.

cies are but secondary instruments in developing men—they depend almost entirely for their efficiency on popular opinion. When popular opinion is against them in any substantial degree, if it is only lukewarm in their support, they become ineffective and contemptible. In attempting to make the people of this country teetotalers by law we have thrown aside the only machinery by which men and women are really developed—the machinery of education and moral training. I want to see that machinery in operation again. It can never be effective as long as the Eighteenth Amendment stands. Men and women will not listen to arguments and prayers if they are convinced that those who make them are taking from them their right to make decisions.

When the Eighteenth Amendment was adopted in 1918 this country was on the road to temperance. If we go back seventy-five or a hundred years and compare the drinking habits of all classes of society with those which we had in 1918, we will find that our most impressive advances had been made. Go back to the days when Abraham Lincoln was first taking an active part in the political and social affairs of Illinois, back to the eighteen thirties and forties. Why, Lincoln, himself, when for a short time he ran a country store, had a barrel of liquor beside his barrel of molasses and sugar, and the liquor barrel was in the cellar of the very minister of the Gospel. The abuses were general and frightful. One of Lincoln's earliest published speeches was made for the Springfield branch of the Washingtonian Temperance Society, one of the great organizations of his day.

"Although the temperance cause has been in progress for nearly twenty years," he said in beginning, "it has only just been crowned with a degree of success hitherto unparalleled." He found the chief reason for this success in the fact that men were using new tactics—a sympathetic appeal to men's better natures. There had been too much denunciation—this was impolitic because, said Lincoln, "it is not much in the nature of man to be driven to anything; still less to be driven about that which is exclusively his own business." He believed that the new impetus given to temperance was due to "persuasion, kind, unassuming persuasion."

Certainly from Lincoln's day on the "temperance movement," as it was called, grew in power. All sorts of agencies, schools, churches, societies of various kinds allied themselves and, with varying degrees of intelligence, patience, love of their fellow man, built up in this land a strong sentiment for temperance as a rule of life—temperance in all things. Even in the sections where there was the greatest abuse of liquor there was less of the old brutality, fewer habitual drunkards. The work was far from complete but we had in active operation the only forces which bring man to self-control—persistent line upon line teaching, logic, appeal.

Whatever temporary stirring of a community a temperance crusade may have caused, the solid and lasting temperance work of the country was done by men and women who believed in the power of the human being to correct himself and who believed, too, that only by such self-correction did a man make a man of himself. They did not believe that a man who gave up drinking because he could not get liquor was necessarily a temperate man. What they sought to do was to arouse in him a desire—a preference for decency and self-control—encourage a choice of what was good, help in fixing the choice as a habit.

This is not saying that laws had nothing to do with the growing temperance of the country. They did, but they were effective and helpful only when they were the result of a majority community feeling.

Our old educational temperance work has been almost completely ousted by the coming of prohibition. I would see it restored to its former activity—the necessity of it recognized—its methods improved. It has a more serious task on its hands, should it be restored, than before the days of prohibition. It must deal with a youth which has learned to drink, sometimes in a home bar room, again in certain classes in a home speakeasy, which has developed a thirst for fiery liquors, is not content with a glass of wine or beer. It must deal with a new lawlessness born at least partly from the effort to make this not a temperate country but one in which what a man drinks is proscribed by law.

Whatever method is finally decided upon to restore to the people of this country a practical method of developing their one-time ambition to make themselves temperate, whether the first step be by repeal of the amendment or a modification of the Volstead Act, it must not be forgotten that either change means the establishment of some kind of legalized selling place for whatever forms of liquor are allowed. What are we going to do about that? We rightly fear and hate the old saloons, yet the old saloon at its worst was less to be feared than that which has replaced it. The speakeasy, the blind pig—whatever you choose to call it—is an institution outside of all control, slippery as an eel, irresponsible and defiant. Moreover, it is a secret place and the old-fashioned saloon was open. You knew it was a saloon. The men who went in and out did so openly, as a rule. That is, we were dealing with something which we could see.

The speakeasy has no distinguishing mark. As a matter of fact, it may exist on the floor above or beneath you in your exclusive apartment house. It may set itself down in the house next to yours in a neighborhood long highly desirable for residences. Your own doorbell may be clanged by a would-be patron. I know of at least one man in New York City who has sold a home long beloved, because his block has become so infested with speakeasies that his butler was kept busy turning inquirers from his door. There is a story going around, of one house owner who put up this sign, "This is not a speakeasy."

I am afraid that any effort to handle the kinds of drinks which may be finally legalized, if any ever are, is going to meet strong opposition from many men and women who prefer that which they hate to be kept out of sight. It hurts them less and they can delude themselves into a conviction that if they do not see it, it must be negligible.

A few months ago, coming down the street of a college town with a woman of the faculty, she told me that once, in the days before prohibition, she had passed three open saloons every time she went into town. "Now you see they are all gone. Today our boys have no temptations."

But at that moment a group of students, under the direction of a professor in the Economics Department, was making a detailed survey of the town, a bit of laboratory practice. They were finding out how many automobiles were owned and of what makes—they were tabulating school children, church attendance, men and women who owned their houses and, among other things, they were tabulating the town speakeasies. I saw that chart—the drinking places marked in red—there must have been three times as many as there had formerly been open saloons. These boys, who my friend said were growing up without ever seeing a saloon, into which if they wished they could drop, had discovered that throughout the community there were concealed places, into which they could go and drink without danger of detection. Which condition was safer for the boys? Undoubtedly the first saved the lady anguish of mind. Will she ever consent that an evil which she can see, which cannot hide itself, is less to be feared than one which can sneak into corners and multiply freely?

One of the most insidious and alarming features of these drinking places, developed under prohibition, is that women have become patrons, decoys, and in industrial centers, manufacturers and distributors. The "home speakeasy," as it is called, familiar enough particularly in sections of the foreign born, uses children freely in making and handing out the brew, and it is children the country over, not only among the foreign born, but among natives, that deliver stuff sent out by speakeasies. Here is a development in the traffic quite unknown to the old saloon. No one was more rigid about keeping out women and children than the saloon keeper, and for good enough reasons. Even if he had no personal objection to their presence he knew that nothing would arouse the public against him quicker than seeing a woman or child enter his place.

One of the chief reasons for getting away from prohibition, after the moral reason—that it is inconsistent with our contentions as a Christian democracy—is to put an end to the truly awful concoctions of hard liquor that are made and distributed. Merely allowing free sale of beer and wine is not going to do that, at least for a long time. And how about beer and wine? Are we to allow anything that any manufacturer wants to make? Certainly with the experience of the past in mind, no beer or wine should be allowed sold, except what was made under the strictest Government supervision. It is probable that the brewer and the wine maker, chastened by the revolt of ten years ago against his methods and his products, would now be amenable to strict public supervision. I am not too hopeful about this. Nothing is easy in this terrible situation, but certainly the experience of the brewers should count for something.

The repeal of the amendment means a return to local option, that a community will again be responsible for its own decency, order and temperance. We are inclined to overlook the advance in temperance among communities all over the country where there was a sentiment strong enough to secure a majority against the sale of liquor in any form. I was never more impressed with the quality of a community which had developed under local option, than when, back in 1916, I went through the state of Ohio on what was called a Chautauqua circuit.

Day after day we moved from town to town. One had no more than to touch his foot on the platform of the station, look at the bus or the hotel, before he recognized whether it was a dry or a wet town. The tidiness, the prosperity, order—were all on the side of the drys. The inhabitants in the town where there had been a long term of dryness were plainly the better for their temperance. I made not a few inquiries in these places about the perfection of enforcement. I doubt if there was ever a "bone dry" town—certainly never a dry state in which men were not able to get hold of liquor if they wanted it. But where the majority of the sentiment of a community was plainly and aggressively against the saloon, you had no saloon and you had only an occasional speakeasy. The group was small enough and watchful enough to take care of transgressors. Moreover, it was the people and not agents who were looking after the sobriety of the community. The plain truth is that the community under prohibition has turned over to paid agents a kind of supervision in the interest of order and temperance which it formerly exercised, and the paid agent too often unhappily looks after his own interest. He can make more out of violators of the law than out of upholders of the law. You cannot buy a temperate community—you can only develop it.

Prohibition vs. Character

The amendment is failing and will continue to fail, because it is inconsistent with the political, social and moral contentions of democracy. If man is a puppet, then he plainly must be fitted with strings to be pulled both in his own interests and in the interests of society. But democracy is not possible with a race of mechanical toys. It is only conceivable with creatures capable of growth. Growth results only from the free exercise of the will. Let us admit that men must be made to understand their own power of choice—that they must be given constant examples of good and evil—that the environment in which they find themselves must be made as clean, stimulating, hopeful as possible; all of this is necessary if you are to develop character. And what else is worth our efforts but the development of character? Personally, I feel only profound discouragement when I hear the argument that prohibition must be sustained for the sake of prosperity. What is prosperity in people if character is to be stunted? What goodness is there in a prosperity won by taking away from human beings their power of choice, however wantonly they may at times abuse that power of choice?

Is Our Generosity
Wearing Thin?

There is no surer way of finding out what is going on in American towns and cities than to listen to the talk of those informal groups which come together at annual national conventions. For a year now there had been in the discussion of town affairs by such groups a sober and anxious note.

I heard it expressed outspokenly last August by one of a group of what we call "solid citizens"—business men of high type who all their active lives had taken inordinate pride in their towns, securing everything which made a town "a good place to live." They had worked to make them healthful and beautiful, worked for good schools, for parks, hospitals, for slum clearance, for country clubs, boys' clubs, playgrounds, and they had not merely given money, they had given themselves and were proud of what had been done.

But now the speaker addressed an anxious group: "When there was illness or accident or bad luck we looked on it as a community obligation and there was a lot of pride in what we did, for it was community business, not merely rich men's business. We had always taken care of ourselves in depressions and were doing so this time. Then last year along came the State administrator and told us that there was $100,000 of Federal Relief money coming to us, and along with it a bureau to distribute it, a bureau of politicians helped out by people who mean well enough but who know nothing about those we deal with. What they have done to a lot of the people we have been looking after for years trying to save their self-respect or restore it if they had lost it, you wouldn't believe. We have dozens now on relief rolls that we have kept off for years and there is nothing to be done about it. Business is steadily getting on its feet but the more people we put to work the more go on relief rolls and we don't know how to stop it."

These words are significant because you cannot today get together a half dozen men and women really experienced in the problems incident to the meeting of human needs without more or less of the same complaint. The

From *Scribner's Magazine* (Apr. 1935): 235–37.

crux of the problem lies in the danger that personal social responsibility as well as individual effort on the part of the needy is being dissipated by emergency Federal measures.

Emphasis is given to the point by the disconcerting news that, while there has been a substantial increase in employment since the low level of March, 1933, there has been a much greater increase in the amount spent on public relief. It was estimated that in September, 1934, the first stood at 40 per cent, the second at 76 per cent, and the disparity has continued to increase. In November, 1934, there were 19,017,815 persons on relief rolls—according to FERA reports over 600,000 more than in September. The increase in money spent over that with which we started in 1933—the supposed peak of our distress—was 93 per cent.

But how are we to explain this? There is no manner of doubt that the intrusion by the politically minded, which so disturbs many people experienced in social work, accounts in certain quarters for some of the increase. This was foreseen and voiced when in 1933 Congress made its first appropriation—$500,000,000. The Administrator of Federal Relief, Harry Hopkins, was prompt and emphatic in warning against any attempt on the part of politicians to administer relief:

"You cannot fool with this relief business on a political basis. Some people have tried it. I have no doubt in some parts of the United States that it is done. The Federal Relief Administration has no intention of tolerating political interference in the administration of public relief to the millions of people in this country."

In the same class with the politician Mr. Hopkins classified that individual who generally goes along with him, the man or woman who knows nothing about administration but needs a job and gets it:

"There is a perfectly amazing lack of responsibility of people who are willing to turn the administration over to incompetent people. Why, even a bootlegger hires somebody who knows his business to cut his liquor. Great guns, why aren't we entitled in the administration of $70,000,000 of taxpayers' money a month, used in the care of 15,000,000 people, why aren't we entitled to skilled and competent direction in the care for these people?"

That was the way Mr. Hopkins felt about it in the beginning. It is the way he feels about it now.

Once those great sums were voted by Congress there was no human foresight and force that could have prevented an attack by a certain element, but while their influence accounts for a percentage of the increase in the numbers on the relief rolls, I am convinced it is a comparatively small percentage.

Certain things must be remembered when we complain that a 40 per cent increase on pay rolls does not produce a 40 per cent decrease in relief rolls. It has been reckoned by those familiar with the figures that only one in every ten of those who have been re-employed had been on relief. Those first taken back are properly the substantial workers, long with the industry. In the employer's mind, the job "belongs" to them.

But how had they been getting on? Some had nest eggs, insurance, bank accounts, stock in the industry to which they belonged, membership in fraternities which prepare for the evil days which all human experience proves come and must be provided for if lived through—the seven lean years to be cared for by the seven fat.

Generally speaking, men and women who have had the wisdom to provide for a bad time are people who know how to piece out savings. They understand "subsistence farming." Thousands upon thousands of people who never heard the term until now have from time immemorial looked to it as part of their support. Thousands of little farms and gardens existed throughout the country particularly in the neighborhood of industrial towns.

Savings, subsistence farming, odd jobs account for no small number of the one-half of the unemployed who have not been on Federal Relief. No insignificant number is accounted for by that energy and ingenuity which leads men and women in time of stress to seek opportunity, force it. Hundreds have set up little businesses in the last four years which in more than one case have developed into substantial ones.

But there are many, many people in this one-half pretty well worn out with their struggle. Their savings are exhausted. A garden may keep a family in food, a few hens may give eggs and an occasional "chicken in the pot," but where is the money to come from for taxes, up-keep, or rent if he does not own his place? With what is he to buy fuel, clothes? Probably the largest part of those added to the relief rolls since employment began to increase has come from those who have weathered four years but have nothing left for the fifth.

But if I understand the man whose experience I have quoted, his complaint goes much deeper than the fact that, through the efforts of politicians and untrained workers, people in his town are being put on relief rolls who he thinks have no business there. What alarms him is what they are doing to a fifty-years effort to build up a system under which those in need could be brought back to the point where they could take care of their own needs—a system of rehabilitation instead of one of disintegration.

This alarm is shared by many people. It is one of the phases of relief administration that should be squarely faced. The idea that men and women should not be allowed to go to pieces because they can no longer meet even such fundamental needs as food and shelter, that they should be rebuilt, came in with what we call organized charity. Every man and woman in the country over fifty who once was accustomed to giving to the beggar, the tramp, remembers the struggle he had with himself not give to all who asked, but to give his sympathy, his time, and his money to building up institutions which would help cut off the beggars and the tramps at the source.

Over a period of years there has been developed a fine program for holding together crumbling families, for caring for dependent children, for preventing delinquency by providing boys and girls with clubs, playgrounds, vocational work, and for caring for illness through hospitals and nursing service. Men and women were trained to carry out the program. Between the institutions necessary for this work, institutions largely supported by private funds, and the local relief administration there has come to be increasing cooperation. But herein lies a stumbling block.

Not only is our sound and practical service for meeting human needs being demoralized by the obvious difficulties of mass relief but on all sides the fact of Federal Relief is being seized on by former supporters of such essential institutions as hospitals, nursing services, family restoration as a reason for backing down on contributions. "Let the government do it—we pay taxes."

That is, there is a general weakening of the sense of individual responsibility to support and strengthen the very social agencies which they have helped to build.

Who today is giving 10 per cent of his income to support human welfare? Yet there was a time when men who realized their social responsibility talked in terms of the ancient tithe and many religiously observed it. Before the writer is an accounting of one man's tithing. It is entered in four little books, six by three and a half inches, the ordinary ten-cent paper-bound notebook. On the outside in a clear strong hand—"Lord's Box." Look within and you will find on the title page "Accounts with the Lord's Box." The first account runs from January, '83, to December, '93. The second picks up the account from January, '94, and carries to August, 1903, when the book gave out and a new one was bought. The third carries the Box from September, 1903, to December 31, 1927. The fourth and last begins with January 1, 1928, and its last entry is of November 7 of the same year, within two months of his death. These little books give the accounts running over forty-five years of steady giving of 10 per cent of all money earned by the man who kept them.

This man, David L. Holbrook by name, was a minister whose salary seems never to have been over $1400 a year. Regularly he gave 10 per cent of whatever it was. You find it credited properly month by month in the Lord's Box. And he gave 10 per cent of the little sums that came his way. There was a time when the church paid the parsonage rent and always 10 per cent is credited to the Lord. He sang sometimes and received fees, and 10 per cent went to the Lord, as did 10 per cent of the marriage fees and other small royalties and the whole was painstakingly distributed to those institutions which he believed most useful to his world.

Who can match that today? Certainly it is not to be matched by reading the Federal income-tax reports. Take the records for 1928. The returns included, in the lowest taxable brackets, 111,123 persons whose average income was $1749. Their contributions to human needs averaged not 10 per cent but 2.2 per cent. In the largest income brackets, $5,000,000 and over, there were twenty-six people averaging $10,763,077 each. These persons gave just half of what Mr. Holbrook gave or 5 per cent. It is interesting to note that 1.8 per cent is the average donation made by the entire taxable group. Those in the lowest group with an average income of $1749 are above average in their donations to charity. Whereas those whose incomes range from $3000 to $60,000 are below average. Those whose incomes range from $60,000 up increase their average donation until a peak of 5 per cent is reached by the twenty-six whose incomes are above $5,000,000.

Not to support our needed agencies now, to find excuse in the burden of Federal tax is like hauling down a flag in battle and the worst of it is that it weakens what is the most important thing in the United States, or any democracy, the individual and his collective community efforts. They are and always have been the strength of this country. They are our true experiment stations—laboratories in which we learn how to do things, things industrial, educational, social, philanthropic.

The country is not built from the top, it is built from the bottom by those collective efforts. The great problem in this country is to save what is good in them, to correct what is evil, and go on building. The fundamental criticism of Federal Relief, as stated by the man I have quoted, was not that pork and cotton were dispensed when not needed, nor that money was poured forth to provide work for people when already the community was looking after this need, it was that their local responsibility which they were meeting with courage was invaded, that self-respect at both ends of the line, among those who received and who gave, was weakened, the one reverting to his old begging psychology, the other to his hoarding.

But the day of Federal Relief in the form we have known is passing. It never pretended to be any more than an emergency. What we could have done without it no man can say. It was essential at the moment, like building ships, training men in war times. It was done on a grand scale because the emergency was on a grand scale.

The experience now is chiefly valuable as a guide to the administration of the program with which the government plans to replace it.

The present program proposes to substitute at once jobs for the dole. Four billion dollars are asked to make work for those who have none and can find none. What kind of work? Work that men know is sound and useful, such as the projects of the CCC? Or extemporized jobs like too many of the CWA, the memory of which remains in some communities as a laughing-stock to government improvisation?

How is this vast project of public works to be managed? What are the communities affected by it to have to do with that administration? Men, given jobs and allowed to loaf on them, are as badly demoralized as men who give up jobs if they can, [and] through political intervention, get relief.

How are the responsible citizens of the local community to be used in carrying on these attempts to replace relief money by work?

How are the citizen and his community to exercise their responsibility in the essential programs for economic security which Congress is now considering? That program is planned to take care of the worst suffering which comes with [economic] depressions. It proposes to take care of unemployment by building up funds sufficient to carry those out of work over a reasonable period of time. It proposes that State and Nation combine to make old age secure in all times, good or bad, so that, come a crisis, we have the satisfaction of knowing that men and women, too old for labor, who have for any reason been unable to provide for themselves, will be sure of a pension; it proposes to strengthen the great work for public health already in operation as well as all of the projects for child welfare now being developed. It is an attempt to make general those benefits which communities, industries, bureaus—local, state, national—have proved to be desirable and practical. But the great sums of money to be appropriated for these projects will spread thinly over the vast communities of the United States. The community and the individual must still be the main support.

And here again, how about the administration? The community alone knows its old, its children, its health. Only the community can know its individual problems.

The bill recognizes the need of cooperating with local agencies; the strength of that cooperation will depend more on the insistence of the local authority that this is their business than on any desire of outside authority to work with them. And always there will be the danger, in the administration of these great new national agencies for human welfare, that the politician holding the purse strings will attempt the same invasion of which Harry Hopkins warned when the Federal Emergency Relief began in 1933. And he will succeed if those people of the United States who have been running their local affairs give up the job with the hope that all of these cares that they have been managing with more or less success are going to be taken off their shoulders, that the only thing they will have to do henceforth—and which they can do with infinite grumbling—is to pay taxes. No greater disaster could come upon the United States than releasing the individual and the locality from this fundamental obligation: to look after those neighbors who for one reason or another are out of work, old without resources, sick without funds, those for whom the responsible people of the United States have always regarded it their business to provide.

Work

The most satisfying interest in my life, books and friends and beauty aside, is work—plain hard steady work. It is for work—books and friends and beauty again aside—that I shall be most grateful on Thanksgiving Day of 1936. As I have been at it for fifty-six of my seventy-nine years, I feel that I have given it a fair trial.

What do I get out of it?

I have no illusions about its nature. If work is to be productive—that is, give the worker something he can exchange for the products of other workers—it is no sinecure. It carries with it fatigue, disappointment, failure, revolt.

I have never in my life undertaken a fresh piece of work that I have not been obliged to take myself by the scruff of the neck and seat myself at my desk and keep my hand on the scruff until my revolt had subsided. That is, I know the difficulties in steady work. If there was nothing in it but the fruits of barter, I would rather trust myself to the road. On the road you can at least go South in winter and North in summer.

The ability to barter is the least of work's satisfactions, necessary as that may be, great as may be the sense of dignity which a worker gets from being economically independent, joyous as may be the fun of having money to spend, to give, perhaps to waste.

Highest, perhaps, in the satisfactions work gives is the sense that you are keeping in step with the nature of things. That may sound esoteric, but it is plain fact. This is a working universe. So far as we know, it has been that since the beginning of things. There is no spot in it which stands still. Every star is on the move. Such a reliable universe, too: every planet in its place, doing its task; every eclipse on the minute.

Here on earth everything works—the grain of sand, the oaks, the clouds—

This article was Tarbell's answer to the title question for a panel, "What Interests You Most in This Cosmopolitan World of Today?" From *Hearst's International Cosmopolitan* (Dec. 1936): 19, 82.

works and incessantly changes, passing from one form to another, for nothing dies as a fact. The earth tolerates no deadbeats; it keeps everything busy. If it did not it would be out of step in the universe in which it travels year in and out, never behindhand, never off the track—sunrise and sunset, moonrise and moonset always on schedule.

If I am to be happy in this steady-working world I must work, too; otherwise I'll suffer discomfort, uneasiness akin to that which comes to me when in walking I cannot keep step with my companion, when in talking I cannot follow the argument or catch the meaning, when in singing I am off key.

There is a vast unhappiness, inexplicable to those it afflicts, which comes from idleness in a working world. The idle are self-destructive as would be a star which announced that it was going to stand still for an aeon or two.

What the idler fails to understand is the beauty of rhythm, the beauty and the excitement of being in his place in the endless chain of creative motion which is the essential nature of this magnificent and incomprehensible universe.

There is no mystification about this. It is as plain a fact as anything we know, and we ignore it to the destruction of our peace of mind, if not to the peril of our lives. It is one of the factors in our situation on earth which must be accepted.

Margaret Fuller Ossoli once announced loftily that she accepted the universe. "She better," commented Ralph Waldo Emerson. We better, or the first thing we know the world will spew us out of its mouth as the universe does a revolting star, breaking it to fragments doomed eternally to cruise through space. Fragments occasionally collide with a planet, burying themselves in its surface—meteorites, we call them. They are pieces (probably!) of a star that tried to get out of work assigned it.

Work means health. The very urges of our bodies show that nature expects action of us if we are to be in health. From the time we kick our heels and try our lungs on being released from our mother's womb we cry for work. Watch the child—never still. It is obeying the order of nature to keep busy.

How defeated and restless the child that is not doing something in which it sees a purpose, a meaning. It is by its self-directed activity that the child, as years pass, finds its work, the thing it wants to do and for which it finally is willing to deny itself pleasure, ease, even sleep and comfort.

In such work comes perhaps the deepest of all work's satisfactions: the consciousness that you are growing, the realization that gradually there is more skill in your fingers and your mind. If you work steadily, persistently, with a conviction of the necessity of effort if you are to be in harmony with the nature of things, you grow.

You do more. By giving yourself freely to your work you become a creator suggesting new techniques, new machines, finding new magic in words, new arrangements of facts and thoughts.

Here lies the worker's salvation when the road he has been following suddenly ends—when the factory, the shop, the office closes. The worker who realizes that he has something to do with the making of new work when the old ends does not sit down by the roadside and cry for someone to take down the barriers. He strikes across the open fields, chops a path through the woods, seizes any odd job he spies, labors to set his own notions in operation.

Thousands of men and women have done that in these last difficult seven years and are coming to Thanksgiving Day blessing the Lord for their larger sense of the nature of work, their obligation to create it, keep it going. Thrown out, they refused to beg it—they set about to make it.

They have learned a fundamental truth—that the creative force in work must be constantly exercised, never checked or tampered with, if work is to be kept abundant, if its wornout forms are to be constantly replaced with those which are higher, finer, more productive.

With growth and creation come satisfactions of new kinds. Your work fits in with the work of others. You know yourself to be finally a part of that working world which produces sound things for sound purposes.

But work does more for you. It is the chief protection you have in suffering, despair, disillusionment, fear. There is no antidote to mental and spiritual uncertainty and pain like a regular job.

Here, then, is my philosophy of work—the reasons why after fifty-six years of unbroken trial I thank God for it. It is something which reaches the deepest needs, helps reconcile the baffling mystery of the universe, helps establish order in a disorderly society; which puts despair to sleep, gives experience to offer that youth who is willing to believe you too once were young and had his problems, gives a platter of fruit—small though it may be—to divide with those who for one or another reason have no fruit on their platter.

Blessed work! There will be no finer fruit on our Thanksgiving table.

The Economic Test

I have always been supercilious about the side lines of the author's profession. Take broadcasting. When it came to carrying over what I had to say from the press to the air, it looked easy: write it, talk it off. It had been easy the few times I had gone on the air, always for a cause—ten minutes, fifteen minutes, telling the world its duty about the woman in industry, child labor, the alien with all men's hands against him in this land of the free. I had always put it over well enough to receive generous thanks from the sponsors of the causes. I had always gone from the studio after the experience in a comfortable glow of self-righteousness and self-sufficiency. And then came an invitation to speak two minutes, to say three hundred words, and—"What fee would you expect?"

Never before had anybody hinted to me that there was money for me in broadcasting. I was scared. I might be good enough for a donation to a cause, but was I good enough for a fee? I doubted it. I delayed my reply, but they seemed really to want me. One day a charming, coaxing voice called me up in the country: "Only three hundred words . . . two minutes . . . just anything dear to your heart. . . . How much would you expect?"

"Young woman," I said severely, "I don't know how to say anything dear to my heart or otherwise in three hundred words. It always takes me three thousand. To put a thing of any value in three hundred words, go to a master of the craft, not a working journalist."

But the coaxing voice persisted.

"Well," I said ungraciously, "I'll accept if you give me my price." And I set one which I thought was too much then, but not too much for me if I was to say anything in three hundred words. I was right on both points.

The price did not daunt the owner of that persuasive voice. Promptly and cheerfully she said she would see what she could do about it. But the best she could do was to halve my figure.

From the "Onward and Upward with the Arts" section of the *New Yorker*, Feb. 3, 1937, 40–43.

I have never ceased to wonder at my own susceptibility to flattery. I always end by agreeing if I am sufficiently wheedled. I was now, and said, "Yes."

My suspicion that an economic test was a different thing from a charity test was soon realized. It seems that I was not to speak on just anything dear to my heart. It must be a something of which my sponsor approved, dear to me or not.

"Won't you please submit three or four suggestions?"

I took a day off and did it. If a thing strikes fire with an editor on or off the air, you hear from it right away. If it does not, you can be sure he has his doubts. He had in this case. However, what I had sent in seemed to merit a contract. Apparently there was nothing to do now but put one of my suggestions into three hundred words.

I was wrong. First of all, the publicity department wanted a chatty sketch of my life. The last thing in the world I can do is to be chatty about my life. Ungraciously I set down certain hard facts: age, fifty years of work, confession that I do not smoke cigarettes, that I read detective yarns, do other things that do not seem to have any bearing on speaking on the air.

But my charming voice came back bubbling. "Just what they wanted. Now, won't you tell them how it feels to be at work at your age?"

Nothing to do but give another morning. Measuring it by time given, I had already earned that fee twice over. In an irritable tone I spoke into my dictaphone a thousand or so words on the theme in which they pretended to be so deeply interested.

This time there was no delay. I had struck fire. "Just what we wanted. . . . Three hundred words . . . two minutes."

Putting a thousand words into three hundred is real work. I grimly tackled it; stuck to it until by my watch I could read my piece exactly within the time—two seconds to spare in case of accident.

When you talk for a cause, you drop into the studio before you go on, and have your voice tested, read your piece, and go out with a pleased sense of your generosity. I had supposed my two minutes meant that and nothing more. Again I was wrong. Orders came: "You are to be at the studio at ten o'clock for rehearsal. You will go on soon after eleven; you will be back in the afternoon at three for the Pacific Coast."

That meant a whole working day. I told myself I would do nothing of the kind, that I would slip in a little before eleven o'clock, give them time for a voice test, do my piece, and go home. But my conscience began to trouble me. I had signed a contract. That meant taking orders. The studio had said ten o'clock. There was probably some reason for it. At any rate I was there before ten, and thankful enough I was, for I had not crossed the threshold before I realized that being late would have stamped me as nothing but an amateur.

There was nothing of the amateur about this gathering. I have always been impressed with the difference in tempo, the sparkle, which distinguish those working on a real job from those on a made job. The moment I entered the room, I knew these people considered themselves on a real job. There were forty or more of them—the orchestra, perhaps twenty musicians standing around talking; a half-dozen more or less pretty girls, though for what purpose I could not guess; a distinguished-looking baritone; a body of important and worried-looking inspectors and broadcasters.

Fascinated, I watched the animated confusion crystallize into a pattern. A sign from somewhere—I did not see where—and they flowed into their places. The microphones were the magnets drawing them—microphones obviously suited to the needs of what each person or group of persons had to offer. Tall, gangling ones for the orchestra—marvelous how they pick up and blend all those instruments. Others suited to the height of the announcers, to the soloists, to a group of pretty dark and light heads which went into a huddle around a singer's instrument and crooned an accompaniment to his song. As for the speakers, like myself, we sat in state at a table, very comfortable, the announcer on the other side of the voice transmitter.

It was different indeed from the first time I went on the air for somebody's cause, fifteen or more years ago over in Newark. You found your way there at night through a dark and forbidding warehouse; you stood before a big, round platter which both mystified and antagonized you. There was nothing of that sort now. Here you sat intimately and quietly, and at once, curiously enough, had the feel of the radio's real audience. You knew that it is not a million people, as they bombastically tell you. No, your radio audience is two or three or a half-dozen sitting before the fire or around the living-room table, sewing, knitting, looking over the paper, stopping long enough to listen when you drop in. Very informal, and the more deeply one realizes this, the better one's voice, I fancy.

At ten o'clock exactly the rehearsal began. And then I saw why a rehearsal. We ran over our time by something like five minutes. That five minutes had to be cut out of a program of perhaps a dozen numbers, each item of which had beforehand been given its exact time. It came out literally second by second—ten seconds there, thirty there, a minute somewhere, perhaps. The pleasant speeches of the head announcer probably suffered most. I had come within my time. Everybody sacrificed without complaint, probably sympathizing with the harrowed, anxious, responsible time heads—everybody but me; I had my two seconds to contribute.

The rehearsal and editing over, something very amusing happened in the minutes left—a general pepping-up process, a preparation for the public performance. The group broke away, stretched their legs and arms, cut pigeon wings, chucked a pretty girl under the chin. That is, everybody did, save the harrowed ones making sure their scripts as cut were clear enough to read. All the other ones were tuning themselves for the performance. And they were interested in each other's performance. Before I realized it, I was twinkled at by members of the orchestra—friendly smiles. "Your first time here, isn't it? Good luck to you, old girl." The bosses came around and patted me on the shoulder: "You'll do all right."

And then we went on. I could have gone home, I suppose, at the end of my reading, but I was too interested and went instead into the visitors' box, and through the big window watched these colleagues, for so I now called them, put through their work and come out on the second. I felt as if I had been victor in a race; I realized that for two minutes I had been part of a highly developed mechanism; highly developed mechanically and, more difficult and important, humanly. For here were forty or so people, many of them temperamental artists, submitting themselves to the plan of the whole and getting so much fun out of it.

No use to tell me that I must be back here before three; I was there twenty minutes before. All I wanted now was to be sure I was earning that fee. All the self-complacency of giving for nothing had gone out of me. For it been substituted the self-respect of earning. I was no longer an amateur; I was a professional. I had stood the economic test.

On Old Age:
Script for a Radio Address

The Editor of the Magazine of the Air seems to think that you his subscribers will be interested in a greeting from one whose chief claim to be heard is that though entering her eightieth year she is still at work. In this he differs from the editors of the magazines of the earth who all agree that the interests of their readers are strictly limited to the doings of youth and of active middle life.

The species of embargo that is raised against old age sometimes amazes, sometimes amuses and sometimes chagrins me. I see nothing exceptional in being as active now in my eightieth year as I was at thirty, forty, sixty. Look about you and I doubt if there is one of you that will not recall some man or woman older than I am leading quite as active a life. There are plenty of people, however, who think that all of us oldsters should be out of the game. Some of them even warn us that we are defying the Lord by over-staying our time so busily and cheerfully. Holy writ is against you, they say, it limits us to three score years and ten and tells us that if by reason of strength we run on to four score years there still will be labor and sorrow. They seem to think that ought to scare us to inactivity. After three score years and ten, streaked with more or less labor and sorrow, why should we expect anything else in our last decades? And what poor stuff we must have been if we have not learned to take it.

Then there are the people who are rearranging the Social system. Anybody who works after sixty five is taking bread out of the mouth of the unemployed, they tell me. By sixty five you either should have provided a sufficient competence to live without productive work or you should have seen to it that you are taken care of by some of the many pension schemes in operation. But supposing you haven't been able to set aside enough to provide for your living and so fulfill your obligations without piecing out work and supposing you have been a free lance and are not eligible for a pension—even

Untitled, undated manuscript [Jan. 1937?], Tarbell Papers Collection, Pelletier Library, Allegheny College, Meadville, Pennsylvania.

under the present far-flung Social Security Act—are you a poacher if you work? Should I feel guilty?

When I insist that I find in these late years of activity a peculiar and satisfying adventure my younger friends hoot at me. They too seem to see life after seventy-five as sterile—no fresh experience—no zest—no enjoyment of its own. They think I am putting up a bluff, that at best old age can be nothing more than a camouflaged middle age—a pathetic and sometime a ludicrous imitation of youth. But I am not patterning my present years after any decade gone before. I find the period interesting and fertile in itself. It has its own pleasures, its own possibilities, its own needs of adaptation to the new situations which a changing world produce. It is just as full of problems and hopes as any other decade, only the problems are peculiar to late life. The hopes have a security in them those of youth lack. They are less delusive, more tempered by experience, more serene.

No, I refuse to accept the silly taboos against old age which have grown up in the past. I am too busy following the adventure, making the most of that which comes to me, whether it be grave or gay.

Man-Afraid-of-the-Cars

I knew him well when I was twelve or thereabouts, though I had never seen him—only heard my father and his friends talk about him. I called him Man-Afraid-of-the-Cars.

He was a farmer living on a hilltop not so many miles away from where we lived in Titusville, Pennsylvania. His father had cleared that hilltop; he had been born there, inherited the land, stayed by it. He was a good farmer, my father said. Until the Man-Afraid-of-the-Cars was forty-five years old, the nearest railroad had been some twenty-five miles away. He had never been to see it. Why should he? He had all he wanted at home. There were two terms of school each year for his children, and the schoolhouse was so near they could walk. There was a church and a general store, where every Saturday he went to barter produce for groceries, hear the neighborhood news, pick up his copy of the "Weekly Tribune"—"Mr. Greeley's paper." What more could a man want? Besides, he was too busy farming to "go gadding about."

Such were his life and satisfactions when his part of the countryside was turned topsy-turvy. Less than twenty miles away a man drilled a hole some seventy feet into the earth and began pumping up large quantities of petroleum. The news spread, and overnight men from all directions came hurrying into the country to try their luck. They even hauled their engines and tools and boilers over his hilltop, cutting up the roads, tearing down his fences. Many of his neighbors turned teamsters or drillers. He thought the whole business impious and applauded when the preacher declared that taking oil out of the earth was interfering with the plans of the Almighty, because He had put it there to use in burning up the world on the last day.

According to my father's story, the business had been going on five years or so when there appeared in the valley over which the Man-Afraid-of-the-Cars looked, and into which he had never descended, gangs of men cutting

From the *New Yorker,* July 3, 1937, 45–46. © 1937, 1965 The New Yorker Magazine, Inc. (formerly the F-R Publishing Corp.).

down the trees, laying a roadbed, and bridging the streams. They were bringing in a railroad. From the first he looked on it as an outrage, but when a train actually ran over the tracks below, shrieking at the crossings, belching out smoke as engines did seventy-five years ago, the outrage turned to terror. It was a thing out of Hell, he said. One day, when this thing out of Hell picked up a careless friend of his as he drove over the tracks and scattered him and his horses and wagon in pieces right and left, he grimly said the devil was getting in his work.

I treasured every word I heard of him. To think there should be such a man in the world! How superior I felt!

I grew up, and forgot all about my Man-Afraid-of-the-Cars. If I had ever thought about him, it would have been to say the day had passed when there was his like in the United States. Then, suddenly, I discovered we were rearing a new generation of the breed, and of all places here in New York City.

It came about this way: I was walking up and down the platform of an upstate railroad station, getting a bit of exercise before I took the late-afternoon train to town, when I suddenly came upon a pretty girl sobbing on the shoulder of a handsome man. First parting of young lovers, I reflected, and felt a little sorry for myself that the day had gone when I could sob so heartily on anybody's shoulder.

It was a blistering hot day, and I found that the chair cars were not air-conditioned. The conductor, however, found me a seat in a cooled Pullman sleeping car, which I took, much as I detest a sleeper for daylight travel. I was hardly in with my bags when a porter put the pretty girl I had seen crying outside into the seat facing mine. She was trying to check her tears, but settled into her corner, she buried her face in her handkerchief and started in again.

I was too hot and tired to feel either motherly or officious, so I hid behind my magazine, peering out now and then to see if there was any prospect of recovery. When the waiter came in announcing dinner in the dining car, I seized the chance to escape. Leave her to herself, I thought, and she will be all right when I come back. And that was true.

When I came in an hour later, she was showing no sign of tears, even if her eyes were still a little red. Very prettily she made room for me, obviously not averse to speaking. I remarked casually that in spite of the crowding it was much more comfortable here in the sleeper than in the chair car through which I just passed.

"Is this a sleeping car?" she asked with interest.

"Why, yes," I said, surprised. "Have you never been in one before?"

"No," she said. "Where are the beds?"

Now, I am an authority on life in sleeping cars. I shudder to think of the nights I have spent in them as I have gone about the country on lecture tours. Here was a time to use my knowledge to divert the child, and that I did.

She looked a bit shocked after I had explained the process, particularly the climbing into the upper berth.

"It must be dreadful," she said, "getting up in the morning with all these people. How do you do it? It doesn't seem nice."

And with the memory of the process in a crowded sleeper, the indecency of it, the near nausea, I said heartily, "No, it is not nice."

But I was curious. Here was one who looked the travelled young woman; her gown and accessories smacked of the Rue de la Paix, her luggage was the top notch of exclusive smartness. How could it be that she was unfamiliar with Pullmans? I ventured the question.

"Oh," she said quite simply, "I was never on a train before. We always travel by plane, or by car if we are not in a hurry. But this time it could not be arranged. I am sailing back to school tomorrow. There was no other way. That is why I was crying. My brother" (not her lover, then) "said I was fool- ish. But it seemed so dreadful not to know how to act and to be with people I did not know. I was afraid."

As she talked, my Man-Afraid-of-the-Cars came to life. And with him trooped others to whom I had never given a second thought, but whom at that instant I recognized to be of his kind. There was my friend who blanches at the idea of going into the subway. She will drive her car seventy-five miles an hour and skip warning lights, but to walk into an underground tube, to be crowded in with a multitude of strangers, makes her sick with terror and disgust. And I know women to whom a taxi is a degradation. Who may not have been before you? And how can you trust an unknown driver? I know men who stay in town over the weekend if chauffeur or car or plane is out of commission rather than trust themselves to the dangers and the confusion of a railway. I even met a millionaire once who said he never went abroad unless he went in his own ocean-going yacht. "How awful," he said with genuine distaste, "to spend a week with strange people, and to have no control over route or speed."

But when I submit to my sophisticated and experienced friends these little exhibits, I find them either looking at me with surprise that I should be so ignorant of the ways of the great world or matching my exhibits with multitudes of similar ones. Certain it is that our strange new ways of conquering space have not taken from human beings the fear that earlier men had of things they did not know. Men are still afraid of cars.

Plus ça change, plus c'est la meme chose.

My Religion

I cannot remember the time when I did not have a conviction of divine goodness at work in the world. The core of my religion has always been an inward certainty that the central principle of things is beneficence. This conviction has held in spite of the succession of rude jolts that it has received from growing familiarity with the operations of life.

As a child I supposed myself the center of things, with a Good God ready to give me what I wanted. I found from experience that that was not true, but the Good God remained, and I reconstructed my notion of the nature [in] relation to [him].

Later I found myself struggling under the discovery that I had been preceded on the earth by countless generations of men and women and that the civilization of which I heard so much boasting was simply the last of a succession and that it probably in certain respects was less fine than some of its predecessors. The knowledge that I lived in a universe and not merely a world bewildered me; but that which shocked me hardest was a continuous series of discoveries about human sufferings, inequalities, greed, ignorance, all so inconsistent with the notion of a merciful force active in the universe. Yet I never lost my sense that this force was at work, and I never ceased to readjust the disturbing outside to the serene stable inside.

It is true that the divine spirit, which as a child I had visualized, lost its human outline; it became more and more a spirit, and I realize now that as the outline disappeared the hold the spirit had on me became more powerful.

It was while I was seeking desperately to understand and square up this divinity from which I could not escape with what I met in life, that I made my first acquaintance with the doctrine of evolution. It was regarded as blasphemy, a denial of religion by many of those who surrounded me, but to me it was a revelation—the divine method or process by which the beneficent

Undated [1930s?] manuscript, Pelletier Library, Allegheny College, Meadville, Pennsylvania.

spirit in the universe was to work out its intent. Evolution has never ceased to be a fundamental element in my religion.

The slowness of the process does not disturb me, for my religion emancipates me from time. It has come to be literally with me as the Psalmist puts it: "A thousand years in Thy sight are but as yesterday when it is past and as a watch in the night."

Of course this leaves me a tiny atom in the universe, but, as a matter of fact, that is what I am, my only business being to be a sound atom, one that works with and not against the beneficent spirit in things—there lies my immortality.

How keep in touch with the divine and let it work its way with me? That is my most important business—also the one which I have most neglected. It has always seemed clear to me that it was only by some form of very personal communion—worship in its purest form—that I could hope for any degree of understanding of the divine. But if you are to have worship there can be no outside interruption or distraction. Real worship requires silence and solitude. The longer I live the more convinced I have become that when I first laid hold of the relation of silence to genuine communion with the divine, I struck a great spiritual truth.

Miss Best, in her stimulating and illuminating stories of "Rebel Saints," as she characterizes certain early Quakers, quotes Thomas Lurting's comment that "as silence is the first word of command in martial discipline so it is in spiritual; for until that is come unto, the will and mind of God concerning us cannot be known, much less done."

Even primitive religions provided for silent meditation—solitary communion. It has not always been easy for would-be saints to command silence—freedom from disturbance; and so we have had monks, hermits, anchorites, withdrawing from the world, even going for long periods without food, sleep, human presence. If there were to be a pure flame lit and spreading in their souls it could only be done by continued silent contemplation.

But this class has always been small. It came into conflict with one of the strongest instincts of man, also one of his necessities, if he was to live on the earth, and that was the need, the duty of remaining with his kind, sharing its experiences. Men had to do that in order to exist. But they could not get away from the instinct to worship, and a certain consciousness, however dim, that worship meant spiritual withdrawal, so they built temples and churches.

But, alas! The temples and churches sooner or later ceased to be places of meditation, even to give opportunity for solitude. They became more or less bustling centres of song, ceremony and preaching. Men felt the need, too, to visualize the spirit. Feeling that there was something in himself akin to the divine spirit he gave it a form like his own, a form with head, legs, arms—he made it talk—he gave it human qualities. Oftimes the gods he created became scandalous creatures that had to be entertained, flattered, sung to, talked to. The centre of religion was no longer the spirit seeking understanding and development in silence and humility. Man worked out a practical substitute for the agony of soul, for the mystical waiting on the Lord.

I cannot but feel that pure religion is frequently talked to death in the very houses of the Lord. I would not be taken as meaning that creeds, ceremonies, man's efforts to make more real to himself the divine nature and the divine method mean nothing to me. A church, a temple, a religious system is and always has been holy to me. It is only when the exponents of the various religions begin to fight over them that I feel the need to withdraw. The debates over Fundamentalism and Modernism affect me as having nothing to do with my religion—they are outside its province. They are activities of the intellect, not of the spirit; they belong to that effort, always so strong among men, to formulate their thoughts and feelings into a creed, which those who do not know it or [who] deny it are to be forced or persuaded to accept. Pure religion forces no man's spirit—its very essence requires that the spirit be free for contemplation, for learning what the divine has to teach it.

Men naturally accept the creed, the forms to which they are introduced as children as the truth and the only truth. If they are to have real spiritual inner life they must find it by groping out from where they stand. Personally I have no inclination to sneer at the Tennessee mountaineer who regards evolution, which, as I have said, came to me as a revelation, as an impious idea. I do not think you are going to get it out of him by ridiculing and lecturing him. I think he is much more apt to grow away from it if he is left free, to believe or not to believe. After all, true religion does not come from believing this or that, however precious, essential, fundamental this or that may be to you as an individual.

It is not in theologies, creeds, ceremonies that we find the most vital and profound expression of religion—it is in the kind of man the religion makes. A man's tolerance, sympathy, charity—a man's relation to other human beings—reflects the depth and genuineness of his spiritual communion.

The Christian religion, in spite of the crimes in human relation that have been constantly committed in its name, emphasizes more clearly, beautifully and satisfactorily than any other what the relation of the truly religious should be to his fellows. According to the Christian system as it is laid out in the Bible, society should be a brotherhood of men—not a brotherhood of white men only but of men of all colors. Moreover, it takes men as they are, pagan, Christian, idolater, scoffer, Catholic and Jew, and it lays down the set of principles which are essential for their living together in a just and peaceful society. These precepts, if they mean anything, mean mutual understanding, accommodation, sacrifice:

"Judge not lest ye be judged."

"Ye cannot serve God and mammon."

"Whatsoever ye would that men should do to you do ye even so to them."

"Love your enemies, bless them that curse you; do good to them that hate you; and pray for them that despitefully use you and persecute you."

Test these precepts by the inner light, the light which communion, worship gives, and they ring true. They satisfy the spirit more and more deeply as it develops. Moreover, they produce the only type of human being that can work out a brotherhood of man.

A few years ago, trying to get down what I really thought about the beneficent influence that the Bible had exercised in the world, I said of the man that it seeks to build up in order to work out Christianity's notion of a brotherhood of man, that he was "the man of the Beatitudes—hungering and thirsting after righteousness; merciful, pure in heart, meek in spirit, a peacemaker, willing even to be persecuted and reviled for righteousness' sake. This is the 'whole' or perfect man in the Bible sense, and to produce him is its continuous concern. By personal histories, by parables, by contrasts of good and evil conduct, by maxims of the highest beauty of form and of the most penetrating moral quality, it warns against those things which would poison the heart and deform the conduct it seeks to establish. Pride, greed, hypocrisy, cruelty, irreverence, cowardliness are moral diseases on which the Bible wars as a great physician wars on physical ailments which, uncorrected, would destroy the body's tissue."

This conception of men in their relations to one another is not the fruit of doctrinal struggle, church organizations, or theologies however sound and essential, but rather of the travail of the spirit. It comes from the striving in solitude and silence to enter into a fuller understanding of the divine.

Road Town: A Vision

He was a tall, pale-faced man, unshaven and carelessly dressed. You knew at once that he needed very much your help. My first thought was that he had an article to sell, or perhaps he was going to ask me for a loan. But before he spoke there was something about his eyes that told me that it was not at all for himself that he had come, whatever his personal need might be—he wanted something for somebody, or something else, some outside thing, very precious to him to be sure—something of his no doubt, but not for himself. I talked a long time with him, and when he went away he left behind him a knowledge of the thing that had made his face so thin, his clothes so careless, his eyes so intent and full of pain.

It had begun, so I found, with a discovery—a discovery of the suffering that heat and crowds and brick and stone bring to thousands of people in great cities in the summer time. He was a hard-working young man, I take it. And, one morning in full July heat, the cruel heat that sometimes swoops down on New York City, he had motored into town. He had spent a beautiful Sunday with friends in a cool, green, seaside place, and the early ride had been a joyful cap to his good holiday. It was only about six o'clock, he told me, when he struck the upper east-side, and when he, for the first time, saw how people lived through July days there. Stretched on the sidewalk, he saw mattress after mattress where women and men and little children sprawled, some of them still asleep, some of them lying with the pale exhausted look that a restless hot night leaves behind. Then he began to discover the fire-escapes and that on them lay little children and over their sides hung exhausted men or women already trying to gather themselves up for the day. He saw that the roofs were inhabited with thousands—then he realized that ten of thousands of men and women had been seeking in the last twenty-four hours on those heated pavements, those still more heated roofs, those narrow

Undated [1930s?] manuscript, Tarbell Papers Collection, Pelletier Library, Allegheny College, Meadville, Pennsylvania.

dangerous fire-escapes, some respite from the cruel heat which enveloped the great city. It all suddenly seemed monstrous to him, impossible. He went to his day's work but he could think of nothing else.

And all that week instead of going with his companions to the beach or to the roof-garden or to some big quiet cool room in the half deserted house of a friend, he had walked the streets, watching the park, the streets, the roofs and the fire-escapes gradually filled. He became conscious, too, [of] the way faces were paling all about him, and worst of all how babies were pining. The young man had made a great discovery and one which he never could forget, and before the weekend was over his one thought was how this monstrous thing could be stopped. Some way to get them out, that was what his idea was, to get them away. So cruel did it all seem to him that the idea of attempting to alleviate the conditions in town was unthinkable. They must be got away. People must not live in a city like New York through the heated time. He had become a man of one idea and that idea was how it could be done. As the days and weeks went on, instead of forgetting, the thought became more impressed on him. People noticed that he had changed and asked what the matter was, and when he tried to explain they laughed at him, or told him he had to get away for a few days, or quoted Scripture: "The poor ye have always with you." But the mania had taken too strong a hold on him. How to get them out, that had become the one thing in life to him—and what he had come to tell me was that he had found a way by which they could be gotten out.

It was the fear, that I might not be willing to listen to the story of the way, that had brought him to me. So many people had evidently driven him away—had pooh hood [sic] his scheme—had told him he was ruining his business chances—that was what had given his eyes the look of fear. And when he saw that I was going to listen, it was with a gratitude that almost brought tears to my eyes, [that] he told his plan.

"It is all so unnecessary," he said. "There is a place, if we could only use it." "You know the Long Island country, you know the limitless fields, you know how easily one gets into the open by a subway. Now here is what I propose. To buy the land, acres and acres, miles and miles. To run one long straight tube through the middle of my purchase, under one long straight street. And then on each side of this street to build miles and miles of houses.

Simple houses, such as the poorest can afford, such as my people who sleep on fire-escapes and roofs and sidewalks can easily afford. These houses shall have through one great conductive tube, electric light, heat, hot and cold water, all that can be so easily carried to houses nowadays. At every mile of my street there shall be one great square tower and in this tower a wonderful cooperative store where at cost they may buy everything they need. Back of little houses there shall be a garden for those that want one, for remember I am to have but one street. There must be green things for my people. They will come from their work in town through my long tube and land at their very doors. There shall be halls for them, music and dancing and plays. All in my long one street. You don't know how little money it costs, my Roadtown, for that is what I call it. I have it all figured out here. There have been one or two big business men who have been willing to listen to me and look at my figures, and they tell me it is a perfectly possible scheme. Mr. Edison listened to me and he tells me that if ever they will buy the land and build the subway, and put in my gas and water and electricity, that he will give me his model for his houses all free, for Mr. Edison sees how it might be, my Roadtown."

I have no time to tell here of all the details that this man, with a look of fear in his eyes, had worked out, for those whom he called "my people"—the poor who in summer must lie on the roofs and sleep in the streets. I looked at his plans for he had them worked out in the greatest detail. It was a great dream, but a dream that might come true. There is nothing impossible in "Roadtown," nothing but man's inertia and money's cowardice and the lack of vision in good people who want as much as my inventor to see those whom he calls "my people" free from the terrible curse of summer heat in a city like New York.

Appendix

Chautauqua Institution: Rectitude and Education

Robert C. Kochersberger, Jr.

Chautauqua's Creation and Mission

Western New York's Chautauqua Institution stood for a singular way of looking at life, always with an eye to innovation, progress, and highest standards
of study. It was at Chautauqua Institution that Melvil Dewey devised his
numbered system of indexing library books. At Chautauqua, Thomas Alva
Edison was spoken of not as a famous inventor but as founder Lewis Miller's
son-in-law. Traveling tent shows that carried entertainment and culture to
the rowdy Midwest took the name of Chautauqua and, in a way, blasphemed
it by adding showmanship and removing its seriousness. And Ida Minerva
Tarbell—biographer, muckraker, social critic—came to journalism through
a Chautauqua connection.[1]

The first official session of the Chautauqua Sunday School Assembly was
held August 4–14, 1874.[2] Its founders, Ohio businessman Lewis Miller and
Methodist Bishop John Heyl Vincent, planned Chautauqua as a site for Sunday school education and took it to the woods of western New York State.
They wanted wide denominational and geographic representation and achieved
both, in no small part because Chautauqua was located on rail lines midway
between New York City and Chicago, facilitating access from two of the
country's major cities and adding a cosmopolitan flair to a very rural place.

The grounds continually were expanded, as Chautauqua's reputation grew
and as it was endorsed by numerous prominent Americans. In spring 1878,
William Cullen Bryant wrote to Vincent, "I perceive this important advantage in the proposed organization, namely, that those who engage in it will
mutually encourage each other. It will give the members a common pursuit,

which always begets a feeling of brotherhood."[3] Vincent also received a note from John Greenleaf Whittier, who, in a rather convoluted way, said that he approved of the way the Chautauqua Literary and Scientific Circle was running: "I have been watching the progress of the Chautauqua Literary and Scientific Circle . . . and take . . . blame to myself for not sooner expressing my satisfaction as regards its object and its working thus far."[4] Whittier also has been quoted as hoping that Chautauqua's beneficent influences would touch the entire country.[5] Other prominent individuals also commented.[6]

Frederic Perry Noble in 1890 compared Chautauqua to utopia, and in 1883 the *New York Times* took careful note of the institution: "It is only within a few years that this lake has sprung into prominence as a Summer watering place, and even yet its merits are scarcely known in the East, although the name Chautauqua is a 'household word' in every section of the country in relation to the National Sunday-school Assembly and the Chautauqua Literary and Scientific Circle."[7]

Chautauqua, for all its reputation as a place for learning, was first of all a human institution, and it was the people there who, with their quirks and their knowledge, made the institution what it was and what it would be. It has been said that the conscientiously inquiring mind of the Chautauqua student—such as Tarbell clearly possessed—existed long before the institution, and that Chautauqua members were among those Americans who planned always to grow.[8]

As the institution's name and reputation spread, so too did its interest in the issues and problems of the country and the wider world of which it was a part. In 1880, Standard Oil was the topic of a debate on the Chautauqua platform; this was the first time a debate on a public issue was held at the institution.[9] (This debate was held three years before Tarbell joined *The Chautauquan*, so it is unlikely that it had any direct influence in her later Standard Oil work.)

Jesse Hurlbut, Bishop Vincent's successor, said that the Chautauqua leaders made an effort to have the "burning questions of the time" discussed by representative speakers. Some exceedingly radical statements were made at Chautauqua, but the fact that audiences were attentive and even applauded did not mean that the institution agreed with the claims made.[10]

Chautauqua Literary and Scientific Circle

Chautauqua Institution was a major source of innovation in education, as shown by its creation of the Chautauqua Literary and Scientific Circle (CLSC). Bishop Vincent never attended college, but his education continued to the end of his life; he read widely, never ceasing to thirst for knowledge. Although Vincent had been able to educate himself, he felt sympathy toward others who, like himself, had missed the opportunity of "dwelling in college-cloisters." Thus, as Vincent said, the CLSC was geared toward workers on the farm, at the forge, in the store, in the office, in the kitchen, and in the factory.[11]

Vincent's plan was to assemble, and to distribute to those who registered, a course of study to be carried out over four years, on a college-like schedule. In the various branches of study, each day's task entailed forty minutes' reading, for nine or ten months of the year.[12]

Vincent announced the formation of the CLSC on August 10, 1878. His inspiring address had a special effect on the women of Chautauqua. The movement for women's rights had intensified the natural desire for knowledge felt by women of that generation, and the Chautauqua women shared a special devotion to Vincent. But Vincent's persuasiveness and popularity cannot account for the sweeping success of the CLSC.[13] Its first class, dealing with "The Pioneers," enrolled a total of some 8,400 persons, pioneers themselves.[14]

Journalism historian Frank Luther Mott called the CLSC "an extraordinary movement, by which more than three-quarters of a million adults, over a third of a century, pursued one or more annual courses of reading." *Review of Reviews* editor Albert Shaw called the CLSC "the greatest popular educational movement of modern time."[15]

The CLSC had a pioneering spirit that engendered enthusiasm and support. Its founders set out to challenge the notion that education ended when traditional schooling did. For them, education was a lifelong venture.[16] Arthur E. Bestor, Jr., compiler of the invaluable *Chautauqua Publications,* believed that the institution's most significant social contribution was the way it permeated even the smallest units of American life.[17]

Most adherents of the CLSC method of higher education were women. Hurlbut, in dealing with a procedural matter at the institution, recorded that "each graduate was able to receive his own (mostly her own) diploma."[18] Another work on Chautauqua emphasized the predominance of women even more strongly:

> Older women who had looked wistfully toward colleges opened too late for their instruction welcomed the guidance of the systematic reading course. So did the members of the newly organized women's clubs scattered thinly over the country. . . .
>
> Housewives propped the books before them in their kitchens.
>
> Ailing women . . . found the Circle's compulsion to completed work beneficial.
>
> Pastors' wives took a few minutes every day for their own reading—it would give them an interest in common with their better-educated husbands.[19]

Not long after Chautauqua Institution gave birth to the CLSC, Chautauqua's leaders recognized the need for a publication to disseminate the circle's assigned readings. Thus *The Chautauquan* was launched. The magazine was convenient for circle members, reduced the number of separate printings the CLSC needed, and was profitable for its founder and editor.

Such Chautauquan traits as inquisitiveness and open-mindedness were urged upon readers of *The Chautauquan* far beyond the institution's gates. The magazine interested itself in all of the "turbulent and confused life" that surrounded it, and nearly every item of the country's social program was noted and discussed within its pages.[20] This range of interest marked Tarbell for life. Her writing, especially in her later years, seemed almost opportunistic, so wide was her range of interest. But in fact Tarbell was a journalist of the best sort. She identified a topic, did her job exquisitely, and moved on.

Notes

Introduction

1. Ida M. Tarbell, "Editorial Responsibility," speech to the Kansas Editorial Association, 20–21 Apr. 1908, Tarbell Papers Collection, Pelletier Library, Allegheny College, Meadville, Pa. (hereafter cited as "Tarbell Papers Collection").

2. Arthur Weinberg and Lila Weinberg, eds., *The Muckrakers: The Era in Journalism That Moved America to Reform: The Most Significant Magazine Articles of 1902–1912* (New York: Simon and Schuster, 1961), 243.

3. Peter Lyon, *Success Story: The Life and Times of S. S. McClure* (New York: Scribner's, 1963), 213.

4. Ibid., 210.

5. Ida M. Tarbell, *History of the Standard Oil Company* (New York: S. S. McClure, 1904), 1: ix, quoted in Mary E. Tomkins, *Ida M. Tarbell* (New York: Twayne, 1974), 60.

6. Fred J. Cook, *The Muckrakers: Crusading Journalists Who Changed America* (Garden City, N.Y.: Doubleday, 1972), 8–9.

7. Ibid., 9.

8. Ibid., 11.

9. Robert Miraldi, *Muckraking and Objectivity: Journalism's Colliding Traditions* (New York: Greenwood, 1990), 5.

10. John Tebbel and Mary Ellen Zuckerman, *The Magazine in America: 1741–1990* (New York: Oxford Univ. Press, 1991), 108.

11. S. S. McClure, "Concerning Three Articles in This Number of *McClure's,* and a Coincidence That May Set Us Thinking," editorial, *McClure's,* Jan. 1903, quoted in Weinberg and Weinberg, *The Muckrakers,* 4–5.

12. Tebbel and Zuckerman, *Magazine in America,* 108.

13. Norman Hapgood, *The Changing Years* (New York: Farrar and Rinehart, 1930), 12.

14. Shelley Fisher Fishkin, *From Fact to Fiction: Journalism and Imaginative Writing in America* (Baltimore: Johns Hopkins Univ. Press, 1985), 9.

15. Tomkins, *Tarbell,* 158.

16. Tebbel and Zuckerman, *Magazine in America,* 119–20.

17. Miraldi, *Muckraking and Objectivity,* 5.

18. Paul J. Baker and Louis E. Anderson, *Social Problems: A Critical Thinking Approach* (Belmont, Calif.: Wadsworth, 1987), 22.

19. Tomkins, *Tarbell,* 158–59.

20. Tarbell, *A Life of Napoleon Bonaparte, With a Sketch of Josephine, Empress of the French* (New York: Moffat Yard, 1909), 390.

21. Tebbel and Zuckerman, *Magazine in America,* 113.

22. Michael Emery and Edwin Emery, *The Press and America: An Interpretive History of the Mass Media,* 6th ed. (Englewood Cliffs, N.J.: Prentice-Hall, 1988), 186.

23. Ibid., 220–21.

24. David M. Chalmers, *The Social and Political Ideas of the Muckrakers* (New York: Citadel Press, 1964), quoted in Marvin Olasky, *Central Ideas in the Development of American Journalism: A Narrative History* (Hillsdale, N.J.: Erlbaum, 1991), 180.

25. Ida M. Tarbell, *All in the Day's Work* (New York: Macmillan, 1939), 399. All subsequent information about Tarbell's life comes from this autobiography, unless otherwise noted.

26. Mark Sullivan, *Our Times: The United States, 1900–1925* (New York: Scribner, 1927), vol. 2: 478n.

27. Philip F. Lawler, *The Alternative Influence: The Impact of Investigative Reporting Groups on America's Media* (Lanham, Md.: University Press of America, 1984), 2.

28. Miraldi, *Muckraking and Objectivity,* 32.

29. Dan Noyes, *Raising Hell: A Citizens Guide to the Fine Art of Investigation* (San Francisco: Mother Jones, n.d.), quoted in Philip F. Lawler, *The Alternative Influence,* 38.

30. Tarbell, *Day's Work,* 205.

31. Kathleen Brady, *Ida Tarbell: Portrait of a Muckraker* (New York: Seaview/Putnam's, 1984), 6.

32. John Chamberlain, *Farewell to Reform* (New York: Liveright, 1932), 140.

33. Jesse Lyman Hurlbut, *The Story of Chautauqua* (New York: Putnam's, 1921), 78.

34. Rebecca Richmond, *Chautauqua: An American Place* (New York: Duell, Sloan and Pearce, 1943), 89.

35. Ida M. Tarbell, "Wellesley Talk," undated, Tarbell Papers Collection.

36. Tarbell, *Day's Work,* 400.

37. Linda Simon, "Introduction," in Ida M. Tarbell, *All in the Day's Work,* 1939, rpt. ed. (Boston: G. K. Hall, 1985), x.

38. Tarbell, *Day's Work,* 30.

39. Ibid., 66.

40. Ibid., 64.

41. Ibid., 72–73.

42. Brady, *Ida Tarbell,* 46–47.

43. Samuel S. McClure, *My Autobiography* (New York: Frederick A. Stokes, 1914), 217–19.

44. Louis Filler, *Crusaders for American Liberalism* (New York: Harcourt, Brace, 1939), 241. Rev. ed. is entitled *The Muckrakers* (University Park, Pa.: Pennsylvania State Univ. Press, 1976).

45. Lyon, *Success Story*, 204.

46. Elmer Ellis, *Mr. Dooley's America: A Life of Peter Finley Dunne* (New York: Knopf, 1941), 214.

47. Lincoln Steffens, *The Autobiography of Lincoln Steffens* (New York: Harcourt, Brace, 1931), 392–93.

48. Robert C. Bannister, Jr., *Ray Stannard Baker: The Mind and Thought of a Progressive* (New Haven, Conn.: Yale Univ. Press, 1966), 160.

49. Ray Stannard Baker, *American Chronicle* (New York: Scribner's, 1945), 98–99, 228.

50. Tarbell, *Day's Work*, 84.

51. Ibid., 242.

52. Ibid., 250.

53. Robert Stinson, "Ida M. Tarbell and the Ambiguities of Feminism," *Pennsylvania Magazine of History and Biography* 101 (Apr. 1977): 217–18.

54. Ibid., 219.

55. Ibid., 227–28.

55. Ibid., 232.

56. Tomkins, *Tarbell*, 26.

57. Tarbell, "Woman as Inventors," *Chautauquan* 7 (Mar. 1887): 355–57.

58. Tomkins, *Tarbell*, 156–57.

59. Ibid., 60; Marion Marzolf, *Up from the Footnote* (New York: Hastings House, 1977), 41; Richard Hofstadter, *The Age of Reform* (New York: Knopf, 1955), 192.

60. Frank Chapin Bray, "Theodore L. Flood," *Meadville (Pa.) Tribune Republican,* 12 May 1938.

61. Ibid.

62. Hurlbut, *Story of Chautauqua,* 69.

63. No headline, *Chautauqua Daily Assembly Herald* vol. 5, no. 1 (n.d.): 1–2.

64. Ibid.

65. Theodore Morrison, *Chautauqua: A Center for Education, Religion, and the Arts in America* (Chicago: Univ. of Chicago Press, 1974), 62.

66. Ibid.

67. Frank Luther Mott, *A History of American Magazines,* vol. 3: *1865–1885* (Cambridge, Mass.: Harvard Univ. Press, 1957), 544–47.

68. Morrison, *Chautauqua,* 62–63.

69. Theodore L. Flood, "The Chautauquan: Twenty Years an Editor," *Chautauquan* 19 (June 1899): 322.

70. Hurlbut, *Story of Chautauqua,* 181.

71. Harrison J. Thornton, "Chautauqua—Adventure in Popular Education," 2 vols., typescript, Smith Memorial Library, Chautauqua Institution, Chautauqua, N.Y., 360. Thornton is a professor at the University of Iowa.

72. "How the Chautauquan Is Made," *Chautauquan* 7 (Jan. 1887): 322.

73. Frances Power Cobbe, "Duties of Women as Mistresses of Households," *Chautauquan* 4 (May 1884): 473–74; and "The Emancipation of Married Women," *Chautauquan* 8 (May 1888): 506.

74. Pattie L. Collins, "Government Employment for Women," *Chautauquan* 5 (Oct. 1884): 27.

75. Mary A. Livermore, "Women's Work in Moral Reforms," *Chautauquan* 7 (Nov. 1886): 72.

76. "The Good Woman," *Chautauquan* 2 (Mar. 1882): 366.

77. Helen Campbell, "Out-of-Door Employment for Women," *Chautauquan* 7 (Jan. 1887): 200.

78. Pattie L. Collins, "Government Employment for Women," *Chautauquan* 5 (May 1885): 467.

79. Frances E. Willard, "Women in Journalism," *Chautauquan* 7 (Apr. 1887): 395.

80. Ida M. Tarbell, "Women in Journalism," *Chautauquan* 7 (Apr. 1887): 393–95.

81. Ibid.

82. J. L. Corning, "What Woman Has Done for Art in 1,000 Years," *Chautauquan* 2 (Oct. 1881): 29.

83. "Women as Literary Forces," Editor's Outlook, *Chautauquan* 9 (Mar. 1889): 366.

84. "A Victory for Women," Editor's Outlook, *Chautauquan* 10 (Dec. 1889): 340.

85. Julia Ward Howe, "Women in the Professions," *Chautauquan* 7 (May 1887): 460.

86. Grace H. Dodge, "Working Girls' Societies," *Chautauquan* 9 (Jan. 1889): 223.

87. "A Business Education for Girls," *Chautauquan* 7 (Oct. 1886): 3.

88. Felicia Hillel, "Working Girls," *Chautauquan* 10 (Dec. 1889): 328.

89. "Work for Women," *Chautauquan* 4 (Jan. 1884): 219.

90. Ida M. Tarbell, "Meadville in the Eighties," *Meadville (Pa.) Tribune-Republican,* 12 May 1938.

91. Ibid.

92. Tarbell, *Day's Work,* 73.

93. Ibid., 73–75.

94. Tarbell, "Arts and Industries of Cincinnati," *Chautauquan* 7 (Nov. 1886): 160–62.

95. Morrison, *Chautauqua,* 63.

96. Tarbell, *Day's Work,* 80.

97. Ibid., 78.

98. Ibid., 87.

99. Theodore L. Flood to Ida M. Tarbell, 19 Mar. 1891, Tarbell Papers Collection.

100. Theodore L. Flood, letter of recommendation, 25 Mar. 1891, Tarbell Papers Collection.

101. Flood to Tarbell, 19 Mar. 1891.

102. Flood, letter of recommendation, 25 Mar. 1891.

103. Tarbell, "Women in Journalism, 393.

104. Thomas B. Connery, "A Third Way to Tell the Story: American Literary Journalism at the Turn of the Century," in *Literary Journalism in the Twentieth Century,* ed. Norman Sims (New York: Oxford Univ. Press, 1990), 6.

105. Baker and Anderson, *Social Problems,* 26.

106. Brady, *Ida Tarbell,* 255.

I. Biography

1. Kathleen Brady, *Ida Tarbell: Portrait of a Muckraker* (New York: Seaview/Putnam's, 1984), 45.

II. A Woman's Eye on Business

1. Frank Luther Mott, *A History of American Magazines* (Cambridge, Mass.: Harvard Univ. Press, 1957), vol. 4: 598.

2. Paul J. Baker and Louis E. Anderson, *Social Problems: A Critical Thinking Approach* (Belmont, Calif.: Wadsworth, 1987), 356.

3. Elbert Hubbard, *The Standard Oil Company* (East Aurora, N.Y.: Roycroft Shop, 1910), 13–14.

4. Peter Lyon, *Success Story: The Life and Times of S. S. McClure* (New York: Scribner's, 1963), 213.

Appendix

1. Theodore Morrison, *Chautauqua: A Center for Education, Religion, and the Arts in America* (Chicago: Univ. of Chicago Press, 1974), 294; Rebecca Richmond, *Chautauqua: An American Place* (New York: Duell, Sloan and Pearce, 1943), 147.

2. Alfreda L. Irwin, *Three Taps of the Gavel* (Chautauqua, N.Y.: Chautauqua Institution, 1977), 15.

3. William Cullen Bryant to John Heyl Vincent, 18 May 1878, Smith Memorial Library, Chautauqua Institution, Chautauqua, N.Y.

4. John Greenleaf Whittier to John Heyl Vincent, 1882 [no specific date], Smith Memorial Library, Chautauqua Institution, Chautauqua, N.Y.

5. Jesse Lyman Hurlbut, *The Story of Chautauqua* (New York: Putnam's, 1921), x.

6. According to Hurlbut, *Story of Chautauqua*, x, these would include Theodore Roosevelt, J. Lyman Abbott, and Edward Everett Hale.

7. Frederick P. Noble, "Chautauqua as a New Factor in American Life," *New England Magazine* 2 (Mar.-Apr. 1890): 90.

8. Richmond, *Chautauqua*, 11–13.

9. Hurlbut, *Story of Chautauqua*, 180.

10. Ibid.

11. Harrison J. Thornton, "Chautauqua—Adventure in Popular Education," 2 vols., typescript, Smith Memorial Library, Chautauqua Institution, Chautauqua, N.Y., 177.

12. Hurlbut, *Story of Chautauqua*, 122.

13. Thornton, "Chautauqua—Adventure," 55–56.

14. Hurlbut, *Story of Chautauqua*, 123, 136.

15. Frank Luther Mott, "The Magazine Revolution and Popular Ideas in the Nineties," in *American History: Recent Interpretations*, ed. Abraham S. Eisenstadt (New York: Crowell, 1962), 230.

16. Morrison, *Chautauqua: A Center*, 11.

17. Ibid., 65.

18. Hurlbut, *Story of Chautauqua*, 205.

19. Richmond, *Chautauqua*, 75.

20. Ida M. Tarbell, *All in the Day's Work*, 1939, rpt. ed. (Boston: G. K. Hall, 1985), 81.

Selected Bibliography

Books

Baker, Paul J., and Anderson, Louis E. *Social Problems: A Critical Thinking Approach.* Belmont, Calif., Wadsworth, 1987.

Baker, Ray Stannard. *American Chronicle.* New York: Scribner's, 1945.

Bannister, Robert C., Jr. *Ray Stannard Baker: The Mind and Thought of a Progressive.* New Haven, Conn.: Yale University Press, 1966.

Bestor, Arthur E. *Chautauqua Publications.* Chautauqua, N.Y.: Chautauqua Press, 1934.

Brady, Kathleen. *Ida Tarbell: Portrait of a Muckraker.* New York: Putnam's, 1984.

Case, Victoria. *We Called It Culture.* Garden City, N.Y.: Doubleday, 1948.

Chalmers, David M. *The Social and Political Ideas of the Muckrakers.* New York, 1964.

Chamberlain, John. *Farewell to Reform.* New York: Liveright, 1932.

Cook, Fred J. *The Muckrakers: Crusading Journalists Who Changed America.* Garden City, N.Y.: Doubleday, 1972.

DaBoll, Irene Briggs. *Recollections of the Lyceum and Chautauqua Circuits.* Freeport, Me.: Bond Wheelwright, 1969.

Eisenstadt, Abraham S., ed. *American History: Recent Interpretations.* Vol. 2: *Since 1865.* New York: Crowell, 1962.

Ellis, Elmer. *Mr. Dooley's America: A Life of Peter Finley Dunne.* New York: Knopf, 1941.

Emery, Michael, and Emery, Edwin. *The Press and America: An Interpretive History of the Mass Media.* Englewood Cliffs, N.J.: Prentice-Hall, 1988.

Filler, Louis. *Crusaders for American Liberalism.* New York: Harcourt, Brace, 1939. Rev. ed. is titled *The Muckrakers.* University Park, Pa.: Pennsylvania State University Press, 1976.

Fishkin, Shelley Fisher. *From Fact to Fiction: Journalism and Imaginative Writing in America.* Baltimore, Md.: Johns Hopkins University Press, 1985.

Flood, Theodore L. *Lives of Methodist Bishops.* New York: Phillips, 1882.

Gould, Joseph E. *The Chautauqua Movement.* New York: State University of New York, 1961.

Hapgood, Norman. *The Changing Years.* New York: Farrar and Rinehart, 1930.

Hofstadter, Richard. *The Age of Reform.* New York: Knopf, 1955.

Hurlbut, Jesse L. *The Story of Chautauqua.* New York: Putnam's, 1921.

Irwin, Alfreda L. *Three Taps of the Gavel.* Westfield, N.Y.: Westfield Republican, 1970.

James, Edward T. *Notable American Women, 1607–1950.* Cambridge, Mass.: Harvard University Press, 1936.

Lawler, Philip F. *The Alternative Influence: The Impact of Investigative Reporting Groups on America's Media.* Lanham, Md.: University Press of America, 1984.

Love, Cornelia S. *Famous Women of Yesterday and Today.* Chapel Hill: University of North Carolina Press, 1936.

Lyon, Peter. *Success Story, The Life and Times of S. S. McClure.* New York: Scribner's, 1963.

MacLaren, Gay. *Morally We Roll Along.* Boston: Little, Brown, 1938.

McClure, S. S. *My Autobiography.* New York: Frederick A. Stokes, 1914.

Marzolf, Marion. *Up From the Footnote.* New York: Hastings House, 1977.

Miraldi, Robert. *Muckraking and Objectivity: Journalism's Colliding Traditions.* New York: Greenwood, 1990.

Moers, Ellen. *Literary Women.* Garden City, N.Y.: Anchor/Doubleday, 1977.

Morrison, Theodore. *Chautauqua, A Center for Education, Religion, and the Arts in America.* Chicago: University of Chicago Press, 1974.

Mott, Frank Luther. *A History of American Magazines.* Vol. 3: *1865–1885.* Cambridge, Mass.: Harvard University Press, 1957.

Noffsinger, John S. *Correspondence Schools, Lyceums, Chautauquas.* New York: Macmillan, 1926.

Olasky, Marvin, *Central Ideas in the Development of American Journalism: A Narrative History.* Hillsdale, N.J.: Erlbaum, 1991.

Peterson, Theodore. *Magazines in the Twentieth Century.* Urbana, Ill.: University of Illinois Press, 1956.

Richmond, Rebecca. *Chautauqua, an American Place.* New York: Duell, Sloan and Pearce, 1943.

Sims, Norman. *Literary Journalism in the Twentieth Century.* New York: Oxford University Press, 1990.

Steffens, Lincoln. *The Autobiography of Lincoln Steffens.* New York: Harcourt, Brace, 1931.

Tarbell, Ida M. *All in the Day's Work.* New York: Macmillan, 1939.

———. *In the Footsteps of the Lincolns.* New York: Macmillan, 1924.

———. *The Business of Being a Woman.* New York: Macmillan, 1912.

———. *The History of the Standard Oil Company.* New York: Macmillan, 1904.

Tassin, Algernon. *The Magazine in America.* New York: Dodd, Mead, 1916.

Tebbel, John, and Zuckerman, Mary Ellen. *The Magazine in America: 1741–1990.* New York: Oxford University Press, 1990.

Tomkins, Mary E. *Ida M. Tarbell.* Boston: Twayne, 1974.

Vincent, John Heyl. *The Chautauqua Movement.* Boston: Chautauqua Press, 1886.

Weinberg, Arthur, and Weinberg, Lila, eds. *The Muckrakers: The Era in Journalism that Moved America to Reform: The Most Significant Magazine Articles of 1902–1912.* New York: Simon and Schuster, 1961.

White, William Allen. *The Autobiography of William Allen White.* New York: Macmillan, 1946.

Wood, James P. *Magazines in the United States.* New York: Ronald, 1949.

Periodicals and Unpublished Works

"Chautauqua Literary and Scientific Circle." *The Chautauquan* 33 (July 1901): 337–56.

Flood, Theodore L. "Old Chautauqua Days." *The Chautauquan* 13 (Aug. 1891): 561–93.

———. "The Chautauquan: 20 Years an Editor." *The Chautauquan* 29 (July 1899): 322–27.

"How the Chautauquan Is Made." *The Chautauquan* 7 (Jan. 1887): 222–25.

Kimball, K. F. "The Chautauqua Literary and Scientific Circle." *The Chautauquan* 11 (Aug. 1890): 611–15.

Noble, F. P. "Chautauqua as a New Factor in American Life." *New England Magazine* 2 (Mar.- Aug. 1890): 90–92.

Thornton, Harrison J. "Chautauqua—Adventure in Popular Education." 2 vols., typescript, Smith Memorial Library, Chautauqua Institution, Chautauqua, N.Y.

Vincent, G. E. "Chautauqua as an Educational Center." *The Chautauquan* 35 (July 1902): 367.

Index